# Art Flick's Master Fly-Tying Guide

# Art Flick's
# Master Fly-Tying Guide

Art Flick · Ed Koch · Lefty Kreh · Ted Niemeyer
Carl Richards · Ernest Schwiebert · Helen Shaw
Doug Swisher · Dave Whitlock

Edited and with an Introduction
by Art Flick

CROWN PUBLISHERS, INC., NEW YORK
Distributed to the sporting goods trade by Stoeger Industries

Inquiries should be addressed to Crown Publishers, Inc.,
One Park Avenue, New York, N.Y. 10016.
Library of Congress Catalog Card Number: 72-85693

ISBN: 0-517-50023X
ISBN: 0-517-521350 pbk.

Printed in the United States of America

Published simultaneously in Canada by General Publishing Company Limited

*Design — Michael Perpich*

*Five printings, hardcover edition*
*Third paperback printing, July, 1977*

*To Bill and Art, Jr.*
*our two boys*
*(and their families)*
*who give us so much pleasure*

# CONTENTS

# Introduction
## by Art Flick

Fly-fishing may well be the fastest-growing sport in the world. An exaggeration? Hardly. When one considers the number of people who are enjoying this fine sport today, compared to those of as recently as twenty years ago, the percentage of increase is amazing. Every year finds more and more fishermen giving up bait and spinning to join the ranks of the fly-rodders. Never have fly-fishing books sold in the numbers they now do, nor have there ever been so many clubs and organizations and even magazines devoted solely to fly-fishing. This is a healthy sign for the sport, because it probably means that more are fishing for *sport* than for meat.

One of the best examples of the phenomenal growth is seen in the number of saltwater fly-fishermen there are today. Only a few years ago, except for bonefish and tarpon, fly-fishing in salt water was almost unheard of. Now, in the famous annual Metropolitan Tournament conducted by Lefty Kreh out of Miami, last winter and spring found twenty-three species of fish entered in the Fly-Fishing Division, and 98 percent of them were saltwater species. Even billfish are now taken by the pros on flies, as are huge sharks. Fly-fishing even for the monsters has been refined to the point where, in order to enter a fish taken on a fly, the International rules require that the fly-fisherman have, just above the shock tippet, a minimum of one foot of twelve-pound-test monofilament. A few years ago, few people would have thought of such a thing as an organization of saltwater fly-fishermen, but today there are a number of them, the largest and most active being the vigorous Salt Water Fly Rodders of America.

It naturally follows, then, that as fly-fishing gained in popularity, so also would the number of people tying their own flies. This number continues to grow by leaps and bounds, as more and more anglers find that they really haven't enjoyed their sport to the fullest until they have caught their first fish on a fly of their own tying; and even more tyers have been added to the ranks, by the general interest in crafts of all kinds that is spreading across America—adding high-school students and disabled veterans and wives who may not even fish. It is only fair to warn those who are thinking of embarking on this interesting and enjoyable hobby that, after the bug has once bitten them, they will be hooked—and it is a disease for which there is no cure.

There are many fine books on the market today for the man or woman who wants to learn how to put together flies. *This* book, however, is unique. It is for the beginner—and the expert; the freshwater and saltwater fisherman; the tyer of eastern and western patterns; the bass bugger and the salmon fisherman; the traditionalist and the experimenter; the tyer of dry flies, wet flies, nymphs, midges, terrestrials, large flies, small flies—just about everything. Also, the tyers contributing their know-how in the pages that follow represent a broad spectrum of styles and methods of tying. Never before has a book presented such a diversity of talent.

This is *not* a comprehensive, encyclopedic guide to the flytyer on *all* patterns or how to tie all flies, but, instead, a means of showing the different methods of the various tyers. No attempt has been made here to standardize fly-tying, for each of us may use a different method to do the same thing. Helen Shaw may put a streamer together in one way, while Dave Whitlock, tying a similar western pattern, may construct his differently. One tyer constructs the bodies or wings or tails of his flies one way, another does it the way he likes best. In fact, I will tell you how I tie on hackle while Doug Swisher and Carl Richards will show you how to tie dry flies *without* hackle. Fly-tying, like fly-casting, is an individual matter; but the man who has mastered his method, no matter what it is, has something to teach. The flies in this book are well tied; they will take fish and they will take abuse. Despite the lack of uniformity of method, the reader can literally "cover the waterfront"; he can learn how to tie at least one or two flies in every category of artificial flies in the way they are put together by recognized artists in their fields. And the composite of all the styles and patterns in this book should provide amateur and professional tyers with hours and hours of fruitful pleasure at their vises.

Because my little *Streamside Guide* has proven so successful, due in great part to its simplicity, I requested all my coauthors to make their contributions as short and readable as possible. Hopefully, what you will have in this book, for the first time, is a concise, well-illustrated, and representative guide to eight different, proven methods of fly-tying—plus an excellent chapter at the end by Dave Whitlock on new fly-tying tools and materials.

Good tying! And how about making a sincere effort to convert one of your bait- or spin fishing pals to fishing with fur and feathers this year? Perhaps a book with the variety this has will lure him to fly-fishing. Fly-tying and fly-fishing are intriguing arts—and I cannot help thinking that they make better sportsmen and men respectful of their quarry, its environment, and the need to protect both.

# Art Flick's
# Master Fly-Tying Guide

# Helen Shaw

## STREAMER, BUCKTAIL, and BASS FLY

Photographs by Hermann Kessler

The patterns for the flies designated as "streamers" are usually tied with wings comprised of feathers, while those with hairwings have been called "bucktails." Both of these terms have been accepted to indicate flies of a type devised for fishing below the surface, and which have the common characteristic, when wet, of assuming the streamlined appearance of the minnows they are thought to represent. Rightfully, they can both be called "streamers."

For those who may be confused by finding that a hairwing fly called a "bucktail" may not contain any deer hair at all, or may contain both hair *and* feathers, I shall refer to the streamer flies illustrated as "feather-wing" and "hairwing," which they unquestionably are.

In both of the accepted categories there is a wealth of patterns, ranging from simple construction to elaborate multimaterial and multicolor designs, yet all of them will, in the water, appear to have a sleek and minnowlike form. All have long wings, and while the proportion of wing to hook may vary greatly with different patterns, the undulating motion of hair- or feather-wing, as the fly is worked in the water by rod action or water current, has proved the undeniable worth and attractiveness of this fly form for underwater fishing.

Popularly tied on down-eyed hooks, the streamer fly may also be tied on ringed-eye hooks to be used with a small spinner, which not only enables a fly to sink quickly, but also offers protection to the leader from the teeth of enthusiastic fish.

Bodies of the streamer-type flies may be weighted or not, depending on the circumstances under which they will be used, and on the preference of an individual fisherman. Some western patterns have all-metal bodies made by winding fairly soft wire, of a desired dimension, around the hook, tapering the cut ends and binding them with lacquered windings. Other bodies may have soft lead-wire wound on the hook before an outer cover of floss or tinsel is applied. These methods can be applied to any pattern popular in any locality.

The principal difference between the western and eastern streamer is found in the angle at which the wing is tied. To cope with the bigger, swifter water of the western streams, the wing may be raised as much as 45° to achieve maximum wing action. Eastern preference is for a wing that lies close to the hook—which may even cover the hook. There are exceptions to this, of course, in both cases. Throughout the country the angle of the wing may vary anywhere between these two extremes. All have been found successful under various circumstances.

## FEATHER-WING STREAMER

*Golden Furnace Streamer*

| | |
|---|---|
| Tag: | gold flat tinsel |
| Tail: | golden-pheasant tail feather (or dark mottled turkey) |
| Body: | bright orange floss |
| Rib: | gold flat tinsel |
| Throat: | light golden-brown furnace hackle |
| Wing: | two pairs of red-gold furnace hackles |
| Shoulders: | jungle-cock eyed cape feathers |

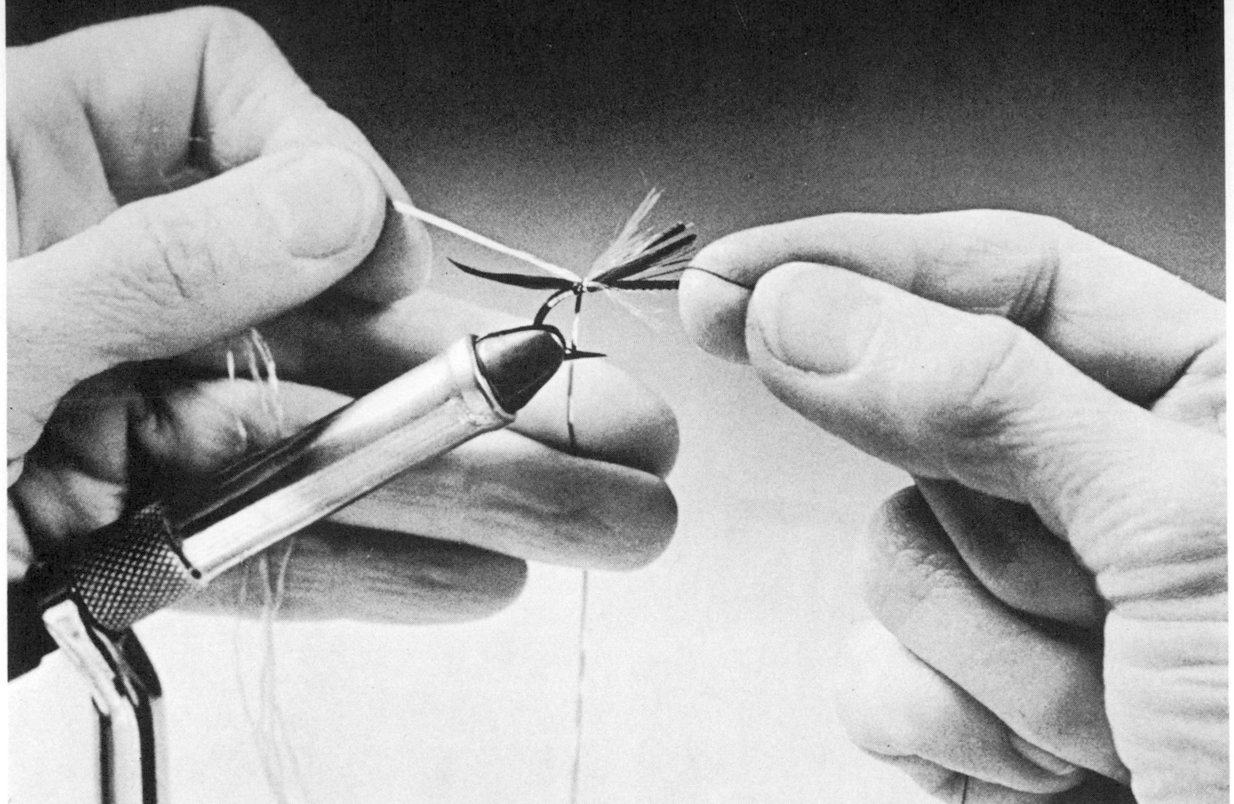

1. Tying thread, attached at "wing position," has been wound evenly back along the hook to just above the barb. The tinsel is attached here and wound down the bend a few turns and back, to form the "tag," leaving an ample amount hanging for the tinsel rib. The tail, a narrow strip of golden-pheasant tail feather, or dark mottled turkey, has been added and the floss is being tied on last.

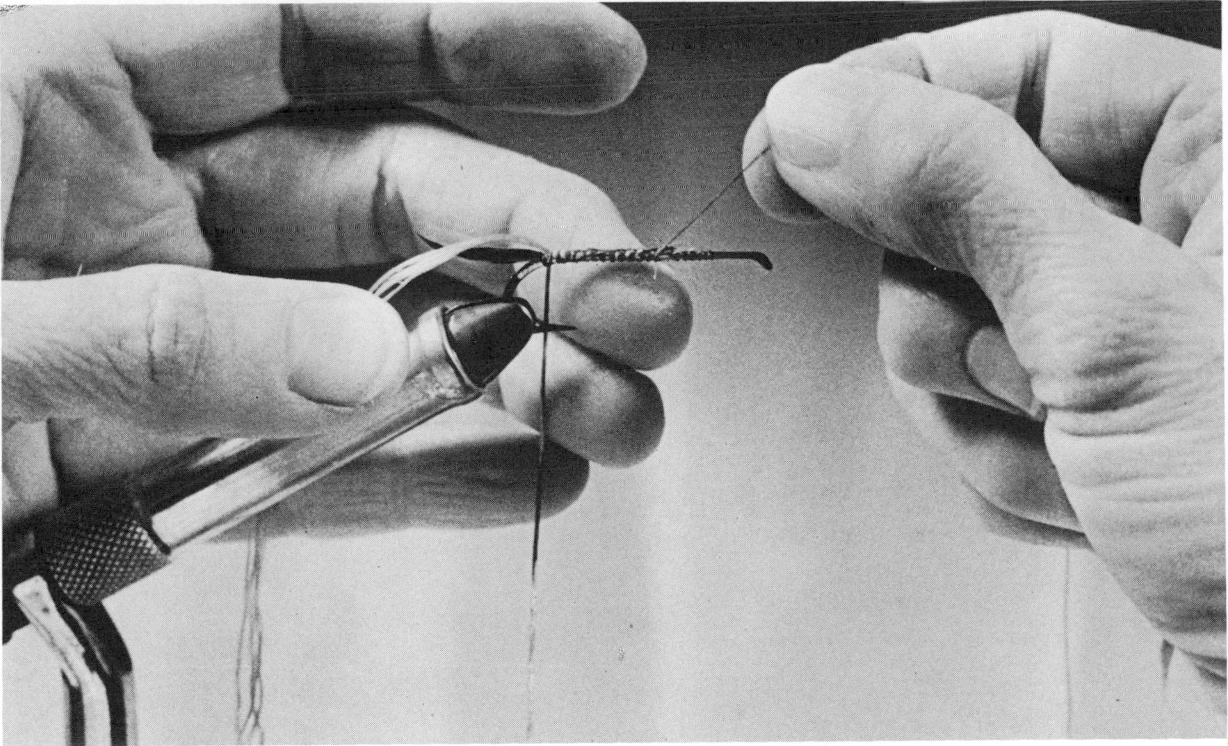

2. Evenly spaced winding of tying thread binds down the cut ends of floss and feather tail together, forming a smooth foundation for floss body.

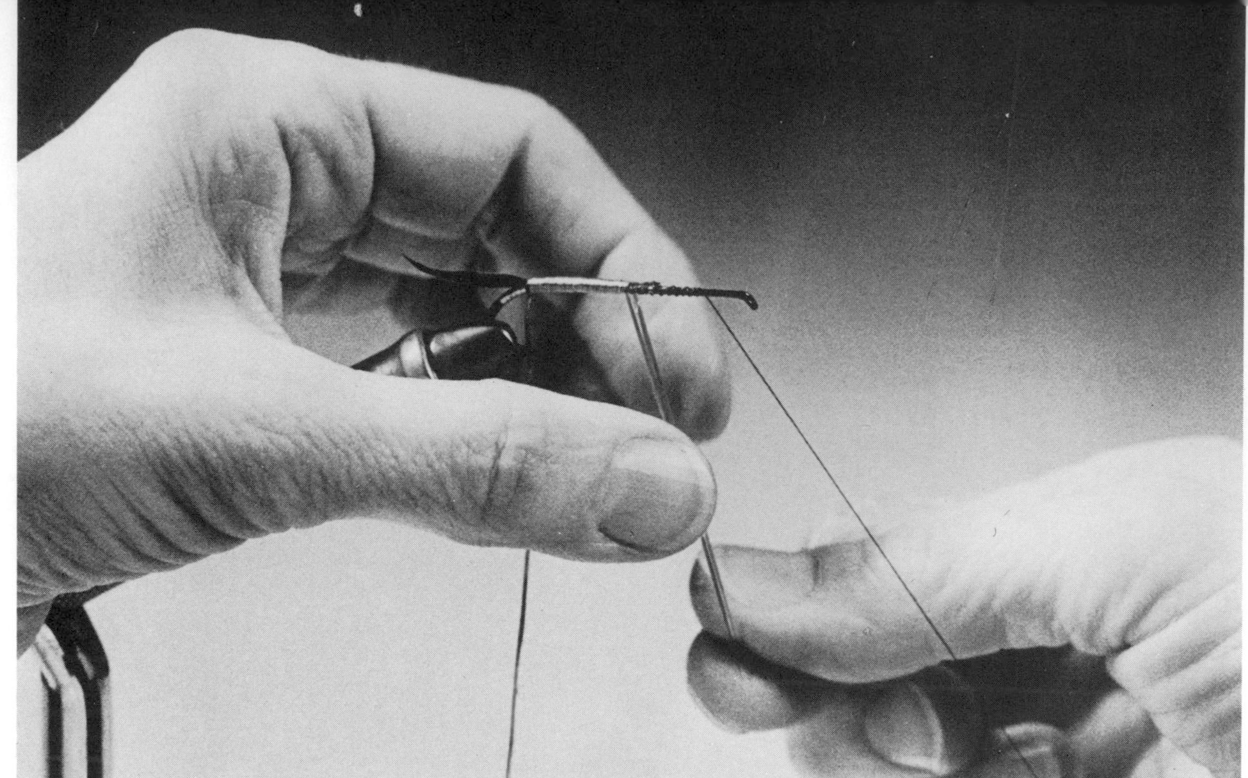

3. Floss is wound on toward the eye, the strands carefully kept smooth and not permitted to twist. (Twisting the floss strands would ridge the body.)

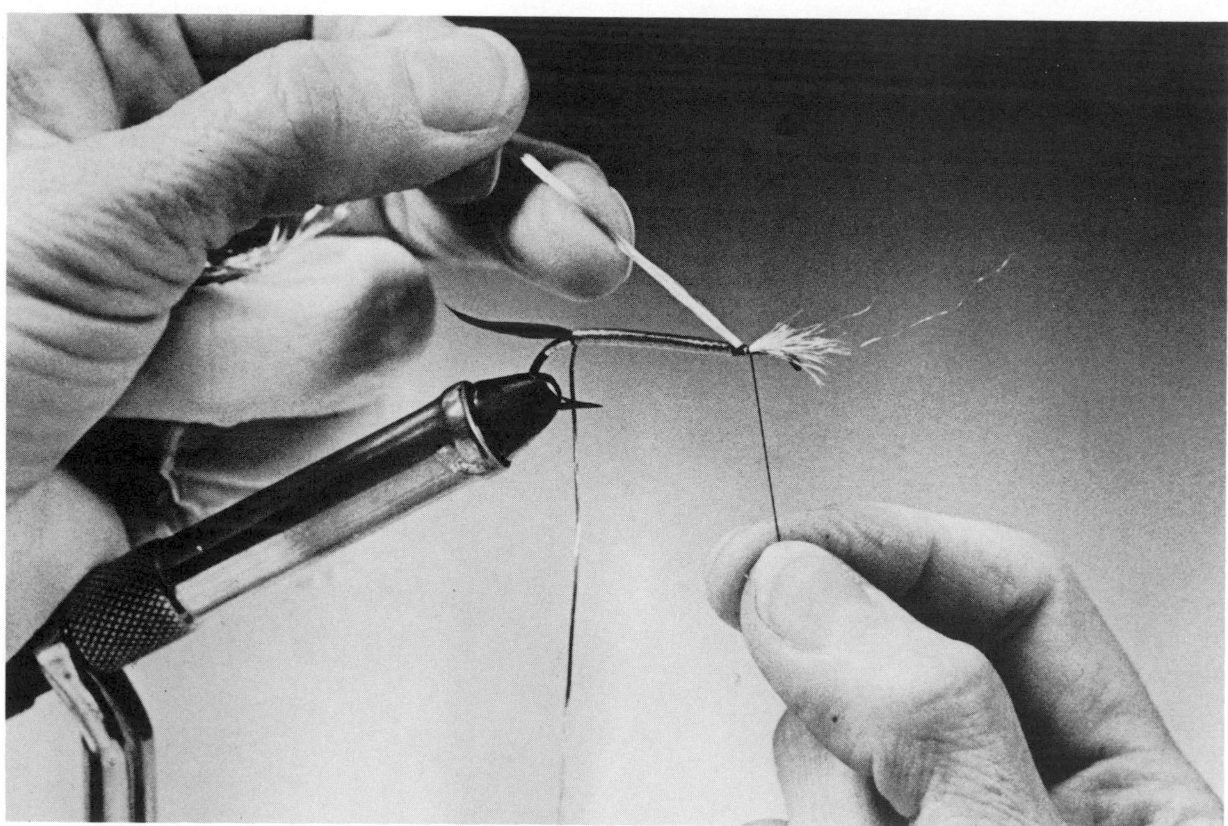

4. If enough floss for a well-shaped body was not estimated correctly, another length is tied in at wing position and excess trimmed away.

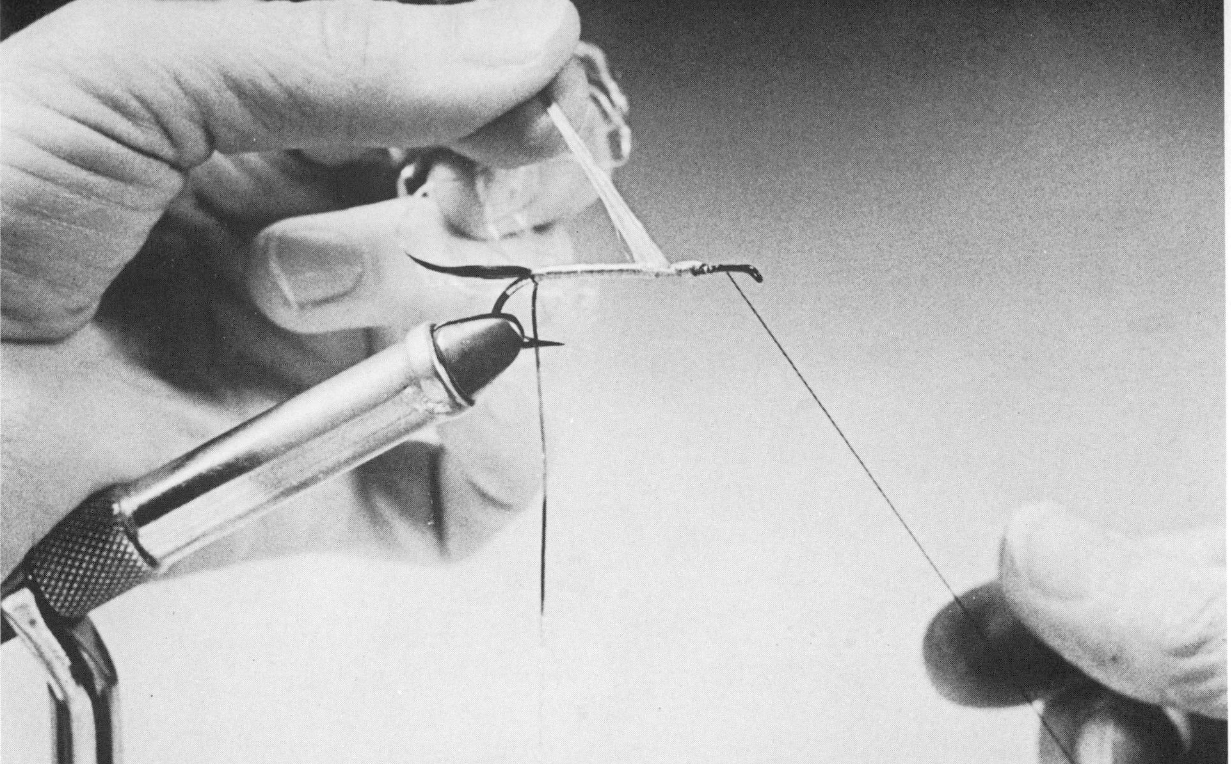

5. This second strand, kept as flat and wide-spread as possible, is wound back toward the tail. The angle at which floss is held will enable it to merge smoothly with the layer of floss beneath.

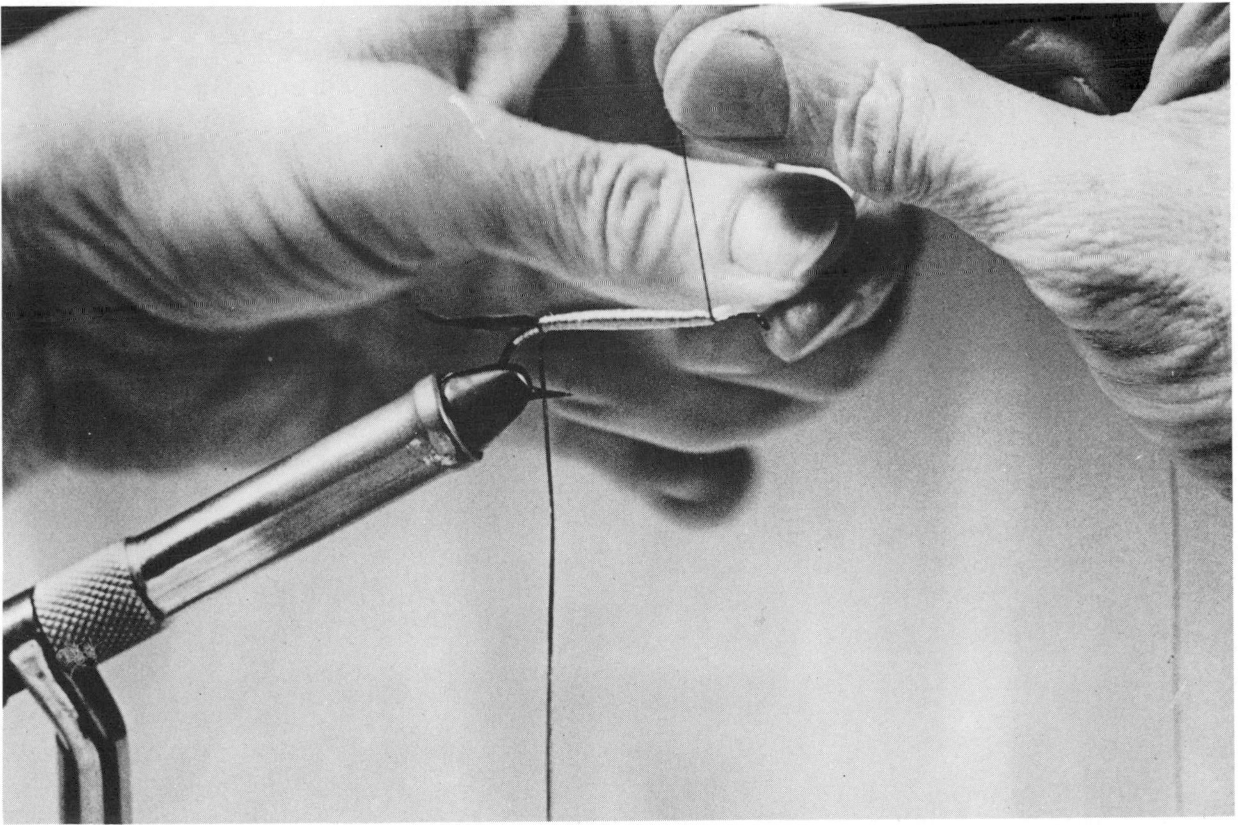

6. When the second layer of floss has been wound on a little beyond the hook point, the direction of winding is then reversed and continued toward the hook eye. This third layer of floss gives the body a better contour—slim, but more oval in shape than before. The floss is then secured at "wing position" and the excess clipped away.

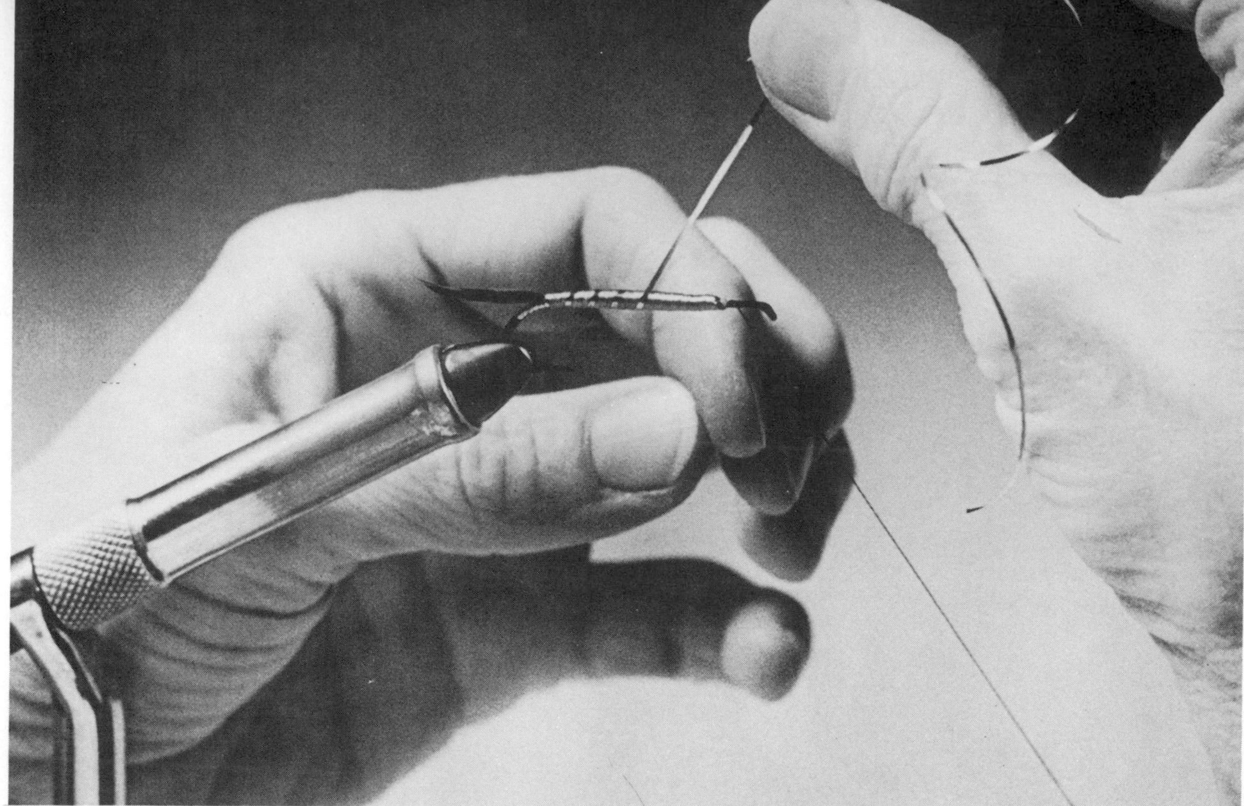

7. The tinsel rib is wound on, the first turn being made at the base of the tail, and successive turns evenly spaced along the body.

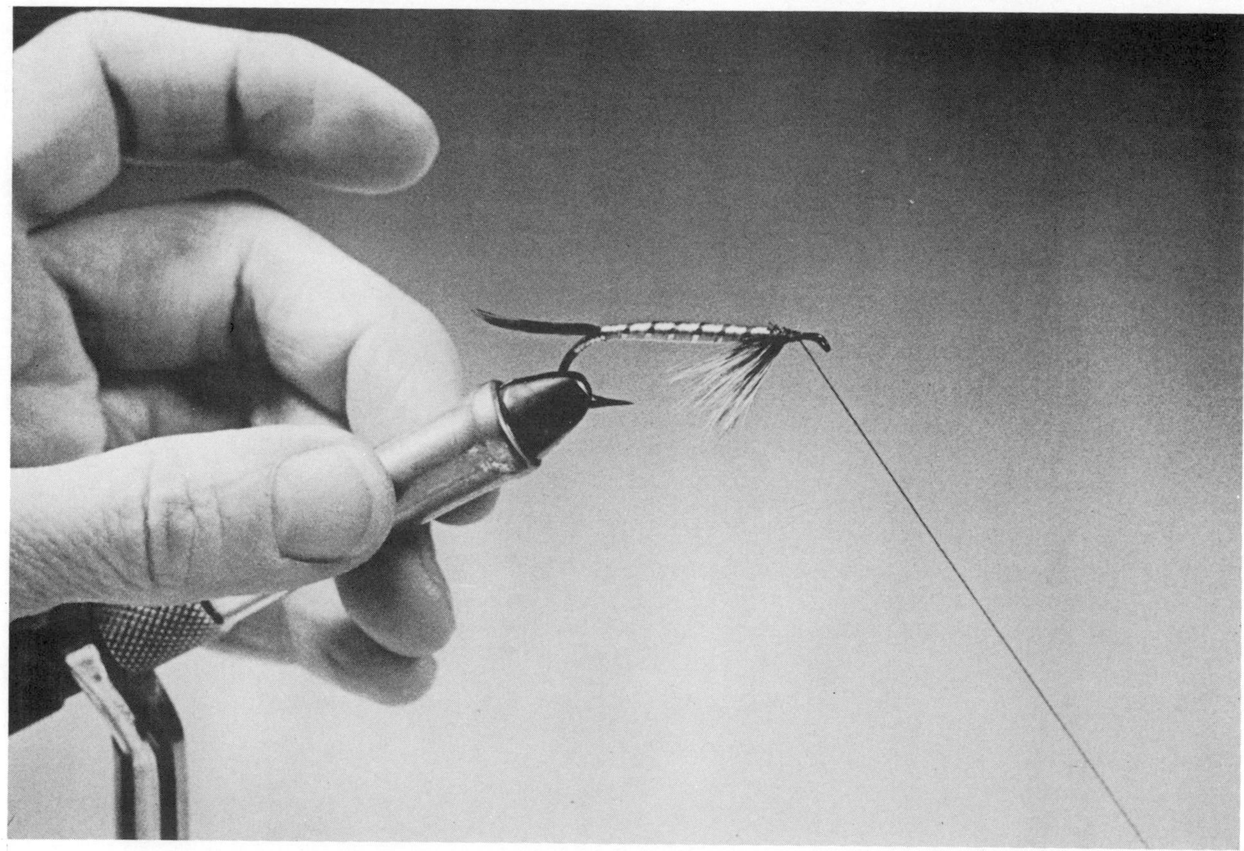

8. A light-golden furnace hackle has been wound on (covering the area where floss and tinsel ended), divided evenly, and drawn down from both sides of the hook to form the throat beneath. (In another method, a small bunch of hackle wisps is tied directly below the hook to form the throat; the resulting appearance is the same.)

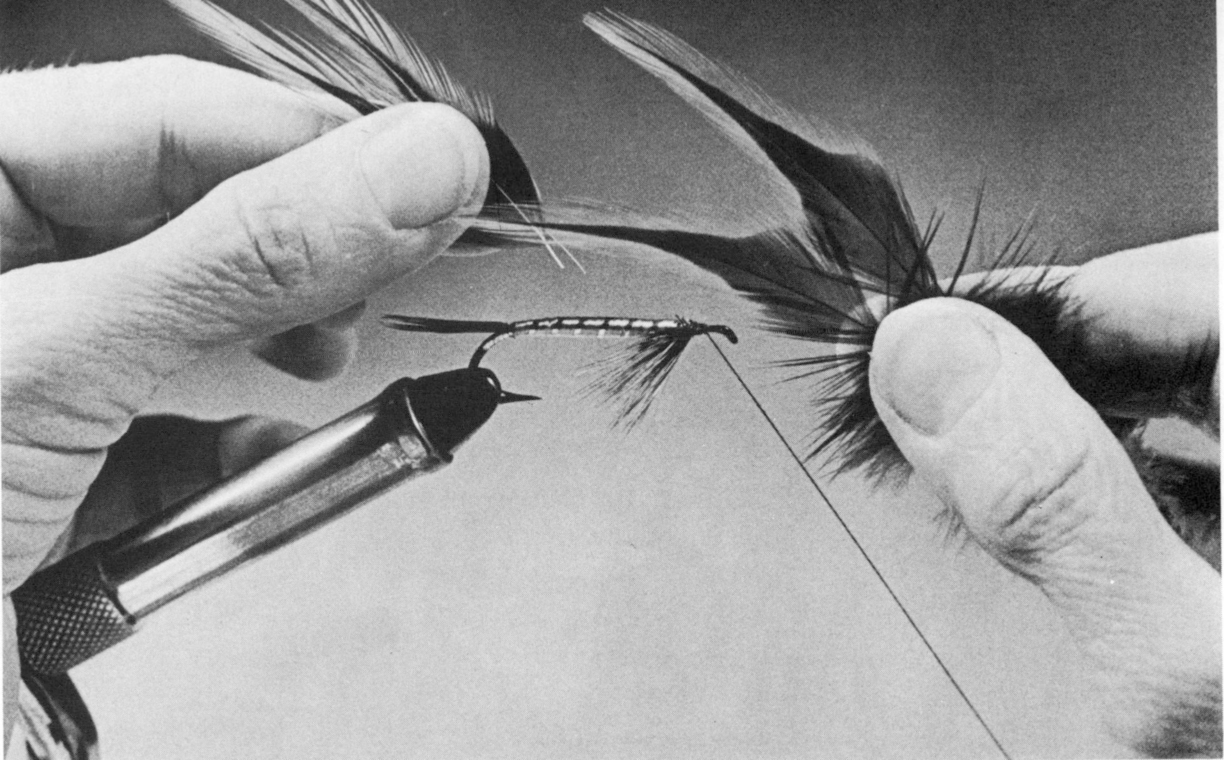

9. Two pairs of red-gold furnace hackles are matched for color, marking, shape, and size. Two "left" feathers in left hand, dull side toward tyer, have had the quills stripped of fluff. Two "rights" in right hand will also have quills freed of webby material and laid with their dull sides against the left pair, to form the wing.

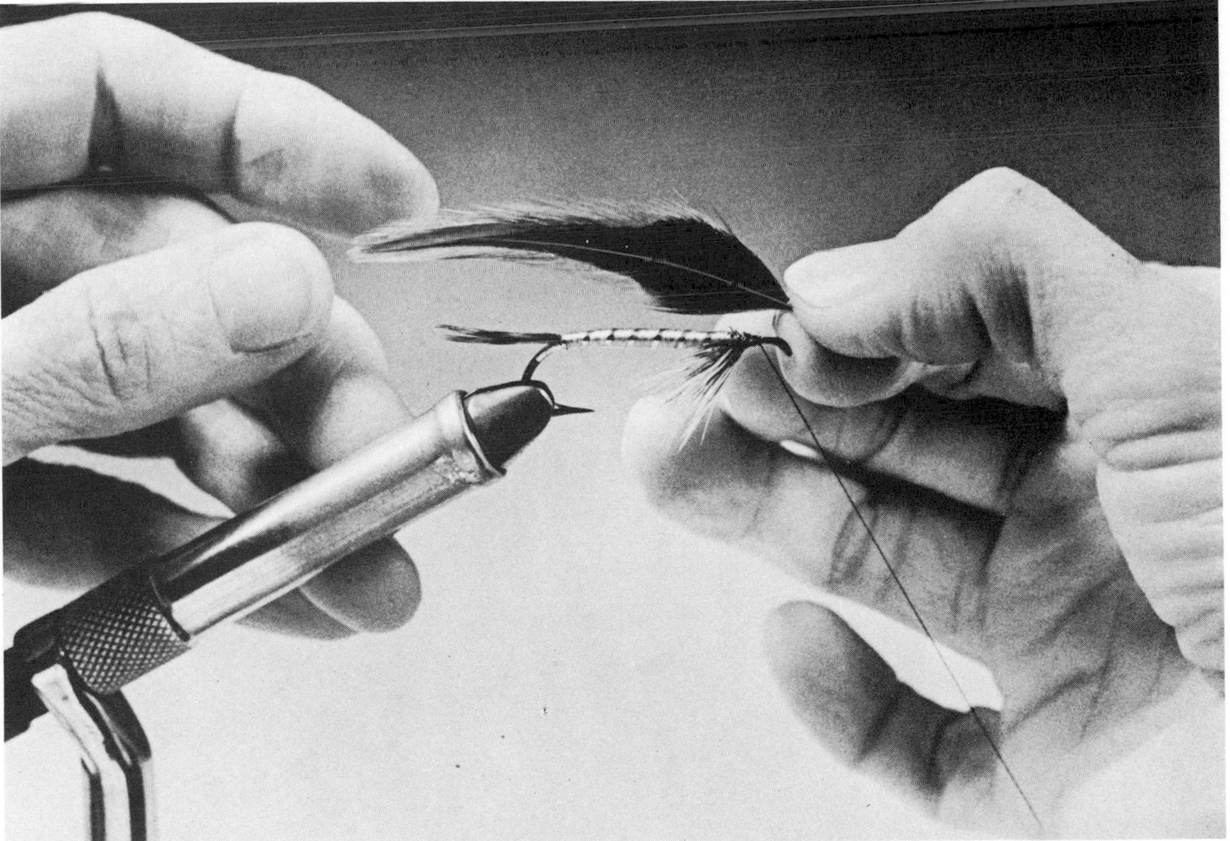

10. All four feathers match perfectly and are measured for length against the hook. Wing tips will extend about twice the length of tail beyond the hook. This pair will have a little more of the web removed from the quills (an amount equal to the space between the throat and the outer end of the eye) preparatory to being tied on.

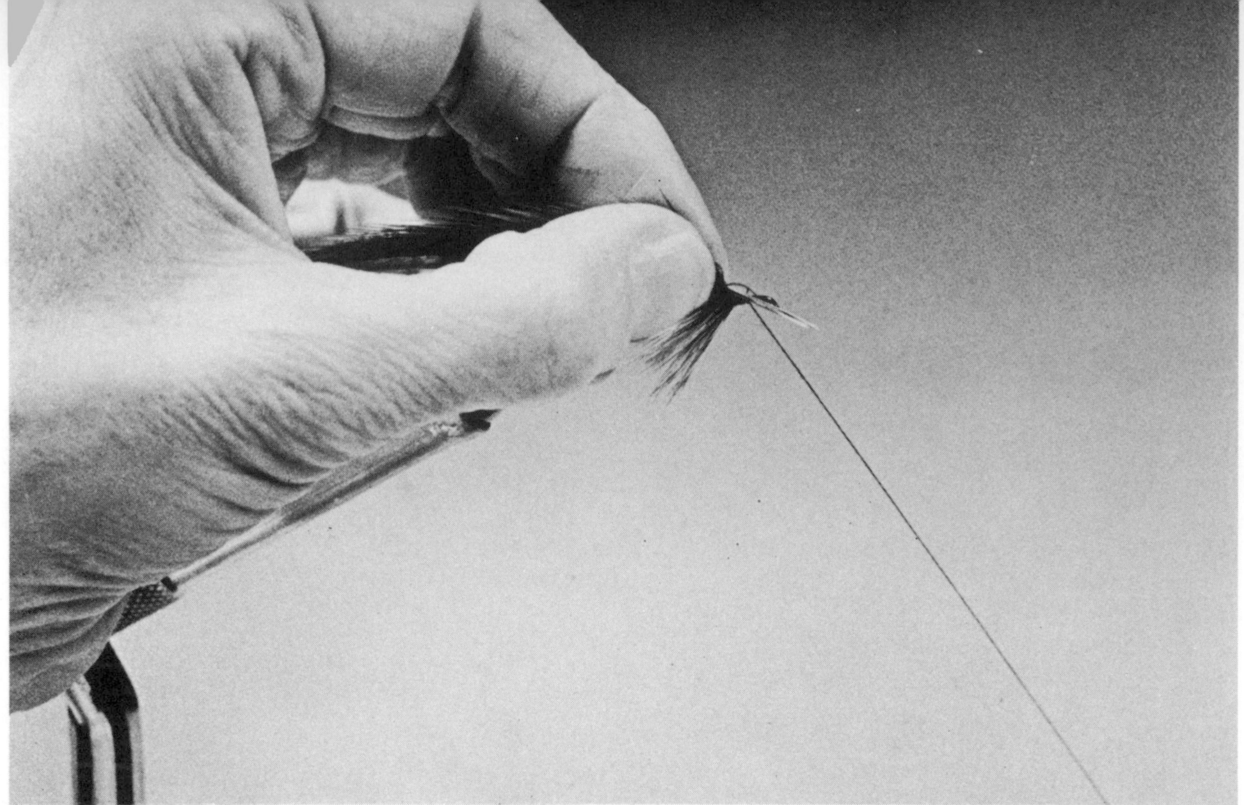

11. Held firmly in the left hand, stripped quills extending beyond the eye, all four feathers comprising the wing have been tied on together in front of the throat.

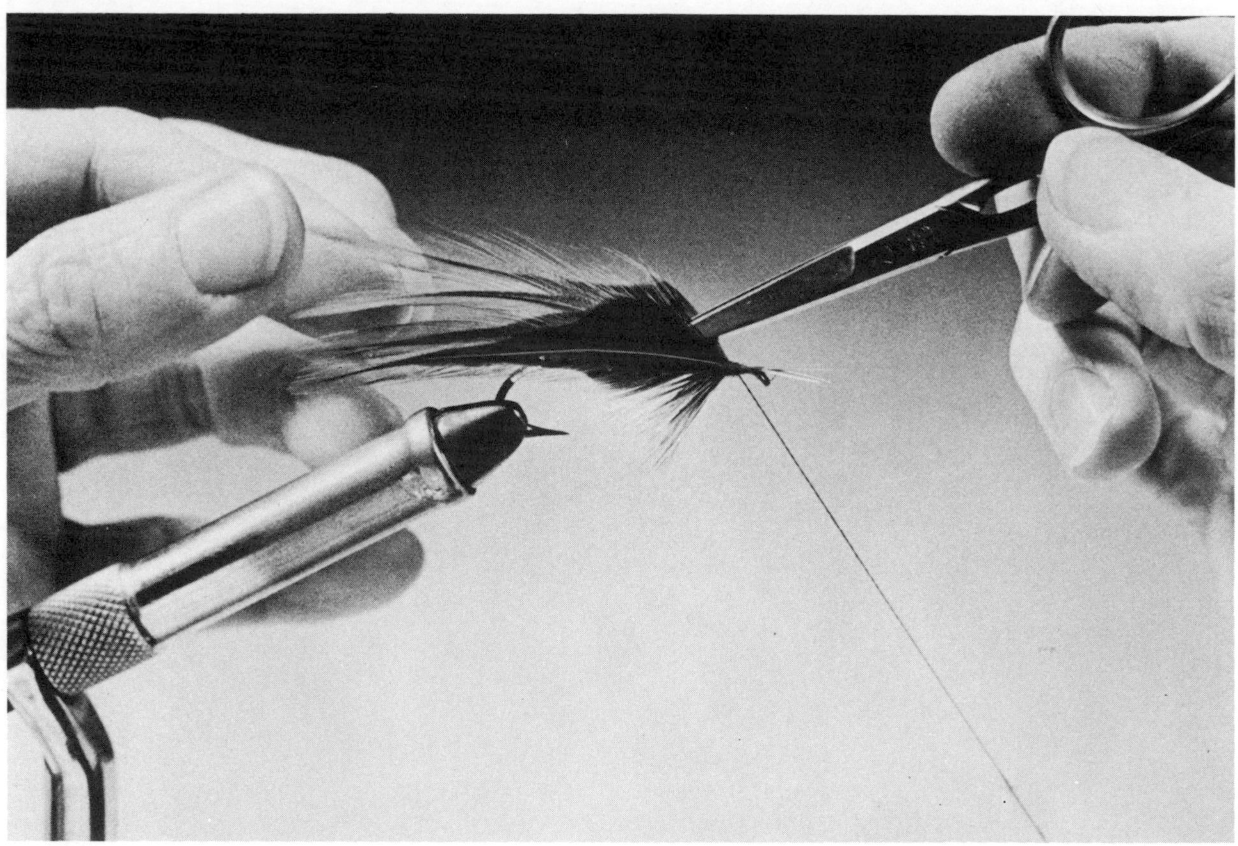

12. Wings, firmly attached, appear as one, but all four feathers are there.

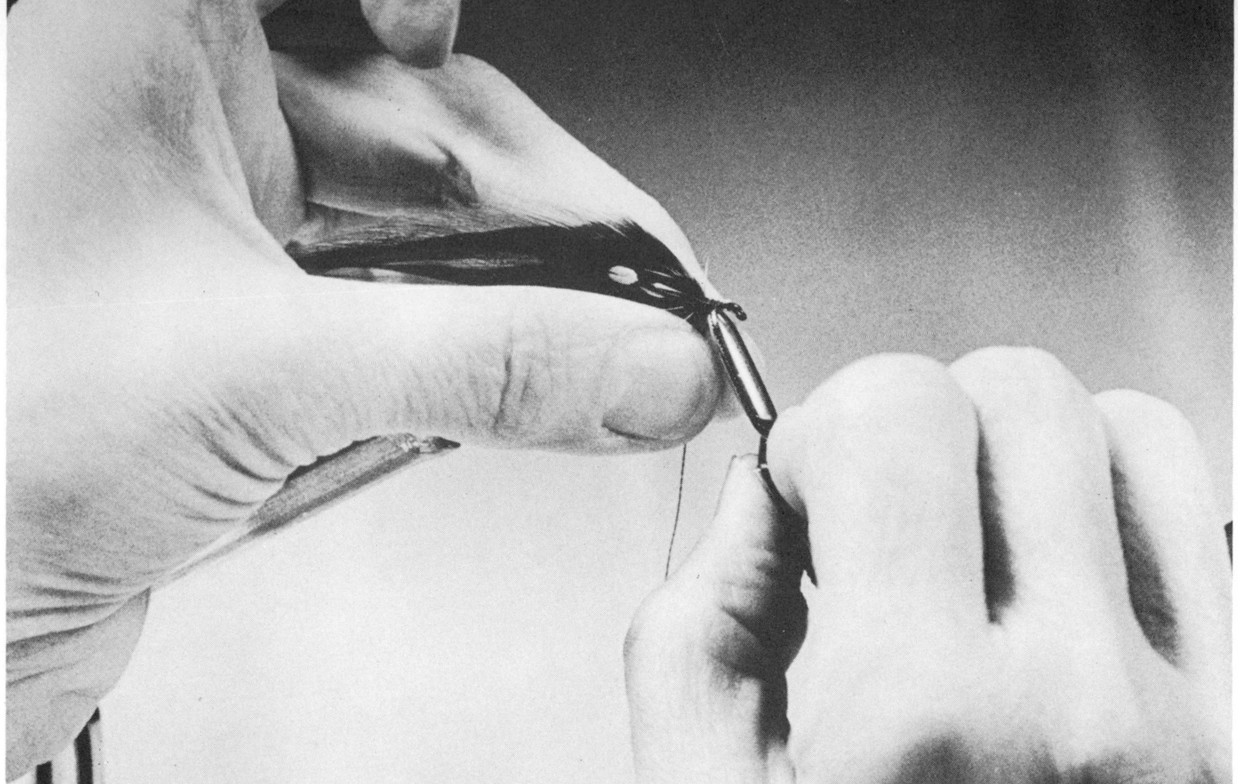

13. The extending quills have been laid back on each side of the hook, toward the throat, and caught there with the tying thread, securely locking the wings in place. Small eye feathers from jungle-fowl cape have been added, one on each side. If one of these feathers does not lie flat against the wing, it can be coaxed into position by gripping its quill with a hackle plier and twisting gently.

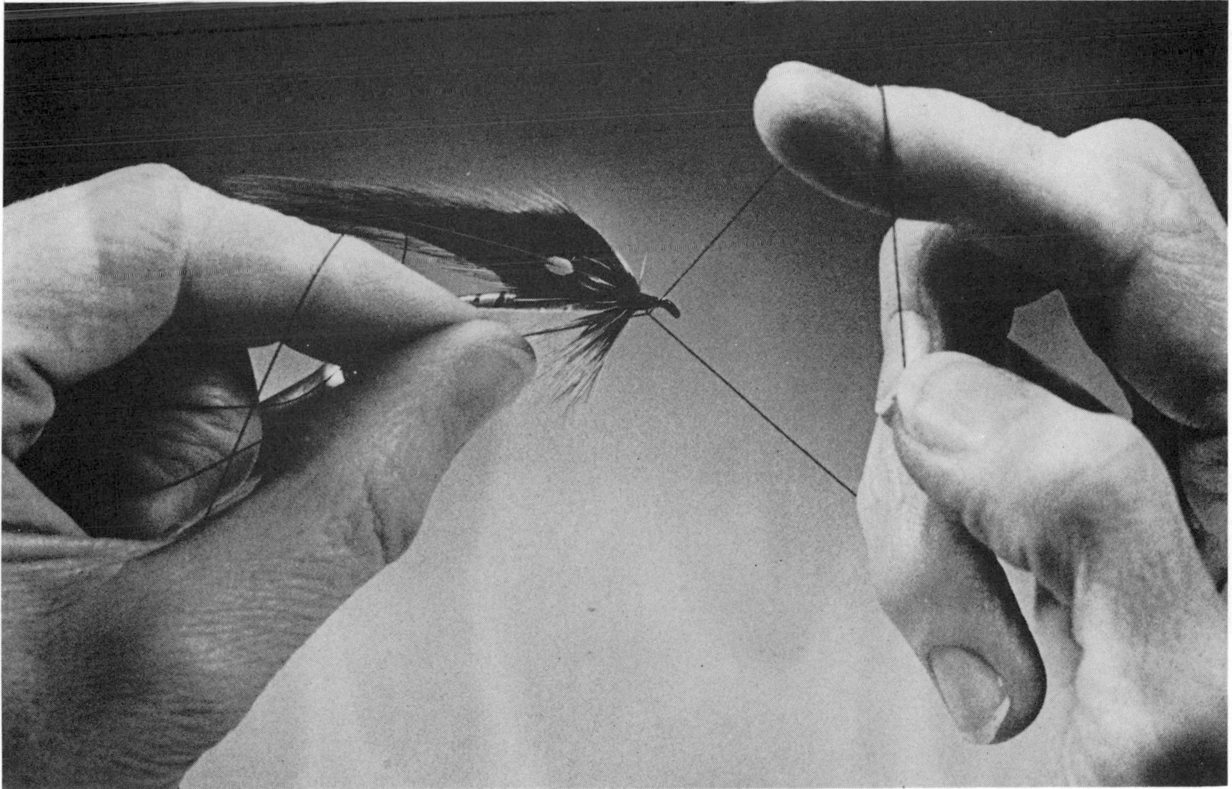

14. The quill is then tied back, as the wing quills were, and the ends of all carefully clipped away. The fly is now ready for the wrap knot, to complete the tying.

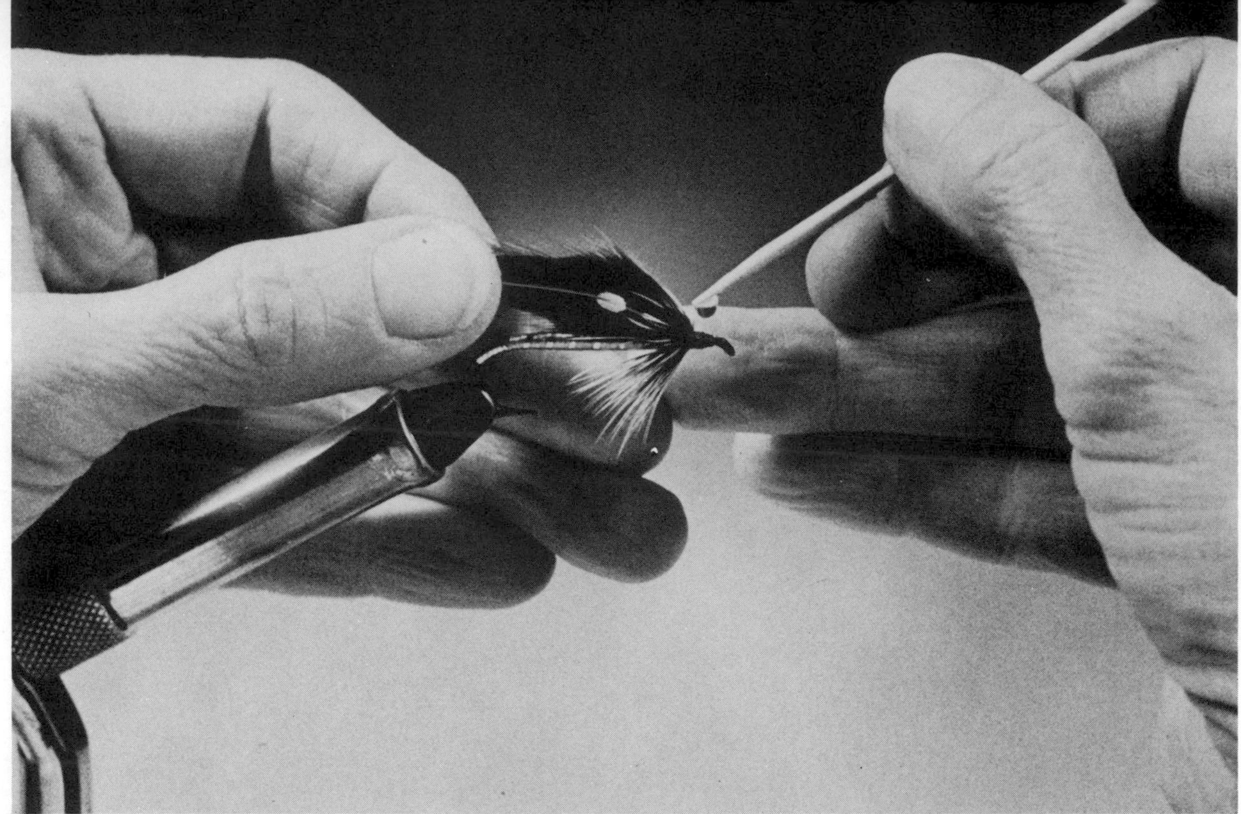

15. A drop of clear, waterproof lacquer applied to the head has a twofold purpose—to protect the tying thread and to give the fly a "finished" appearance. A second coat of lacquer applied after the first has thoroughly dried will make the head practically indestructible.

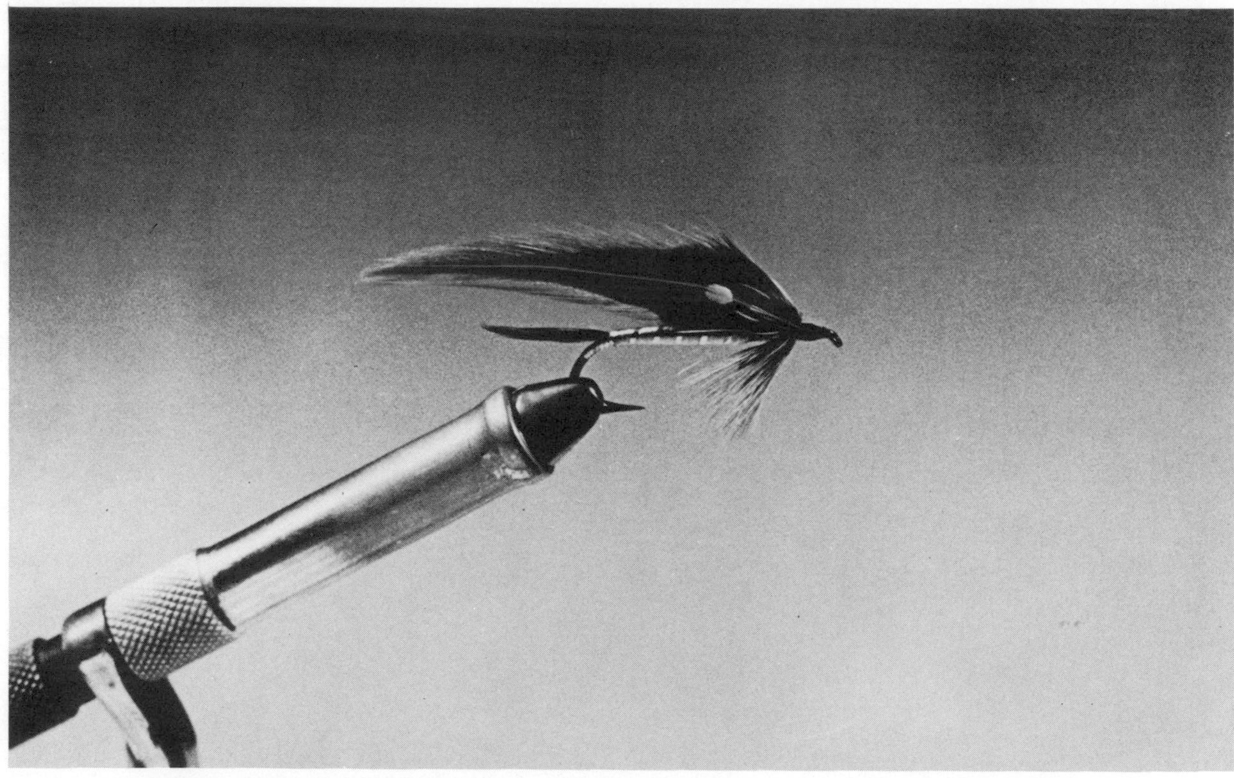

16. The finished fly. Western tying of this pattern could elevate the wing a bit more, perhaps using a weighted body. An eastern version might use hackle with less web to lie parallel with the body, showing no space between.

## HAIRWING STREAMER

*Ambrose Bucktail*

Tag: oval gold tinsel
Tail: white and red deertail hair
Body: yellow chenille
Rib: oval gold tinsel
Hackle: red under black
Wing: white under natural dark-brown deertail hair

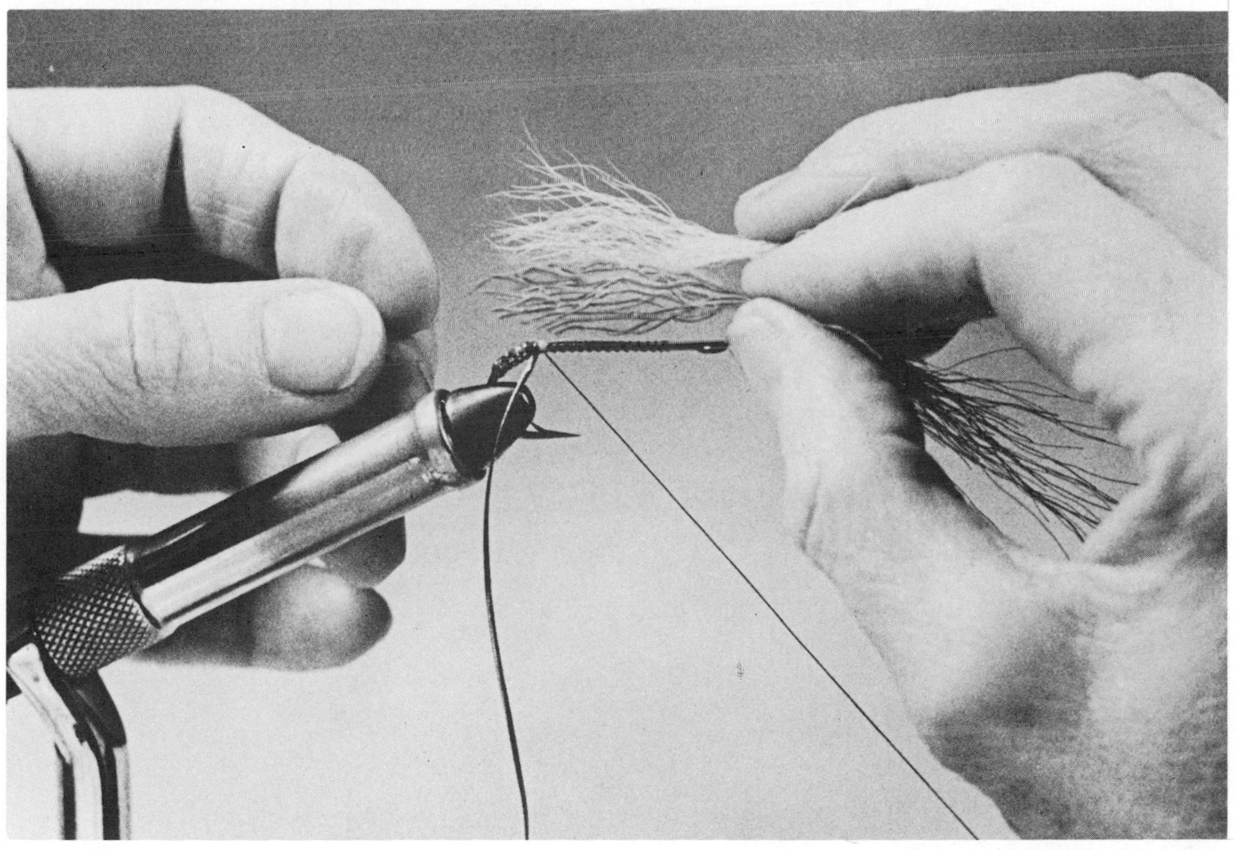

1. Tying thread has been attached to the hook and wound in even turns back to a point just above the barb, where oval gold tinsel has been tied in and a tag made. Tinsel enough for the rib remains hanging. A small amount of white deertail hair, and a small amount dyed bright red, are measured against the hook for length. The natural ends of hair have been sorted and made even to give a neat appearance.

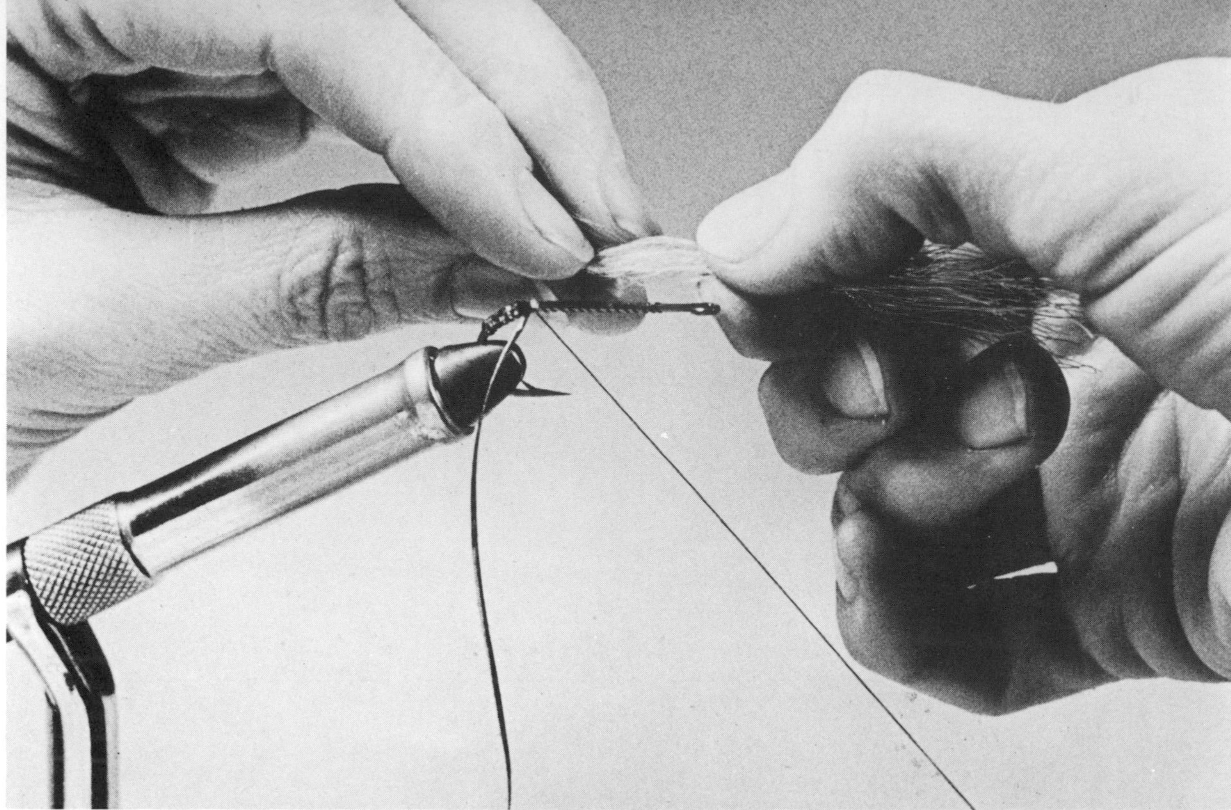

2. The hairs of two colors are not mixed together—the tuft of red is *rolled* carefully *around* the tuft of white, distributing the red hair as evenly as possible around the white center.

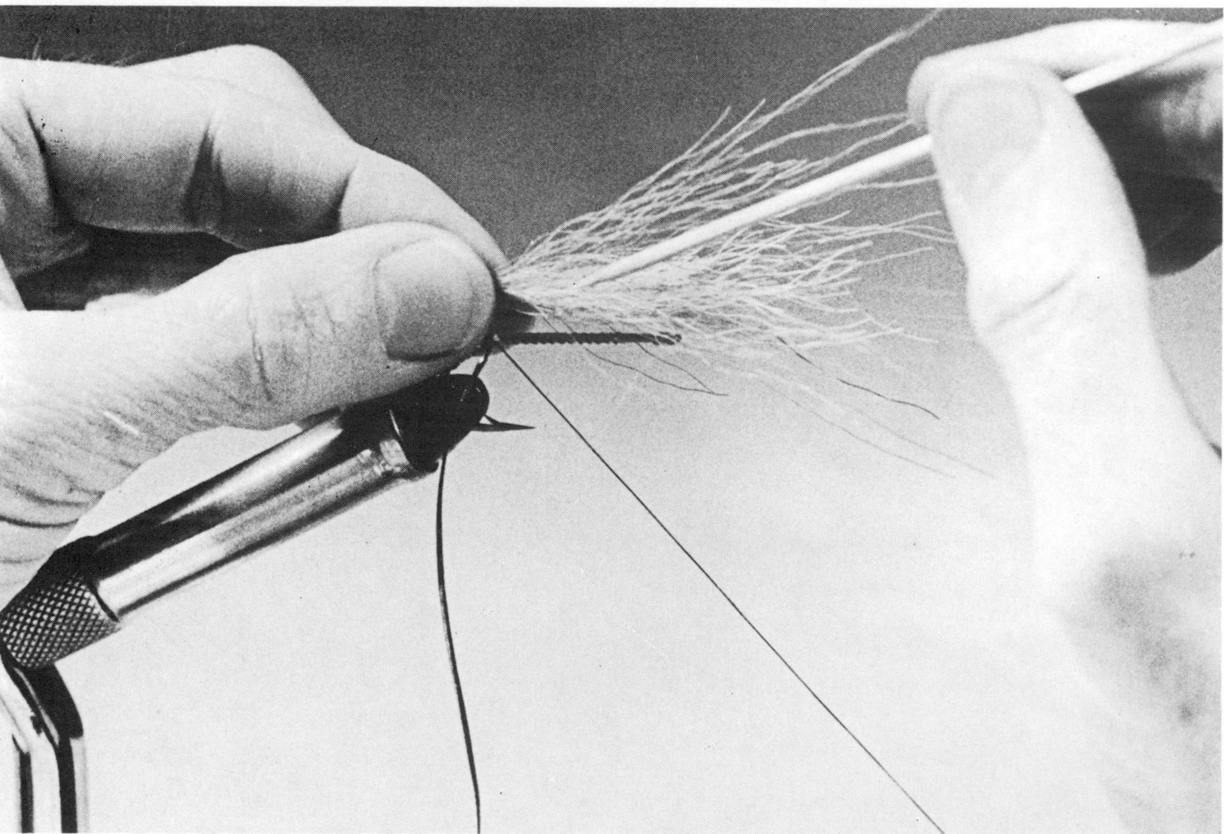

3. With the tail held in position for tying on, brush lacquer through the excess hair, which will be bound down on the hook to form a firm base for the chenille body. Before the lacquered hair has had time to dry, the tail is tied on, and a turn of tying thread under and around the hair will secure it.

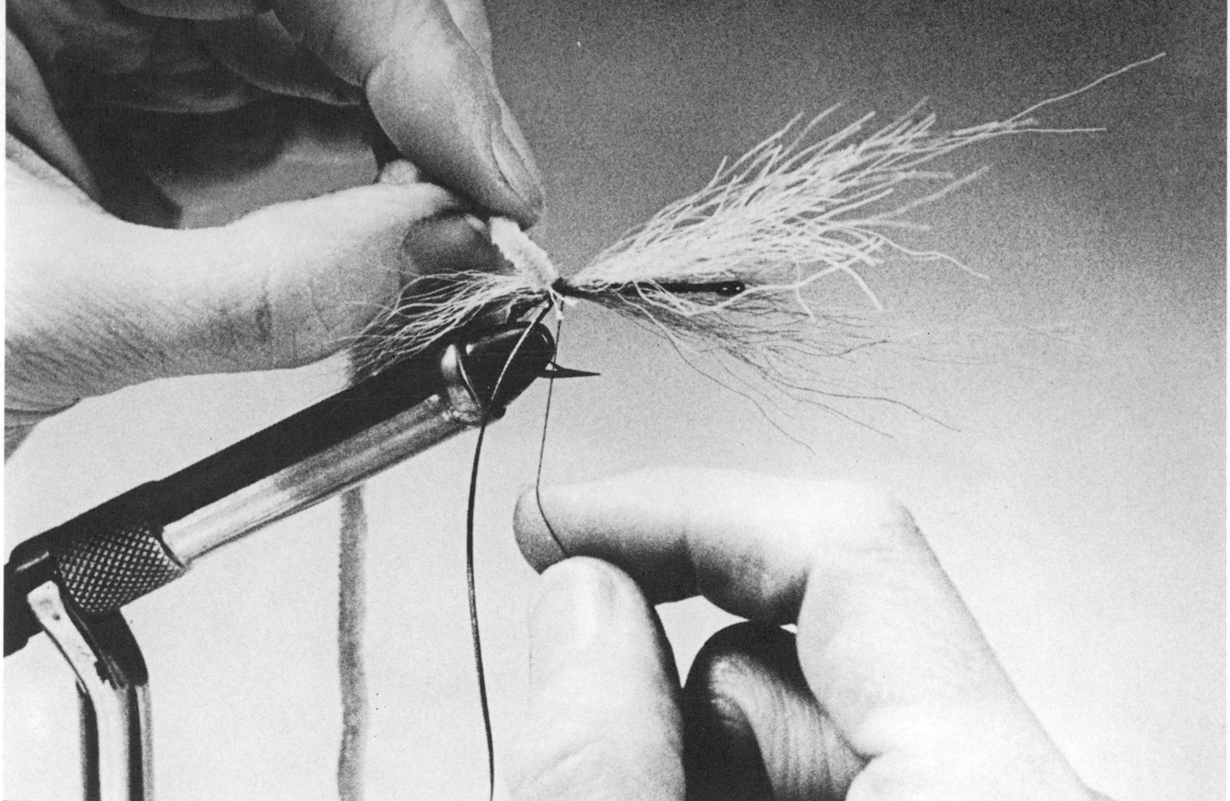

4. Chenille for the body (stripped to expose its thread core, where it will be caught by the tying thread) is tied in quickly.

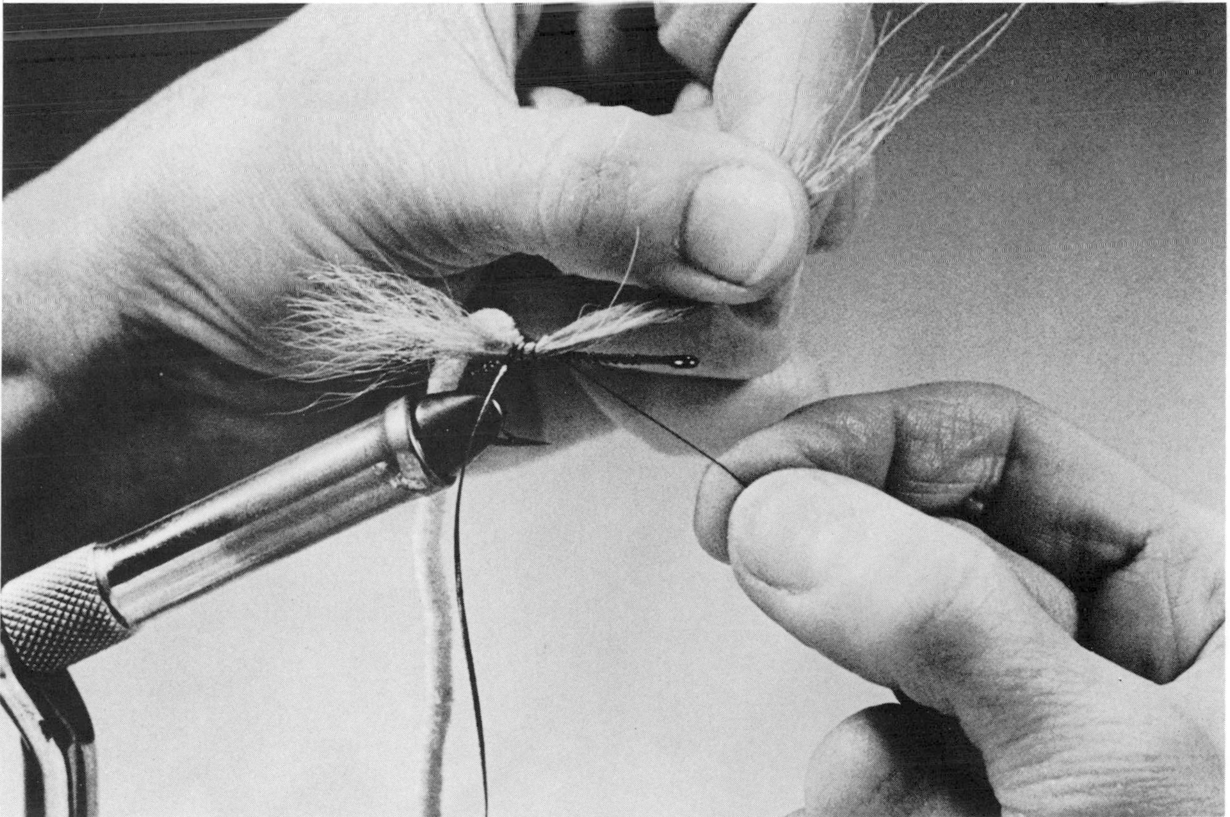

5. The lacquered hair is gathered together and held along the top of the hook shank while it is bound there with evenly spaced turns of the tying thread.

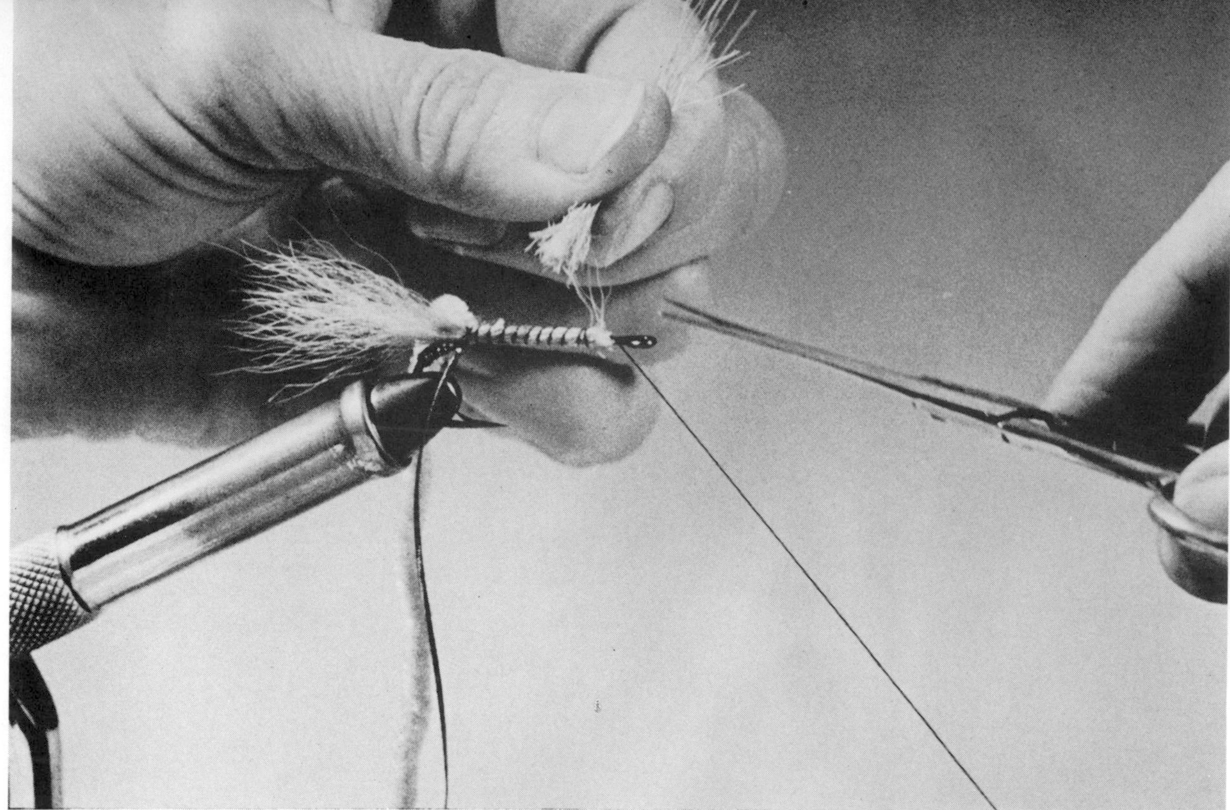

6. The excess hair is now removed, leaving the cut ends neatly tapering to the hook shank. More hair must be clipped away here to achieve this.

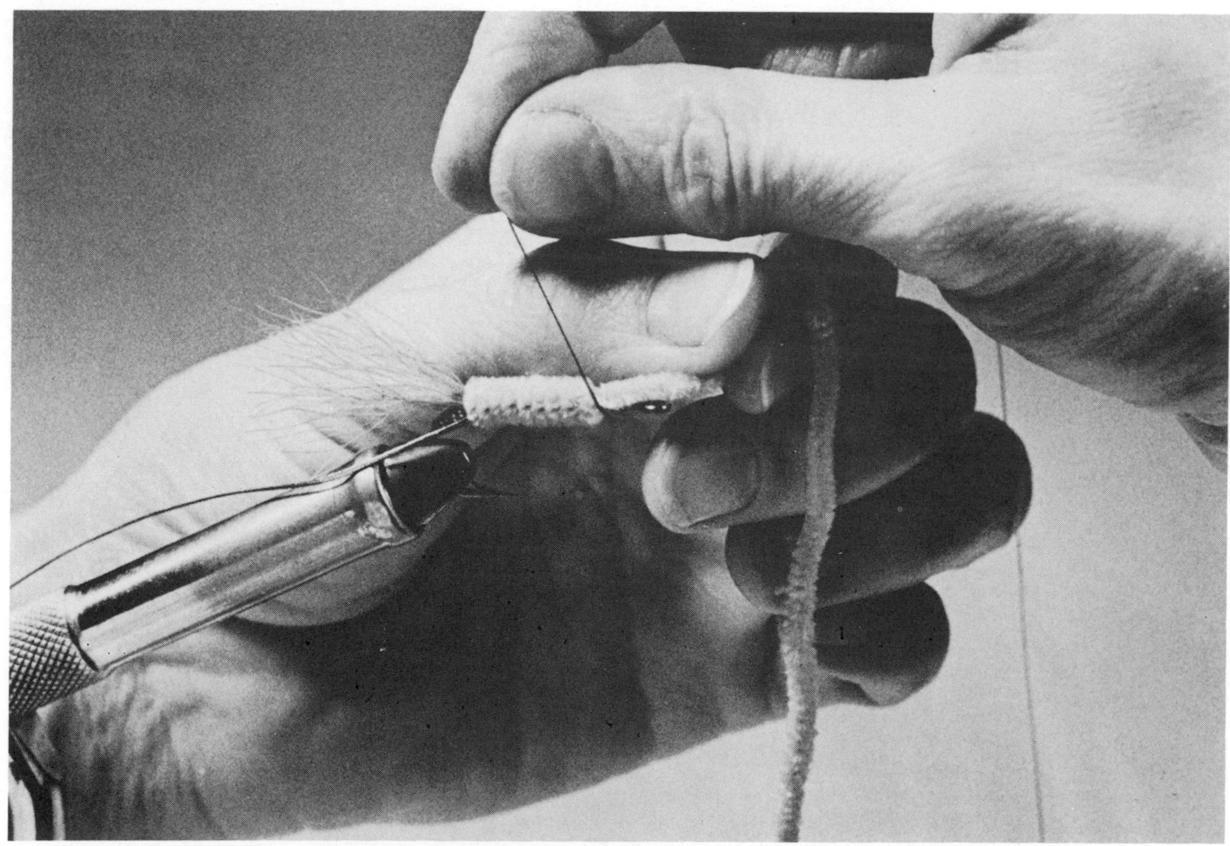

7. Chenille is wound over the hair beneath, and secured with the tying thread. The lacquered hair base adds somewhat to the weight and will help the fly sink.

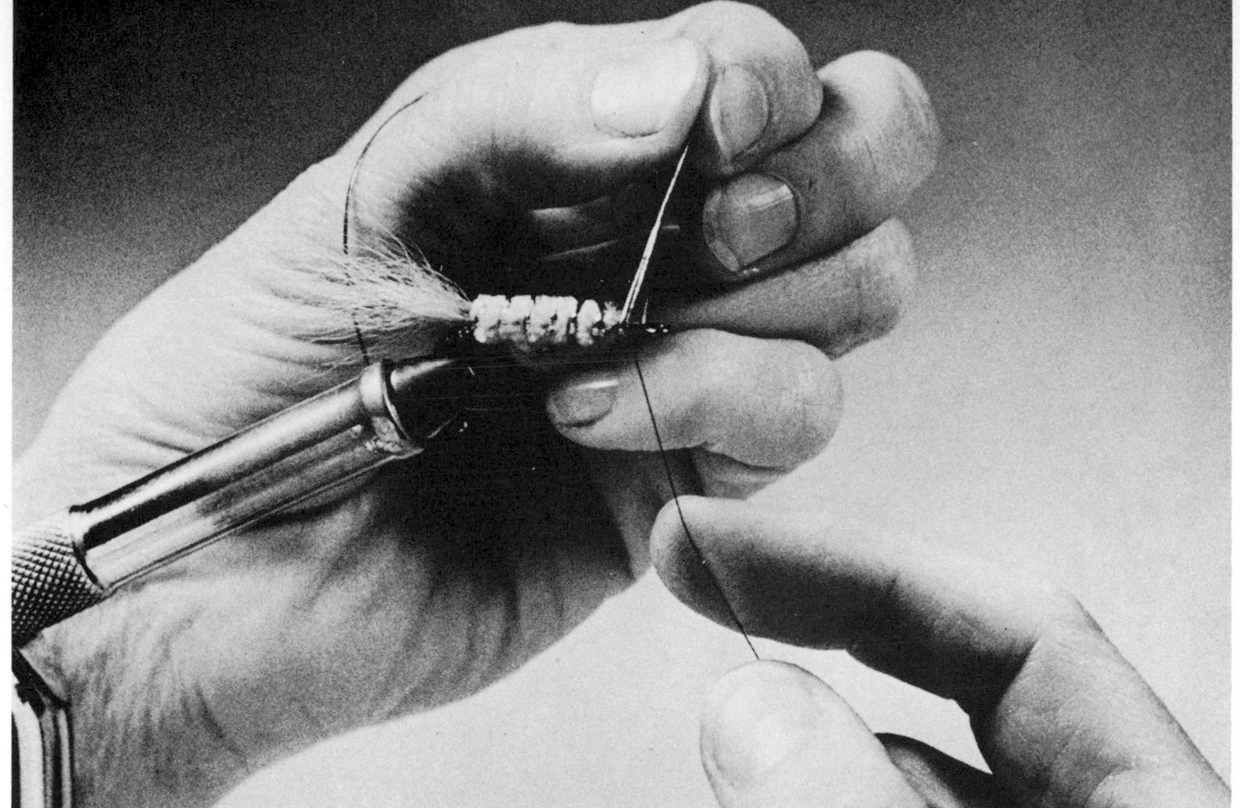

8. Oval tinsel is spaced in even turns along the body and should lie flat against it. Tinsel should be kept snug over its core of threads while being wound on so that the white center will not show through.

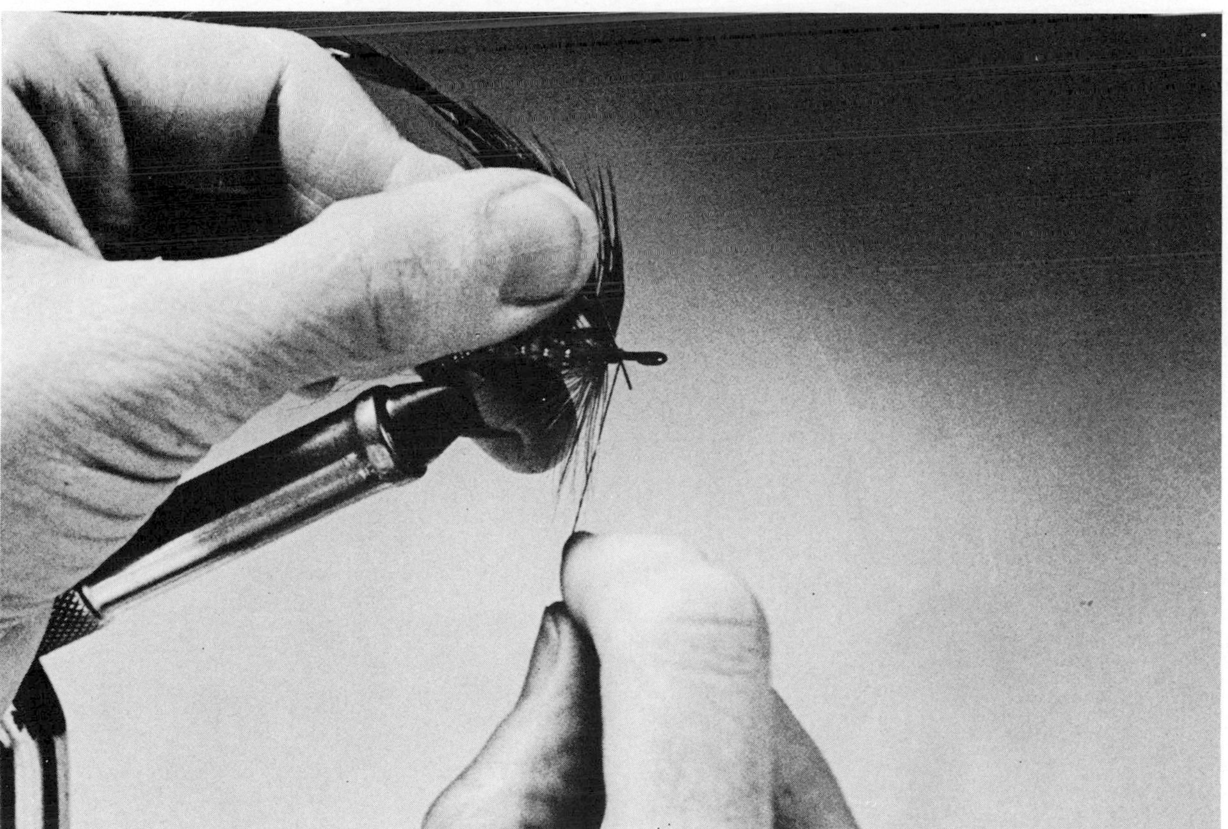

9. A few turns of fairly webby hackle dyed bright red, and long enough to reach approximately to the hook barb, have been tied on. A black hackle is tied in front of it.

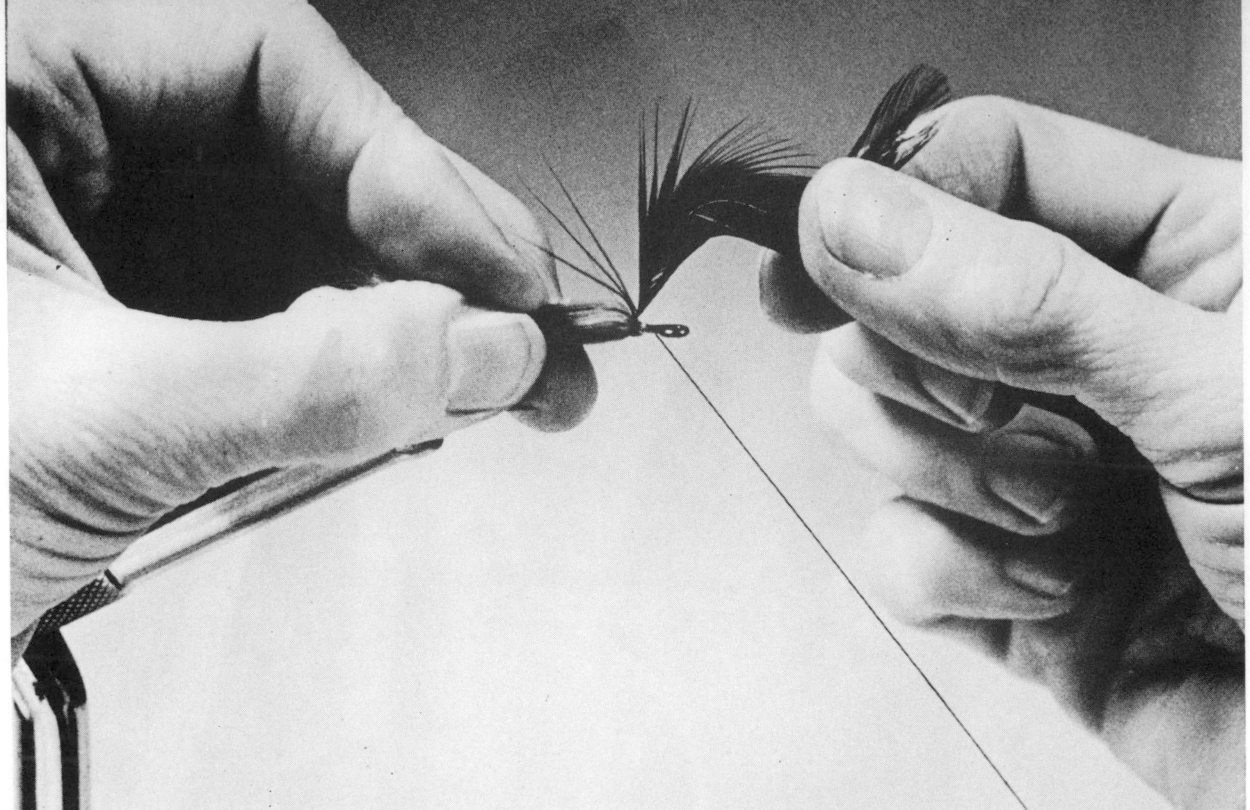

10. The red hackle is held out of the way of each turn of black hackle.

11. A protective finger holds the hackle and keeps it from unwinding when the hackle must pass from one hand to the other.

12. A tuft of white deertail hair is measured against the body for length. (Some prefer to have this wing extend beyond the tail.)

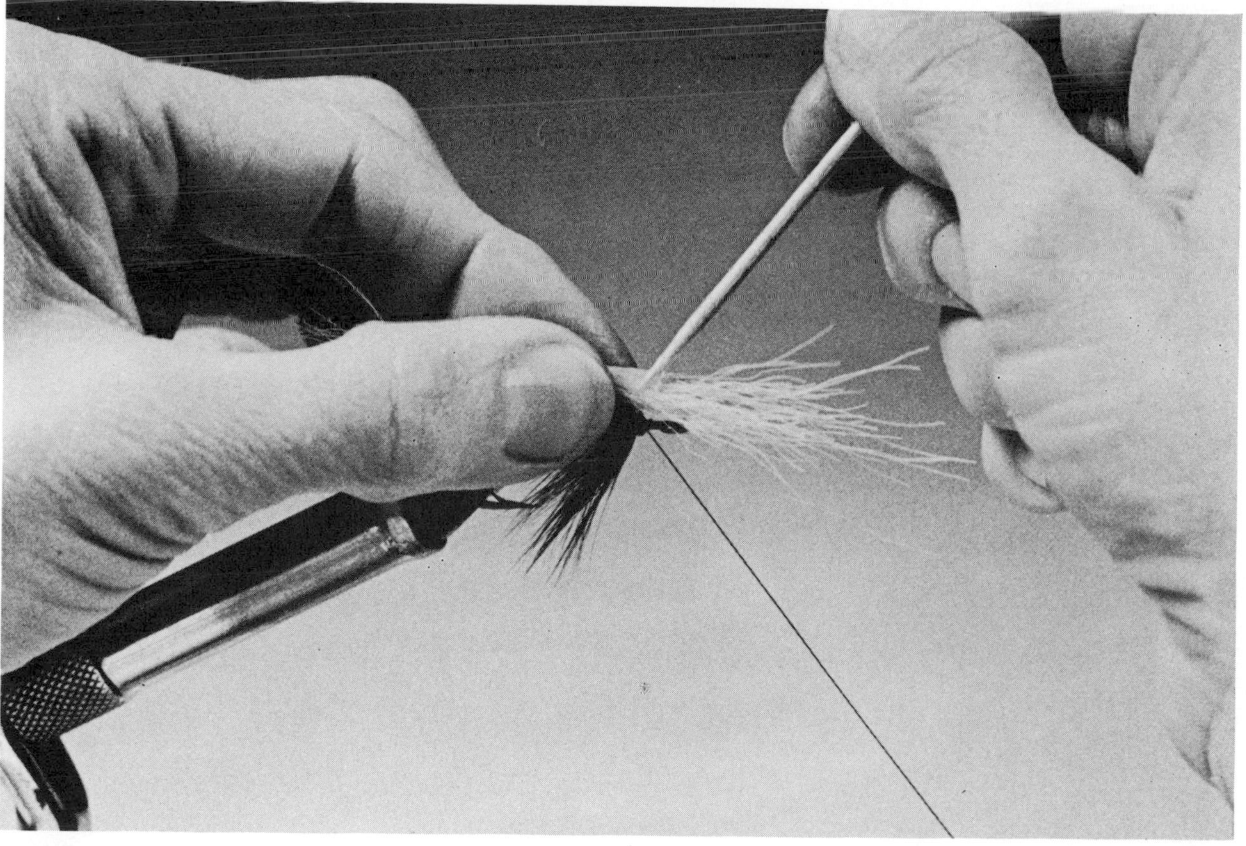

13. Now a drop of lacquer is applied to the hair wing before tying it into position.

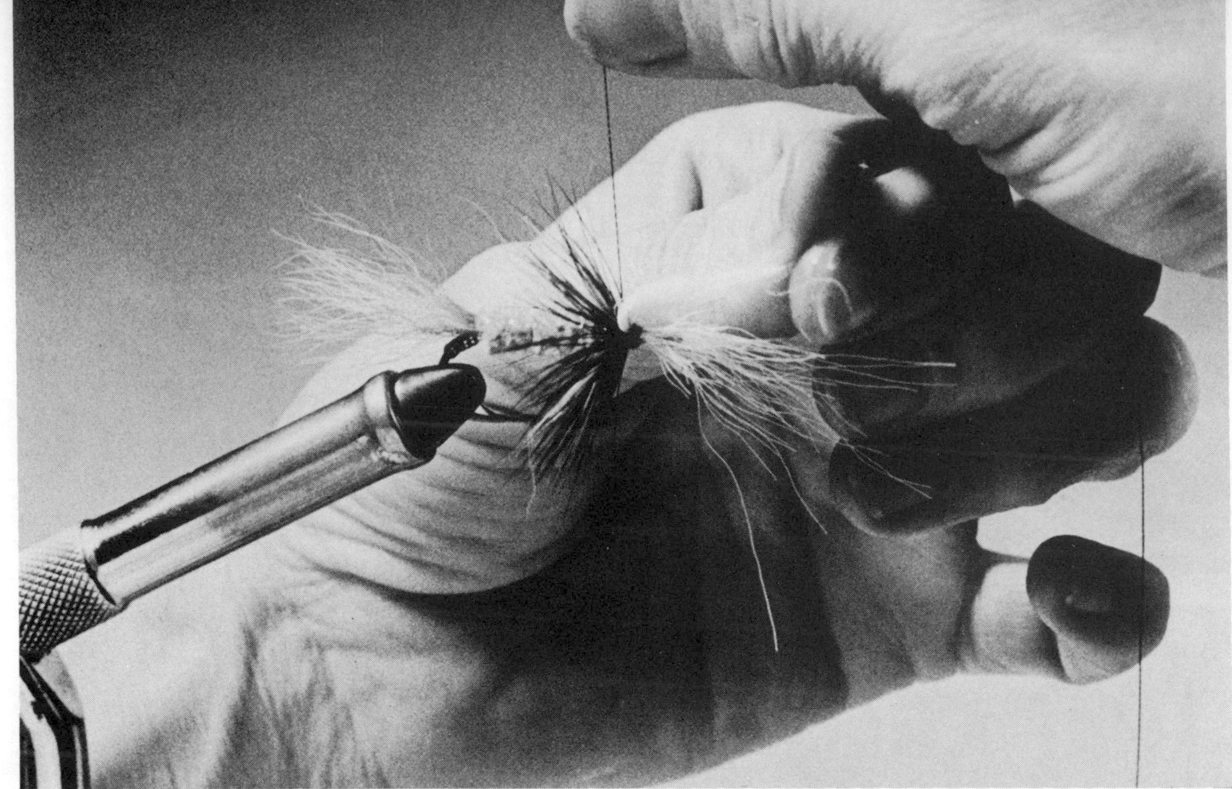

14. Tying thread is passed behind the white wing and around it. Do not be afraid to hold the hair far forward to force taut thread down as close as possible to base of hair next to hook.

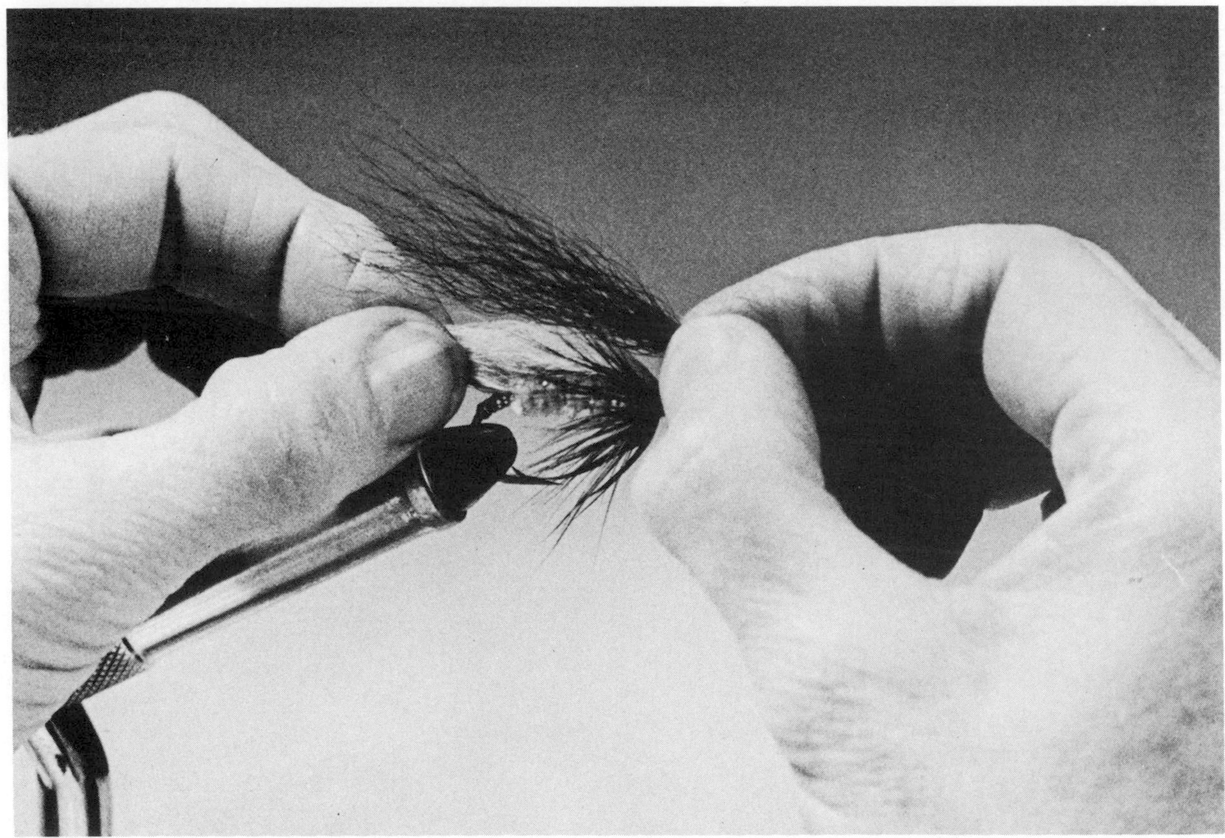

15. Natural, dark-brown hair from back of deer tail is measured against white wing for correct length, tied in on top of white wing and secured.

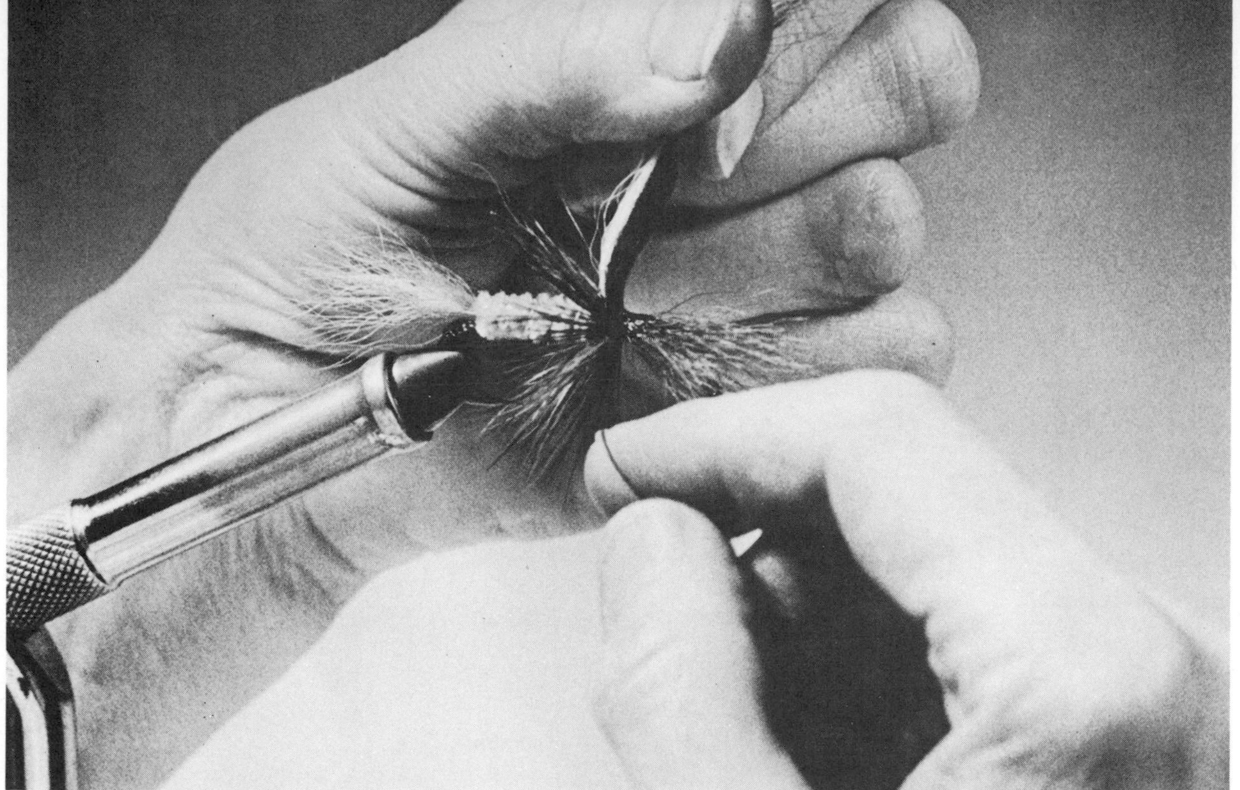

16. The thread is passed behind both tufts of hair and around them. Excess hair will be clipped away, tapering it back from the hook eye.

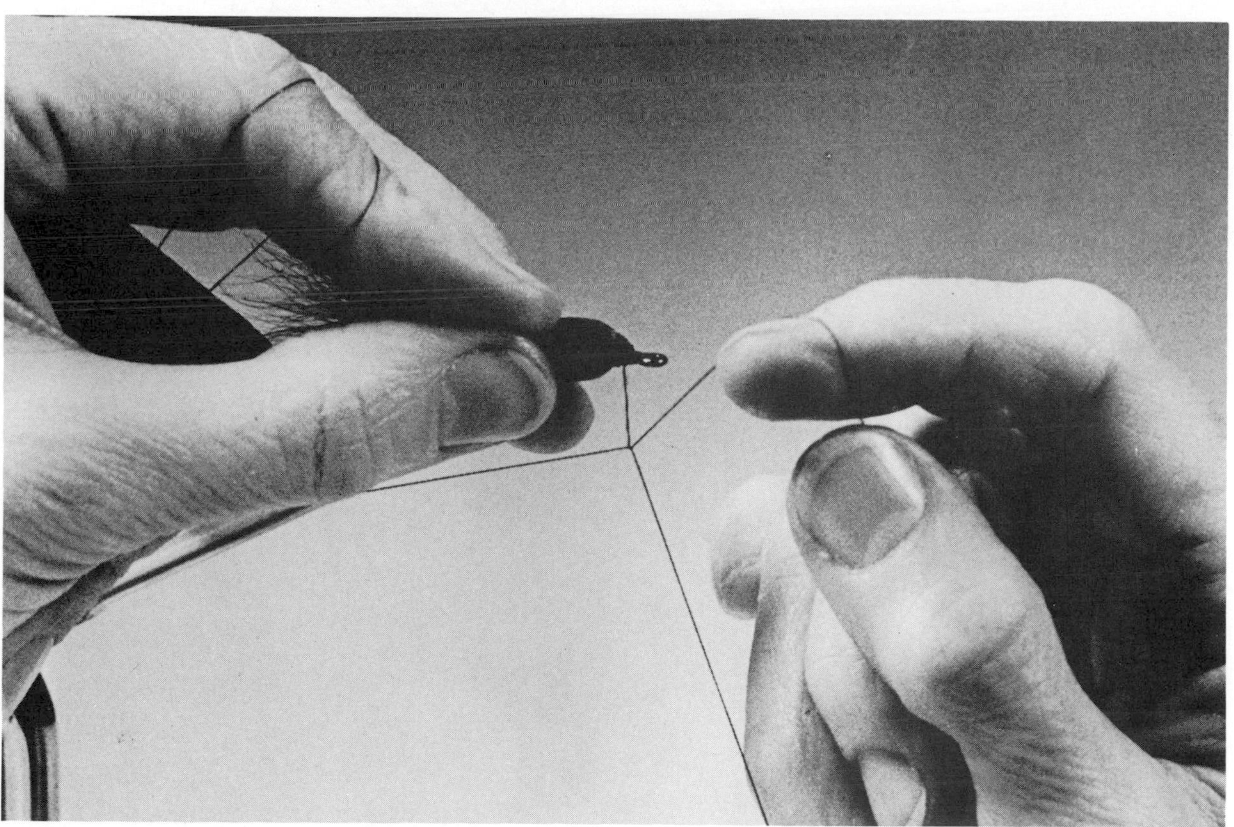

17. With the clipped ends bound smoothly to the hook, the fly is ready for the finishing wrap knot. All the hair and hackle, as well as the free end of tying thread is held out of the way with the left hand, leaving no stray ends to interfere with the wrap knot.

18. A protective finger prevents the thread from slipping as it is being drawn through its wrapped cover. When the loop vanishes entirely and the thread is pulled tight, the free end of thread is clipped away, close to the winding.

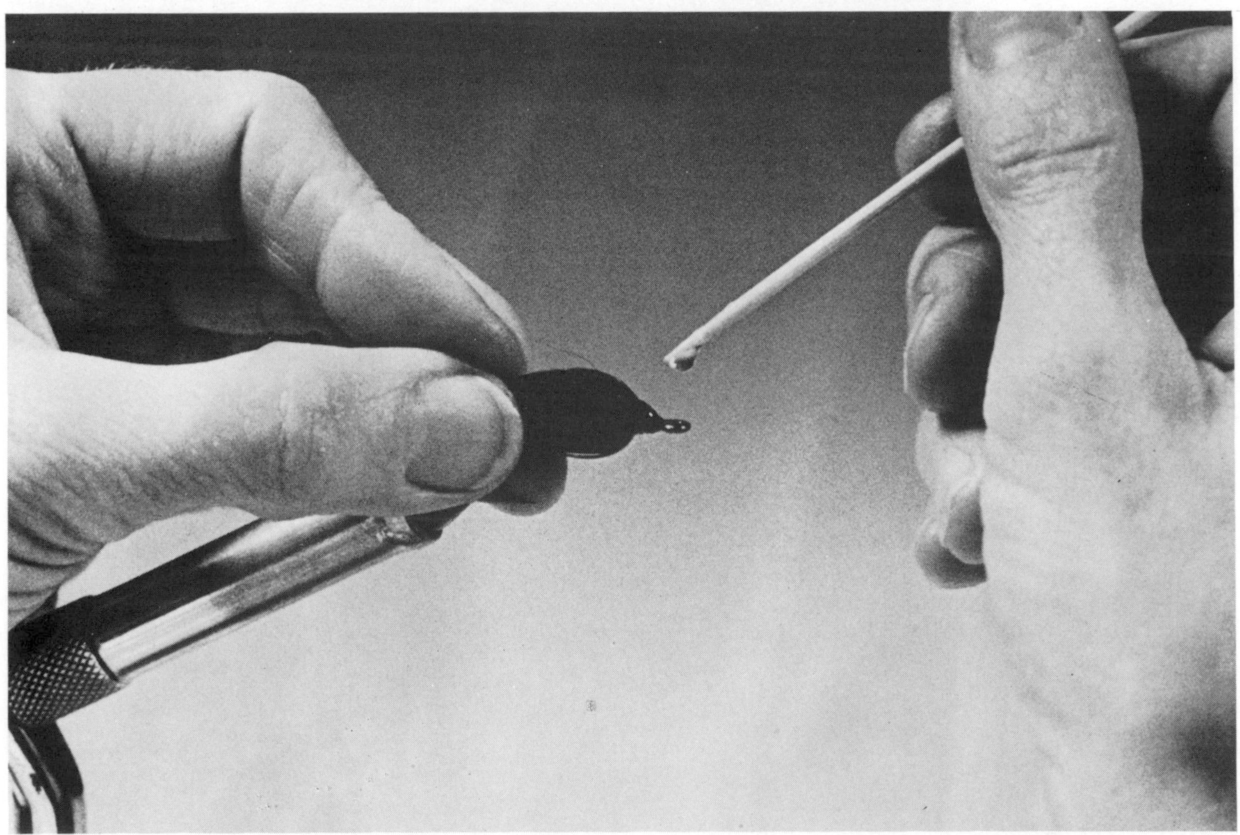

19. All hair and hackle is held away from the head as the lacquer is being applied. When dry, a touch of red lacquer will be the finishing coat.

20. The hair is fluffy when freshly tied. In the water, however, when well soaked, the hair will stream back, close to the body, and will undulate as it is worked through the water by rod action or water current. Since it is tied on a ringed-eye hook, it can be used with or without a spinner.

## THE BASS FLY

Flies suitable for bass-fishing are many—and the type to choose may be dictated by the preference of the angler or the popularity of any pattern in the area where he prefers to fish.

Some waters are particularly suited for trolling, having submerged reefs and sand bars; others with reedy and wooded shores may be excellent for a tantalizing floating lure. Rocky shores, grassy overhangs, or weed beds not far below the surface are also environments for the high-riding surface fly. They can be equally well fished with a sunken fly skillfully manipulated over a rocky ledge or over a sunken log. The temperament and pleasure of the angler will decide "Which fly?"

Many trout-fly patterns greatly enlarged make excellent flies for bass-fishing, and perhaps it would be safe to say that any trout fly of a size large enough to entice a bass would be a good fly to use—with the one proviso that the colors chosen be acceptable in that area. For many bass-fishermen have found that colors do play an important part in the success of their fishing, and, whereas a predominantly yellow fly may work well in one body of water, orange or green may do better elsewhere. The fact may remain debatable, but some color combinations do seem to be more effective on certain lakes than on others. It is left to each fisherman to learn from kindred anglers which is best, or to experiment until he finds which type of fly produces the best results for him. This is one of the many joys of fishing.

One of the nicest dry flies for bass-fishing is the Bubble Pup, a buoyant, airy fly, easily cast and maneuverable because of the frill, or ruff, of deer body-hair that encircles the hook completely, making it almost weedless. It can be cast into reeds and lily pads where it will light gently and respond easily to being coaxed into water openings among them. Its construction is simple and quite durable, and may be made in any color combination desirable. With the front of its hair body stiffened, the little Bubble Pup can be made to "bubble," or gurgle, by a gentle twitch of the rod tip, while riding high at the end of a long cast.

---

*The Bubble Pup*

Tail: black webby hackles
Body: deer body-hair dyed yellow

This simple fly consists of a feather tail, hair "hackle," and trimmed hair body.

---

1. A matched pair of webbed feathers, short, tapered, curving up and outward (away from each other), has been tied on the hook, well forward of the hook point. A wrap knot should be used here, over the feather quills.

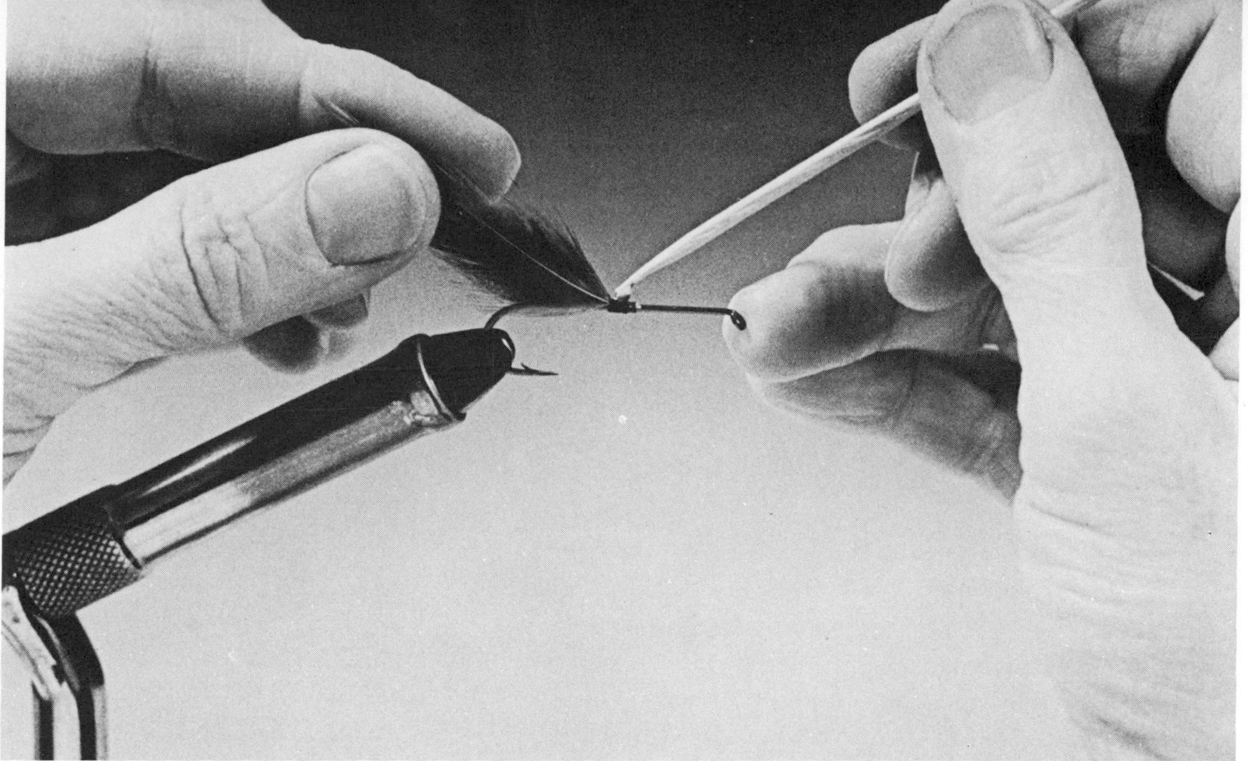

2. When several flies of the same type are to be made at one time, all the tails may be tied on the hooks, lacquered, and permitted to dry thoroughly before tying on the deer hair.

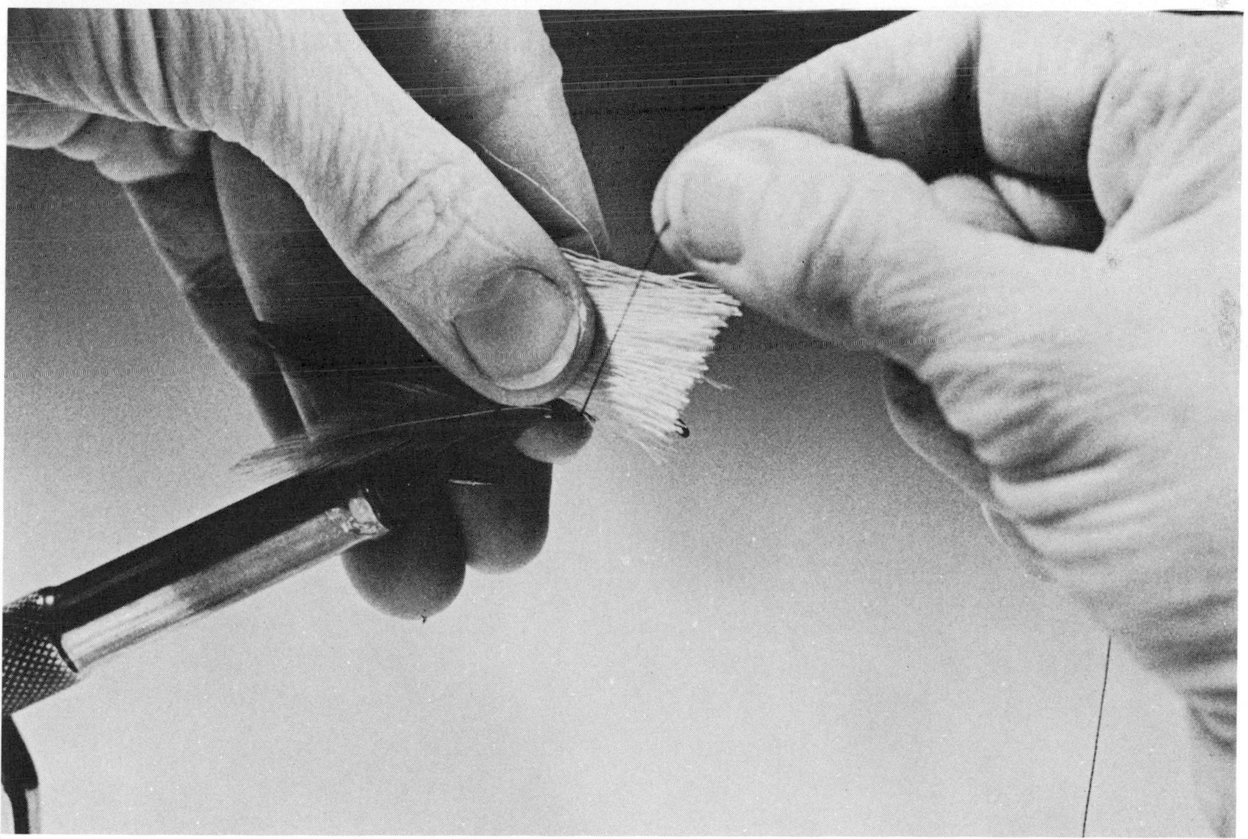

3. The tying thread is attached where the wrap knot ends. A small bunch of body-hair is cut and the natural tips are held back in the fingers, permitting about half an inch of hair to be laid against the hook for tying on.

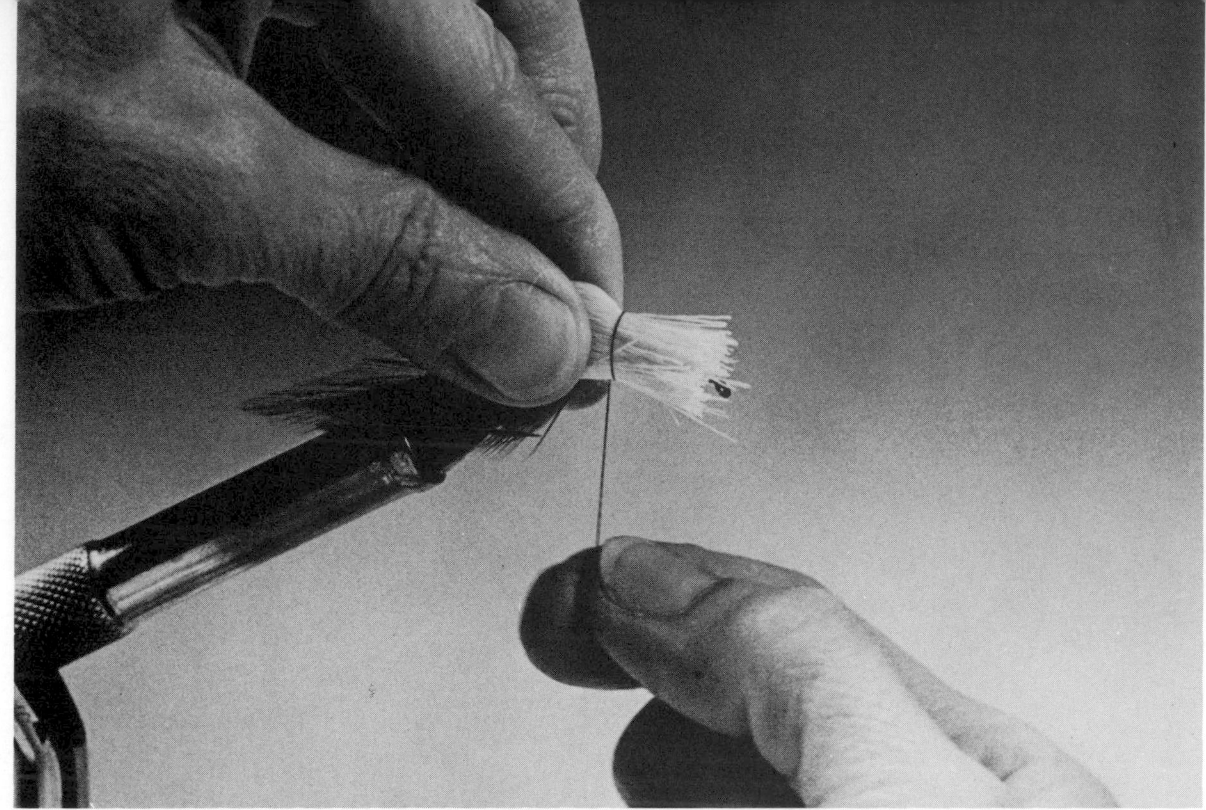

4. Ease the hair around the hook, with the tying thread always taut. The longer part of the hair with its tapered ends is kept arching over the tail and hook.

5. As the taut thread crushes the deer hair to the hook, the short ends will flare up in front.

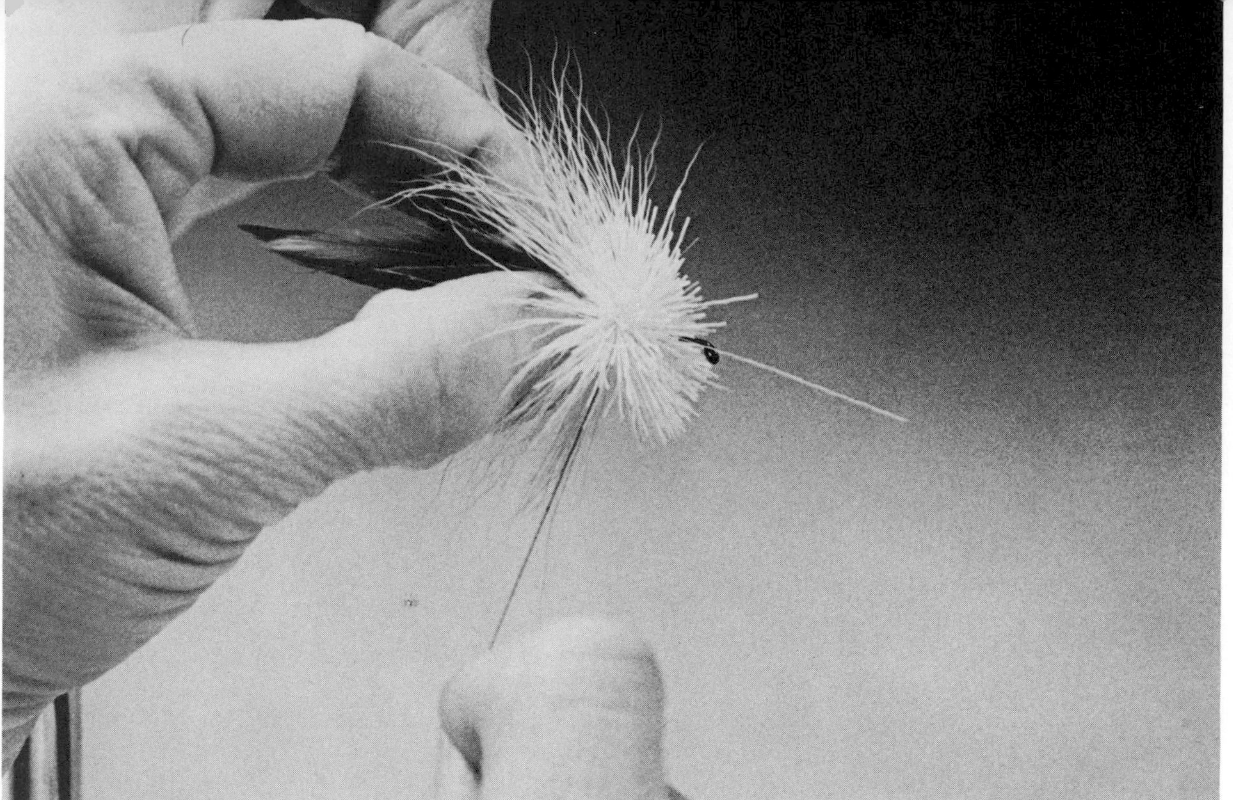

6. Two or three turns of thread should be zigzagged tightly through this first section to secure it.

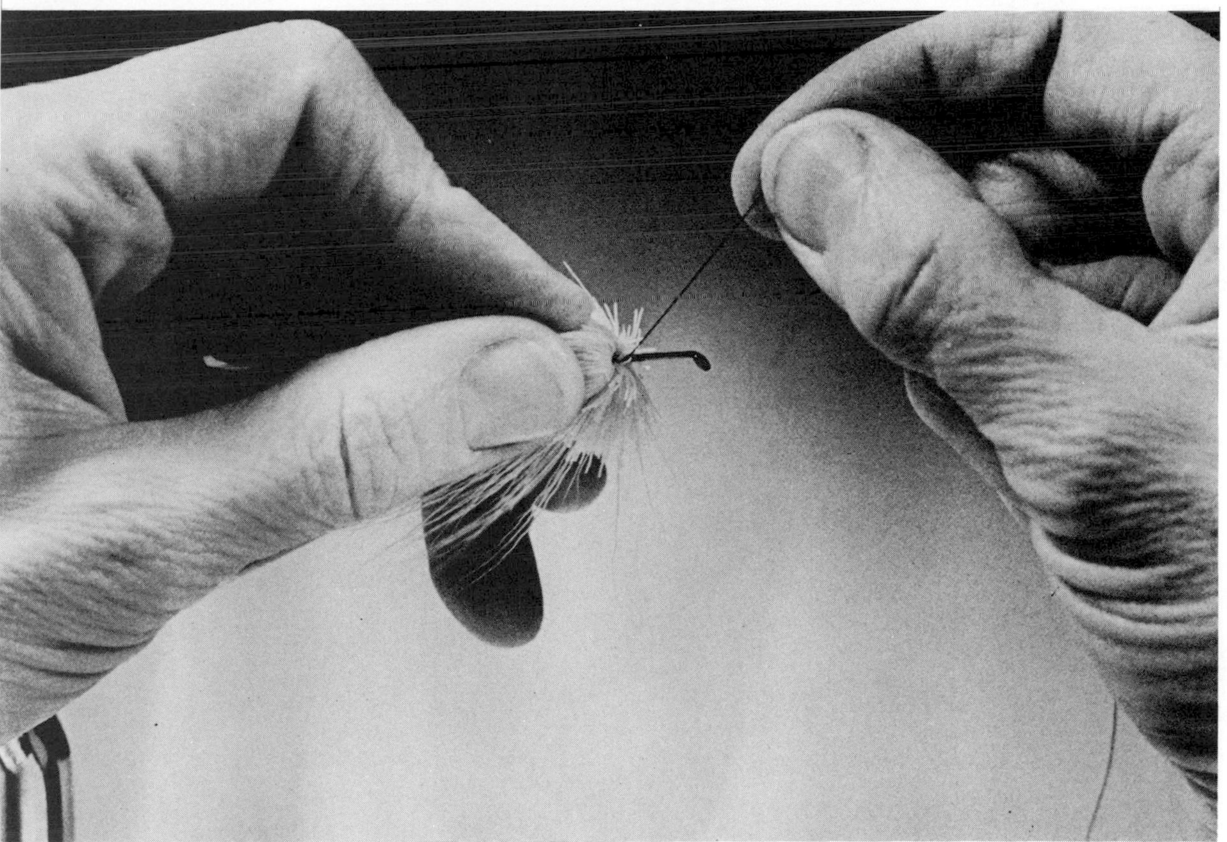

7. The short ends are now brushed back with the fingers and held, so that the tying thread may be brought through the hair and out onto the hook as close to the base of the hair as possible.

8. In order to keep the longer hair out of the way while tying, it is smoothed back over the tail.

9. The next section of hair is cut short. It is approximately an inch in length, with the tapered ends trimmed away, and is tied on as close as possible to the first. Tying thread is zigzagged through area where sections meet. In order to form a tightly packed body, continue to add small sections of the short hair and force them together as close as possible, leaving just enough space behind the eye of the hook for the head.

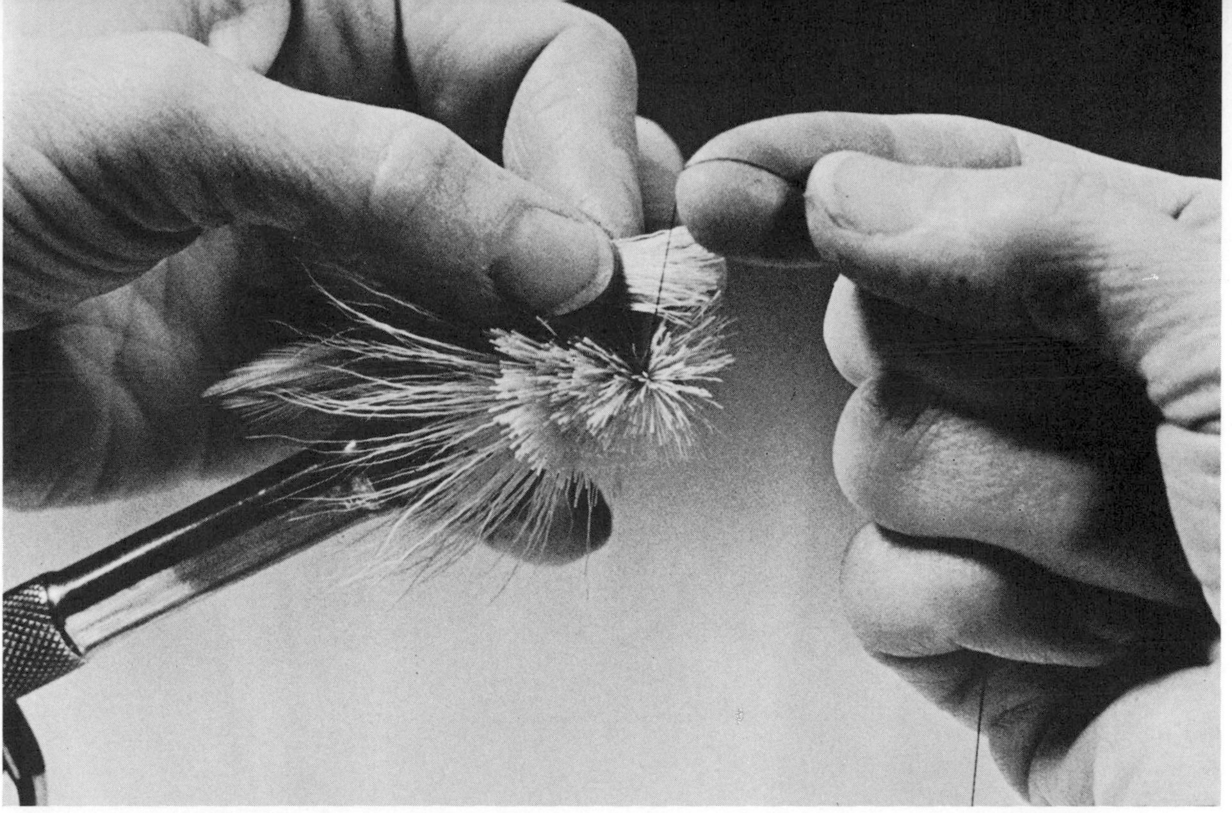

10. Now tie one more section of short hair on *top* of the last section, a space having been made for it by parting the hair with a finger and laying the short hair in the part. This hair will not be distributed around the hook but kept entirely on top.

11. The taut thread is zigzagged through the hair as before. This final section is added to cause the hair above the hook to extend forward over the eye of the hook.

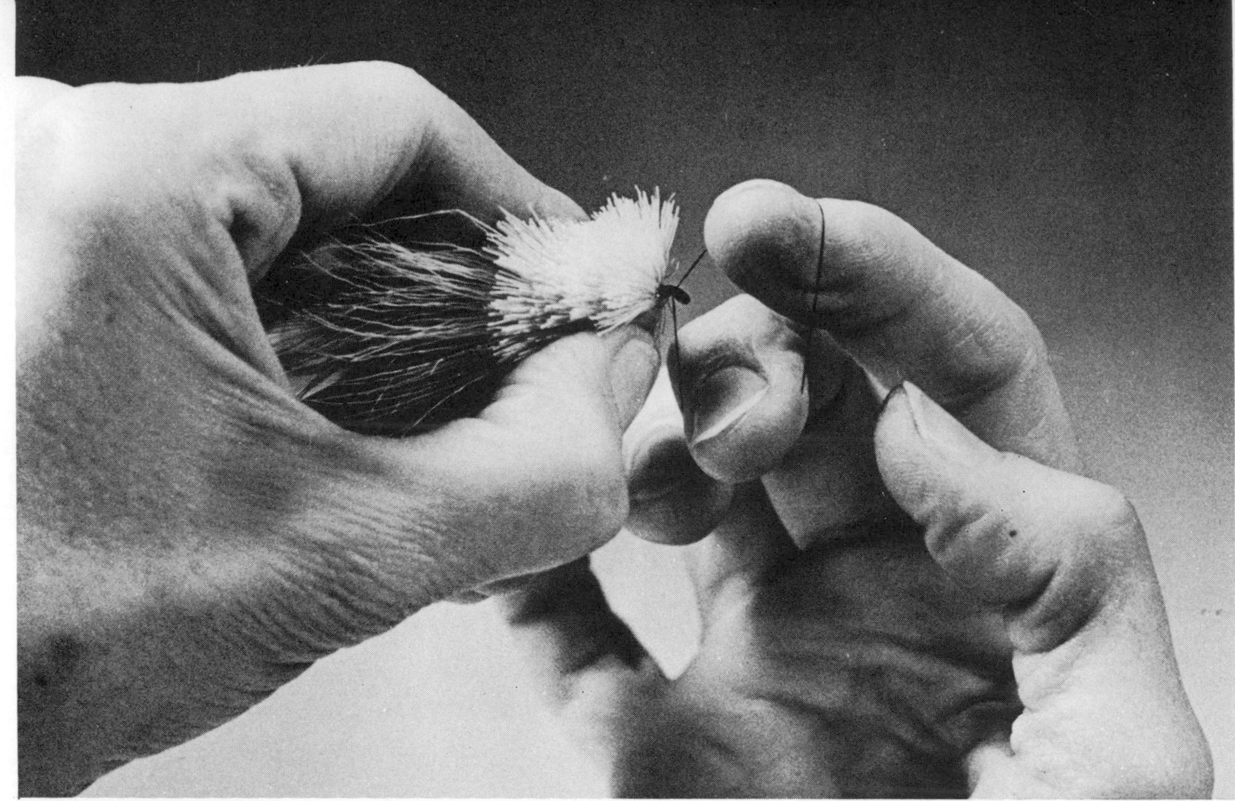

12. With the hair held back, to clear the space left for the head of the fly, the tying thread is brought through it, and the wrap knot completes the tying.

13. Removed from the vise, the fly is easily handled, and trimming begins by turning the fly over and clipping the hair fairly short on the bottom . . . snippets of hair flying.

14. It is advisable to remove only a little hair at a time, turning the fly and snipping as it is turned, gauging the shape, and keeping it evenly balanced on the sides. Note: The hook will be below center when viewed from directly in front.

15. Since the hair for the body of the fly was kept shorter than the "hackle" hair, with its naturally tapered ends, the danger of cutting into it is minimized. If a stray hair with a cut end shows here and there, it should be removed.

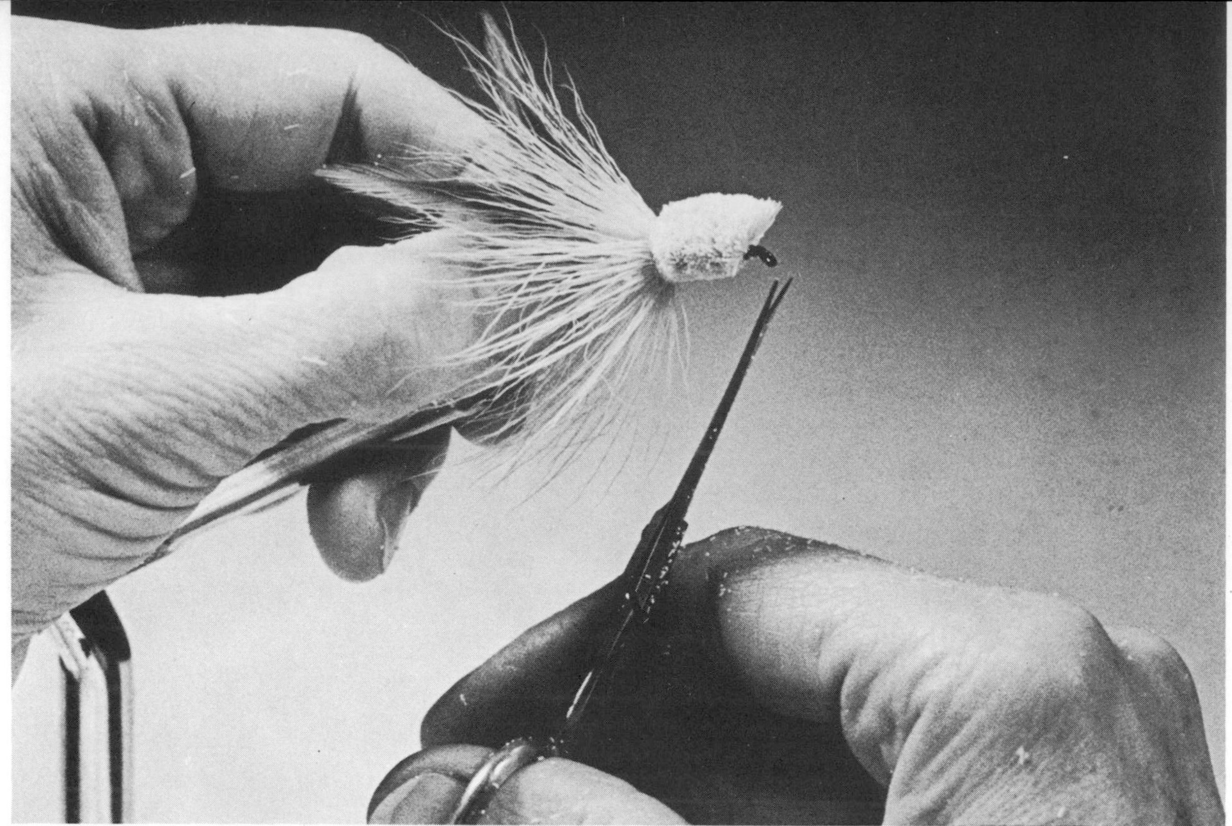

16. The body shape is clearly defined against the ruff of longer hair, and the forward thrust of the top hair is plainly shown.

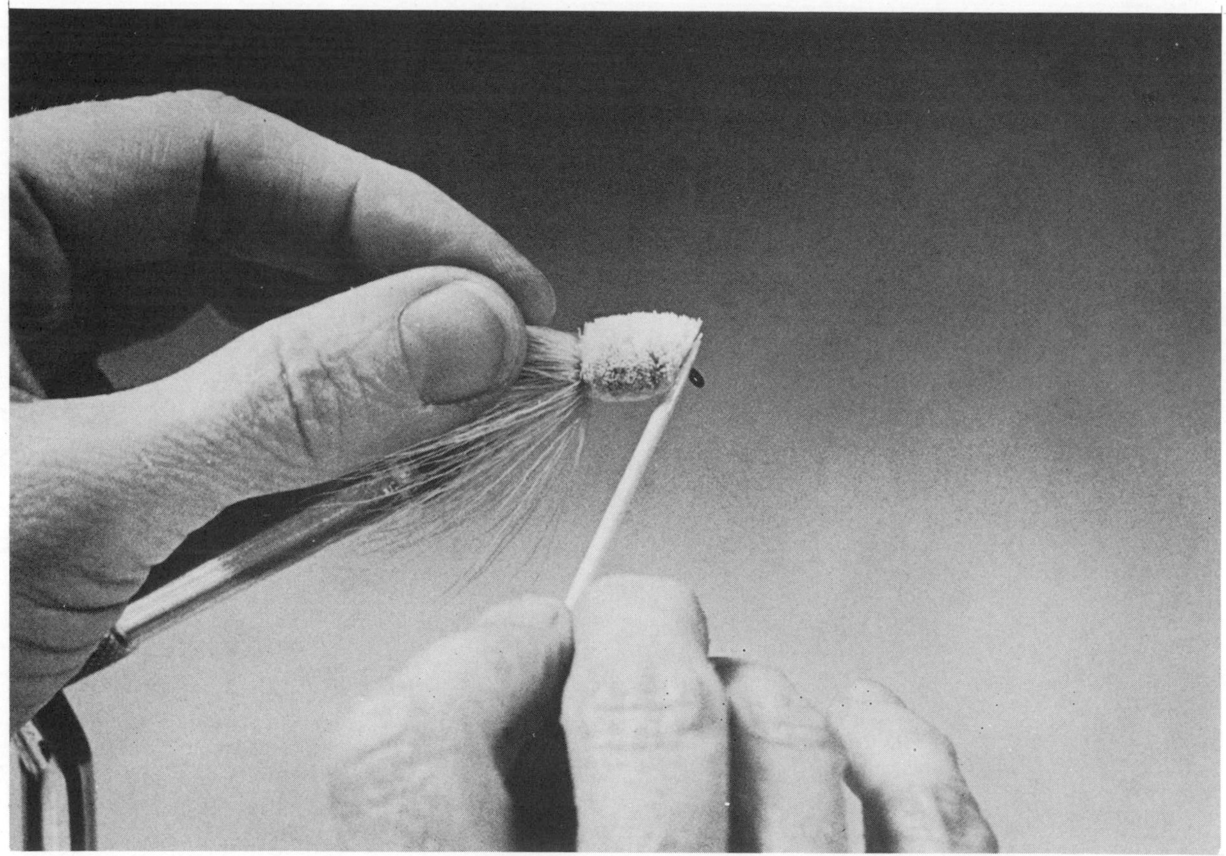

17. A coat of lacquer is applied to the front face of the hair body, as well as to the head. This stiffens the hair and enables the fly to create a burbling sound when fished properly. Only a small amount of aesthetic trimming is still necessary to perfect the contour.

18. Fluffing the hair out around the hook (steaming if necessary) will bring out the full attractiveness of the Bubble Pup.

# Ted Niemeyer

## NYMPH and WET FLY

Photographs by Ren McMann, Jr.

When the hatch is on I find no greater pleasure than opening a small box of specially designed dry flies from the left side pocket of my fishing vest and "flitting the flee" to voracious trout. And when spring waters are high and turbulent I do not overlook the streamer fly that seldom fails me if judiciously selected and properly darted in and out of pockets, riffles, and pools. But my greatest fishing experiences were those garnered through the crafty use of nymphs. Over the past twenty-five years of fly-fishing I have used, without restraint or common sense in some instances, every imaginable concoction representing the nymph life of scores of trout streams.

The tying of nymphs is not easier than tying the dry, wet, streamer, or bass fly, but I think the nymph holds a little more interest for the average flytyer. Since the tying of nymph imitations is relatively new by comparison, new patterns hold considerable interest for me and, I hope, for you. Since most fly-fishermen are aware that nymph-fishing can produce exceptional results if one has the proper patterns and properly honed presentation techniques, an anxious audience awaits the flytyer who says he has developed a new and killing pattern.

The following stone-fly and caddis-nymph patterns will be new to most of you, and it is my hope that they will inspire you to get to work at your vise immediately.

*Atherton Medium*

I have chosen this pattern because it not only produces so very well on all the trout streams from the east to the west coast, but because it provides the fur-body style so popular with a great majority of flytyers and fly-fishermen.

| | |
|---|---|
| Tail: | three fibers from the center tail feather of the Chinese ring-necked pheasant |
| Abdomen: | hare's-ear fur tapered from the tail to thorax; rib with narrow oval gold tinsel |
| Thorax: | hare's-ear fur tied full over a base of lacquered lead wire if added weight is desired |
| Wing case: | English kingfisher wing fiber or other suitable substitute |
| Legs: | brown speckled partridge |
| Tying silk: | 5/0 black or dark brown |
| Hook: | Mustad 9671 size No. 10. |

Secure hook in the vise and complete one full layer of tying silk from the eye of hook to a point opposite the barb. Lacquer the entire layer of silk. Lay three fibers from the center tail feather of the ring-necked pheasant atop the hook at a point opposite the hook barb and secure with two turns of the tying silk *to the left* (see Figure 1). Make sure at this point that all three fibers are of the same length. The two outer butt fibers are now pulled in a counterclockwise motion back along the hook shank. Take one full turn of the tying silk at this point. Hold the two butt pieces that now point in the same direction as the three tail fibers and pull them straight down on each side of the hook shank between the hook and the outside tail fiber on each side.

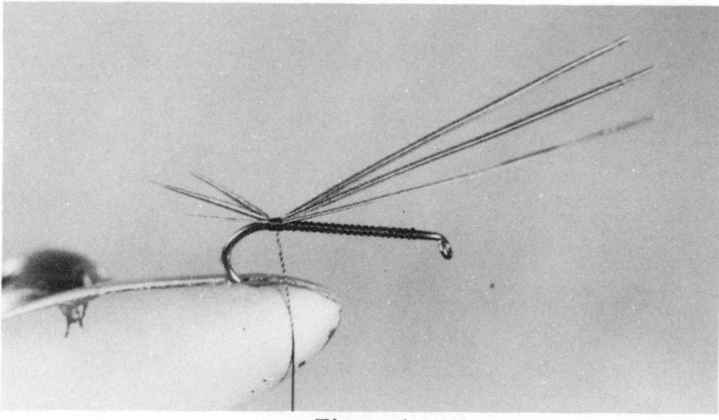

Figure 1

Bring these butts forward toward the eye of the hook and secure with two turns of the tying silk *to the right*. You should now have a well-spread tail that will remain in the spread position even when wet, as with the natural nymph.

Next, tie in a short piece of narrow oval gold tinsel with two turns of the tying silk *to the right* (Figure 2). Wax the tying silk at this time and spin on hare's-ear fur, tapering it from a fine point near the hook shank to a much wider portion near the bobbin. You will be unable to spin the fur all the way up the thread to meet the hook shank, but do not be concerned. When the abdomen is fully spun, commence turning even turns of the tying silk to the left to a point where you wish the fur to start appearing as a body. Turn the fur around the hook shank in close tight turns *to the right,* forming a well-tapered abdomen (Figure 3).

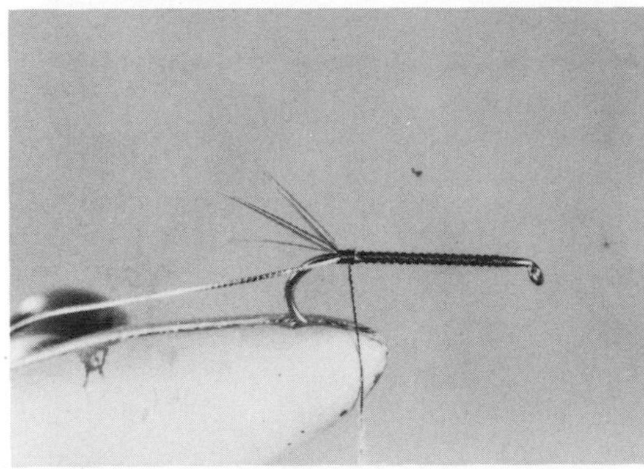

Figure 2

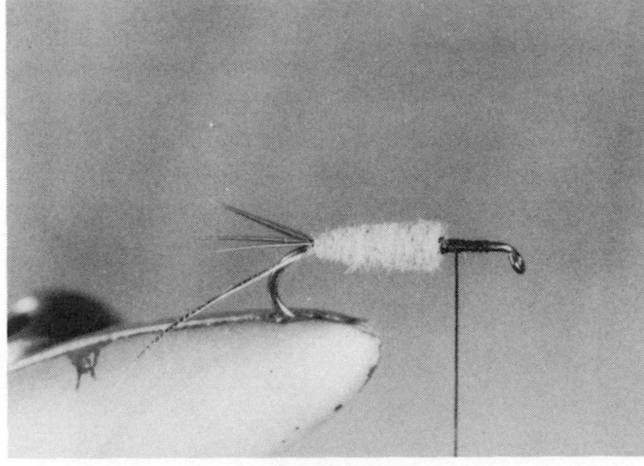

Figure 3

The gold tinsel is now wound in even turns to the right and tied off with four firm turns of the tying silk (Figure 4). Form a double layer of kingfisher-quill fibers and lay flat on top of the hook shank, dull side up. Secure the kingfisher with four turns of tying silk where the abdomen ends (Figure 5). At this same point, tie in a small partridge feather by its tip on top of the kingfisher, dull side up (Figure 6). Wax the tying silk heavily and spin on a heavy amount of hare's-ear fur. The spun fur should now be tightly wound from the abdomen to the eye of the hook (Figure 7). Next, pull the stem of the partridge straight forward to the eye and tie in with three very tight turns of the tying silk (Figure 8). Pull the remaining kingfisher fibers up and forward to the eye and tie off with very tight turns of tying silk. Trim off all excess materials and with the tying silk form a well-tapered head and finish off with a whip-finish (Figure 9). Now apply five coats of thin spar varnish, allowing each coat to dry fully before applying the next.

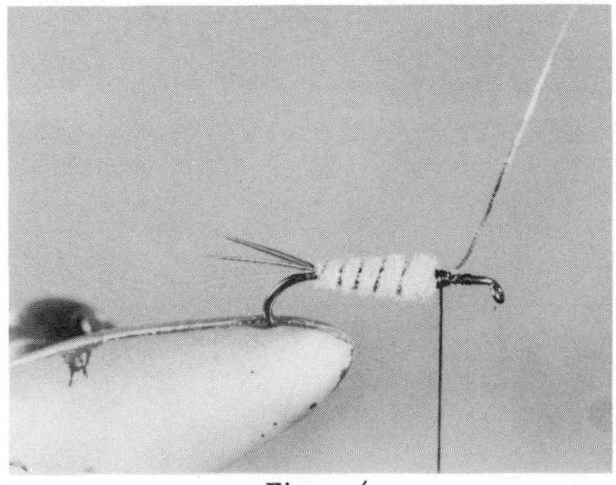

Figure 4

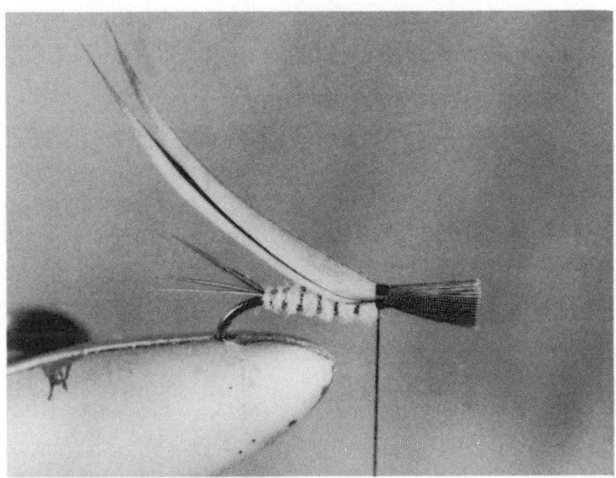

Figure 5

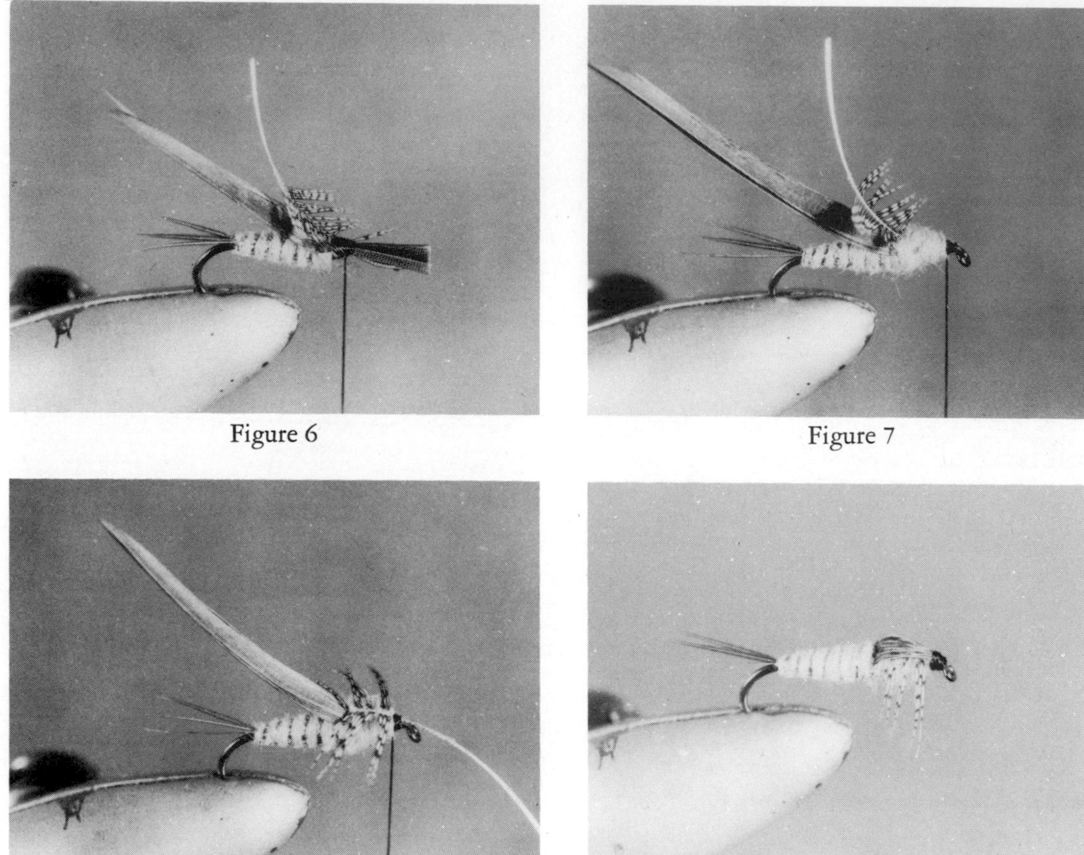
Figure 6
Figure 7
Figure 8
Figure 9

---

*Niemeyer Caddis*

At the very start of my fishing career (age eight), I learned a highly important lesson about the caddis. When fished whole on a bait hook, with the outer case intact, it usually brought me some success, but when I learned to break open the outer case and impale the larva on the hook, I seldom went home without a trout for the table.

During the years of fly-fishing that followed those first experiences, I tied and fished all sorts of caddis larva imitations. Only in the past four years have I found what I was seeking in an imitation. I hope you have as much fun with it as I have.

Tail: fluff or down from the base of any feather; choose the fluff of an appropriate shade for the color of fly you are designing
Body: down off the breast of any waterfowl after the breast feathers have been plucked; rib with the quill stripped from the stem of a mallard primary feather
Head: very dark fluff or down off the breast of any waterfowl
Legs: three fibers from each of a pair of Canada goose black tail feathers
Tying silk: 5/0 black
Hook: Herter's English Bait Hook, quality 707, bronzed, size No. 10

With a small pair of pliers bend the shank of the hook so that the eye is in the same plane as the point of the hook. Secure the hook in the vise and complete one full layer of tying silk from the eye to a point opposite the hook barb. Lacquer the entire layer of tying silk. Strip a small amount of the fluff from the base of any feather and notice that the tips of the fluff are tapered and well shaped. Tie in these fluff tips as a tail with two tight turns of the tying silk *to the left* (Figure 1). Secure the quill rib at its tip with the dull side facing you (Figure 2). This quill is obtained by soaking a mallard primary feather and then with a sharp razor partially cutting through the center stem of the feather near its very tip. With tweezers grasp this exposed quill and strip it from the stem.

Wax a long section of the tying silk and dub on to it a large amount of the down off the breast of a waterfowl (Figure 3). The body is now formed by winding the down in tight turns to a point where the hook shank was bent near the eye (Figure 4). Wind the quill in even but spread-out turns to a point where the

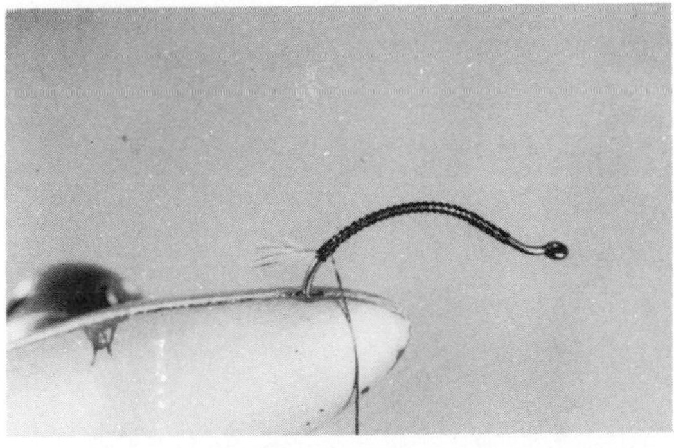

Figure 1

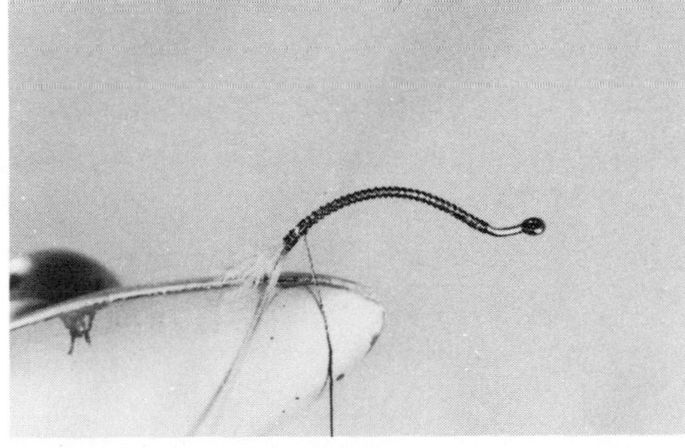

Figure 2

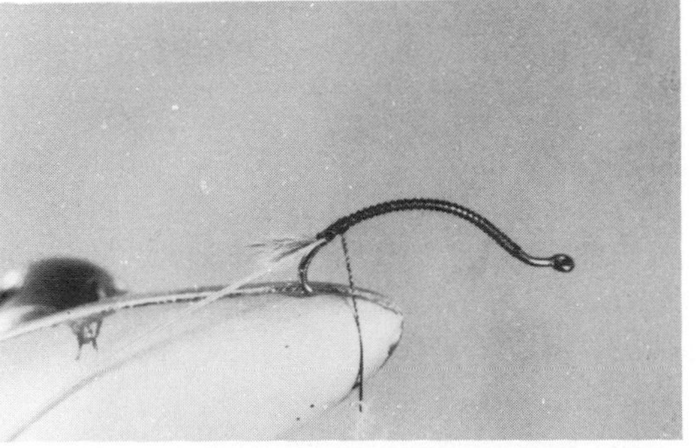

Figure 3

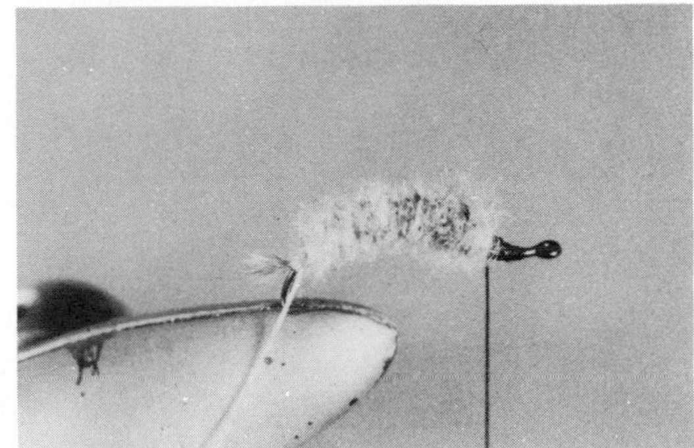

Figure 4

body ends. The down is thus exposed between each revolution of the quill. Bind down the quill with several turns of tying silk (Figure 5). Wax the tying silk and dub on a darker quantity of down from a darker waterfowl. Wind this material in full tight turns to the eye of the hook (Figure 6).

The legs are applied by stripping three fibers from the short side of a Canada goose black tail feather and securing them just behind the eye of the hook. Strip three fibers from a matching goose tail quill (use a right and a left) and secure on the opposite side of the hook shank (Figure 7). Prior to applying the whip finish, you can spread the legs by taking a turn of the tying silk between each individual fiber (Figure 8). Apply five coats of thin spar varnish, allowing each coat to dry fully before applying the next.

Figure 5

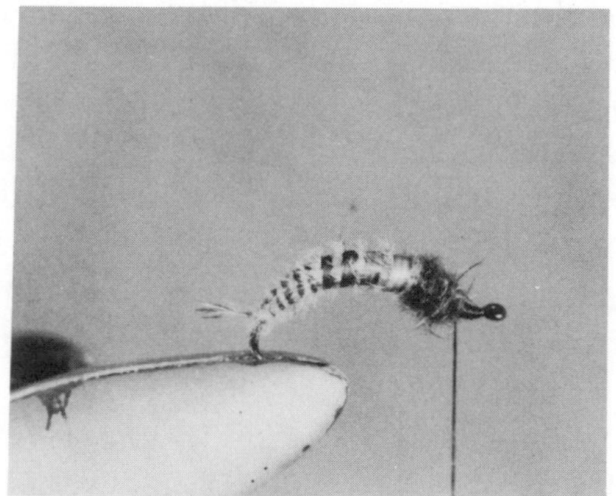
Figure 6

Figure 7

Figure 8

### *Catskill Coiler*

This unique pattern was recently brought to my attention by an eastern flytyer of considerable ability. The coiler represents the large stone flies found on so many of our better trout streams. I vary the size and color to meet the individual needs of each stream I visit during the season.

| | |
|---|---|
| Tail: | two stiff hairs from the neck of the javalena |
| Body: | four-ply worsted wool of cream, yellow, brown, tan, or black; rib with brown-dyed monofilament |
| Legs: | grouse body feather |
| Wing case: | two trimmed and lacquered grouse body feathers |
| Collar: | black ostrich herl |
| Tying silk: | 3/0 black |
| Hook: | Mustad 9575 size No. 6 |

Prepare the legs and wing cases in advance of tying this pattern or I can assure you a mess will result. A single grouse feather for the legs is prepared by holding at the tip and stroking back the fibers on both sides of the stem. With a dubbing needle apply a small amount of thin spar varnish to six fibers on each side of the stem. Repeat the process on the next six fibers on each side. The last set of legs are formed best if you apply the varnish to eight to ten fibers on each side of the stem. Allow the legs to dry thoroughly.

Prepare the wing cases by trimming individual grouse body feathers to shape, and apply three coats of lacquer to the bright side. Allow the cases to dry thoroughly.

Prior to securing the hook in the vise, slightly bend the hook shank as it appears in Figure 1. With hook secure in the vise, wrap the hook shank from the eye to a point opposite the barb of the hook. Two javalena hairs are secured with very tight turns opposite the barb; spread them to a "V" by means of a "Figure 8" with the tying silk (Figure 1). Secure a piece of dark-brown monofilament $\frac{1}{16}$ inch from the tail (Figure 2) and wrap the tying silk to the point where the

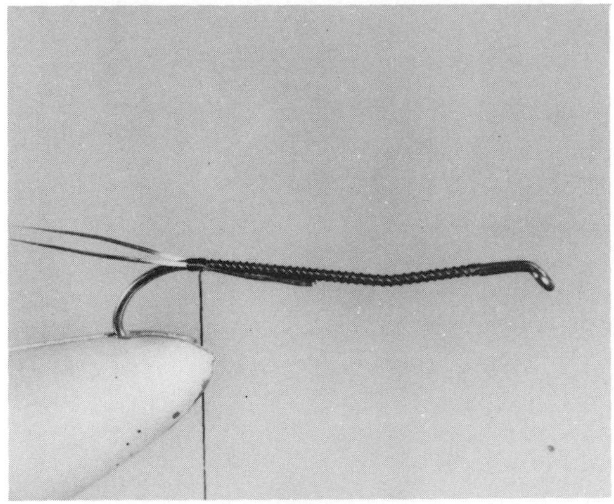

Figure 1

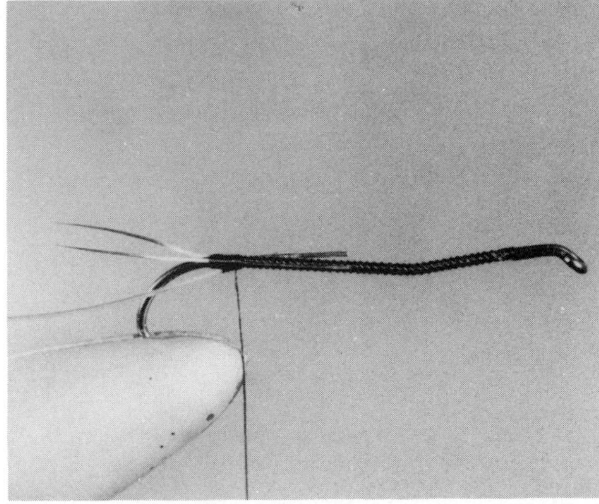

Figure 2

hook shank was bent behind the eye. Secure the wool at this point. Continue the tying silk to the eye (Figure 3). Form a well tapered body from the tail to the head, with the wool ending at the bend of the hook shank (Figure 4). Return tying silk to this same point and bind down wool but do not trim off excess. Rib the abdomen section only with the monofilament and bind in with the tying silk (Figure 5). Cut off the excess monofilament. Return the tying silk to the eye and follow with one thin wrapping of the wool to the eye. Secure the wool and trim off any excess.

A thin coat of Miracle Sheer Magic adhesive is applied to the top of the thorax area. Lay on and press down firmly the previously prepared set of grouse legs. The stem of the feather will extend toward the eye of the hook and should be tightly secured with tying silk (Figure 6). In succession, apply adhesive to the underside of each prepared wing case. Lay each wing case directly on top of the hook shank and secure each stem at the eye with very tight turns of the tying silk (Figure 7). Trim off the stems. Tie in strands of black ostrich herl (Figure 8) and form a collar at the eye approximately ⅛ inch in width. Form a well-tapered head and whip finish with the tying silk (Figure 9). Apply five coats of thin spar varnish, allowing each coat to dry fully before applying the next.

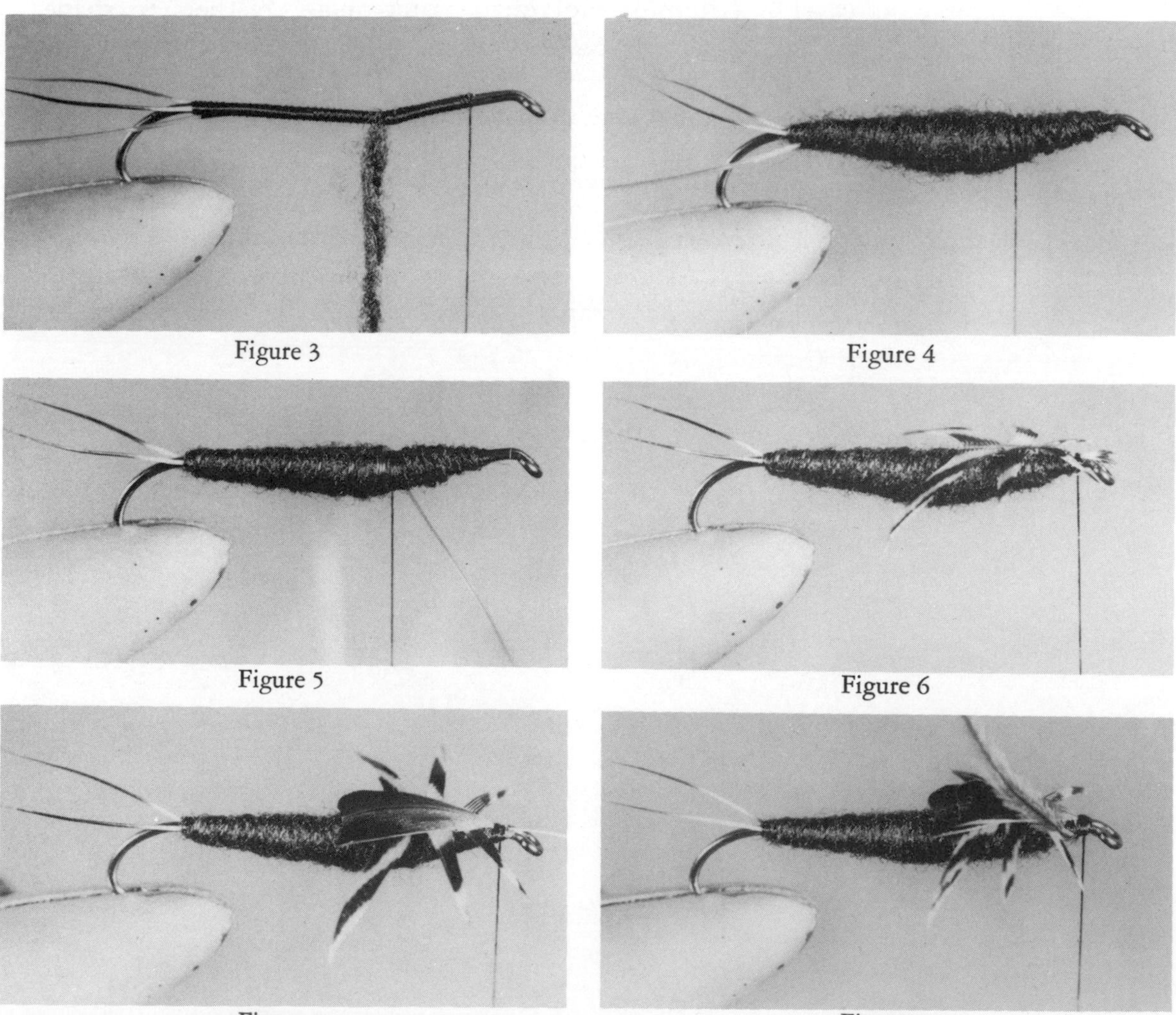

Figure 3

Figure 4

Figure 5

Figure 6

Figure 7

Figure 8

Figure 9

## THE WET FLY

In the beginning God made the wet fly, or so it seems if you are a dedicated fly-fisherman and flytyer. It all began with what we term the "wet fly."

Much controversy surrounds the merit of winging wet patterns. Wings on the wet fly seem to be the rule when seeking the eastern brook trout, landlocked salmon, steelhead, and Atlantic salmon. The exponents of simple hackled wet flies say little about the importance of wingless tying, but if you observe the streamside results of these gentlemen you will find that they are truly the masters of our streams. I tend to follow their lead, and now I fish a variety of hackled flies when stream conditions dictate. This basic pattern can be tied and fished with equal potential by the beginner or the most accomplished piscatorial adventurer.

---

*Badger and Peacock*

Tail: none
Body: bronze peacock herl
Rib: fine flat gold tinsel
Hackle: golden badger
Hook: Partridge No. 12
Tying silk: 6/0 white

---

With the hook firmly in place in the vise, complete one full layer of tying silk from the eye to bend of hook shank. Hold a single strand of bronze peacock herl on top of the hook shank, and then secure it with three tight turns of the tying silk to the *left*. Now take a short section of fine flat gold tinsel and with a spot of lacquer on your left forefinger draw the tinsel through the lacquer, allowing it to dry momentarily before attaching it to the hook shank. Holding the tinsel on top of the hook shank slightly in front of the herl, secure it with two turns of the tying thread to the *right* (Figure 1). Return the tying thread to the eye of the hook.

Hold the peacock herl firmly, and, with close turns to the right, produce a full body to a point 1/16 inch behind the hook eye; three tight turns of the tying thread will hold the herl. Return to the tinsel and lay on three evenly spaced tight turns to the right, ending precisely at the point where the herl was tied off. Secure the end of the tinsel at this point but do not cut off the excess tinsel (Figure 2). Hold the loose end of tinsel firmly between the thumb and forefinger of the right hand and with a side-to-side motion work the tinsel back and forth until it breaks off. This method prevents the tinsel from pulling loose from continued abuse by fish. Trim off the excess herl.

Prepare your badger hackle by stripping off all unwanted soft base fibers. With the brilliant side of the hackle facing you, secure the hackle with five even tight turns of tying thread to the *right*. The tying thread should end 1/32 inch from the eye of the hook (Figure 3). Now hold the tip of the hackle firmly and take three close, tight turns to the right, being sure that each turn butts firmly up against the previous turn. I usually stroke all fibers to the left after each turn so as to expose the hackle stem for the next turn to be applied. With the tying silk, secure the hackle tip with five tight turns (Figure 4). Trim off the excess hackle and apply the whip finish knot. Apply five coats of thin spar varnish, allowing each coat to dry fully before applying the next.

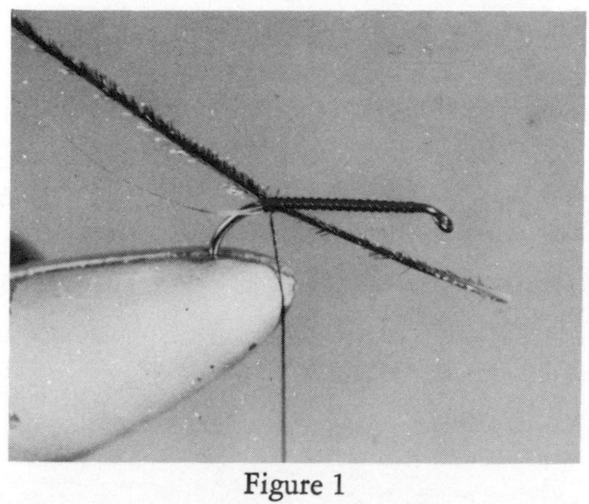

Figure 1

Figure 2

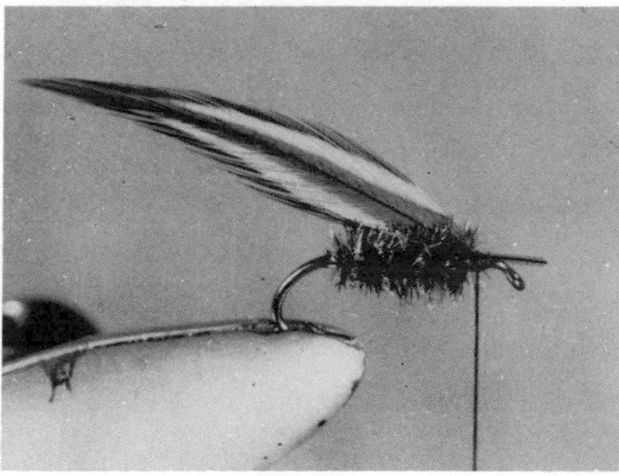

Figure 3

Figure 4

## SOME TYING TIPS

The essentials of good tying should be learned and continuously practiced by those who wish to go beyond mere adequate results. Before you turn to your vise and the unique pleasure of designing your own nymphs and wet flies, I suggest you give some thought to the following points:

1. Determine those materials that you feel will provide the best possible facsimile of the specimen you plan to imitate. It should be obvious from the start that you will have limited success with your patterns unless you thoroughly study the unique properties of the nearly endless variety of materials available to you. This is not really a difficult task, provided you have gathered together a good collection

of tying materials. Two hours a night for about one week should be sufficient investment of time.

2. Study the materials under water if you wish to determine their true color and action. You will be surprised and elated with what you observe. The first time I applied this principle I was forced to alter a number of patterns in order to present materials more akin to the natural insects' underwater appearance and action.

3. Observation of aquatic life in its own natural environment can be invaluable to the flytyer. You have no excuse for lack of knowledge on this score. If you fish in fresh water as I do, then you are footloose in nature's prolific laboratory. Any fly-fisherman worth his salt knows that slack periods of feeding activity occur during each twenty-four hours; pick your time and lay aside the rod in favor of gaining a little basic knowledge of entomology. I can promise that you will add considerably to your knowledge at the vise and pleasure afield.

4. Buy the very best hooks that you can locate. Too many hooks are invariably very soft, or very brittle, or have dull points, or have poorly shaped eyes that are seldom closed properly. I throw out any hook that is too soft or too brittle. Dull-pointed hooks can be salvaged by sharpening them with a fine Arkansas stone and touching the point with gun blue. Be sure to wipe the gun blue clean after ten seconds or less. Open eyes can be closed during the tying process by forming a long tapered head on the fly and allowing the tying silk to work well down on the eye. Several coats of spar varnish over all will secure the fly head and protect your leader.

5. Flies sold at sporting-goods stores and fishing-tackle shops too often have heads that are poorly shaped and finished off. This comes, among other things, as a result of the commercial tyer's using a very heavy thread. With the improvements achieved over the past ten years I find it difficult to understand why so many accomplished tyers continue to use the heavier threads that result in poorly proportioned and finished flies. The most suitable thread is the *smallest and strongest* available, considering the type of fly under construction. For nymphs I suggest 3/0 for the larger size #4 and #6. For nymph sizes #8 and #10 I suggest 5/0. Below size #10 try 8/0.

6. Looking at any of Nature's aquatic handiwork you will see a well-defined smoothness of individual parts and superbly designed body joints to facilitate movement. A failing of most flytyers is the obvious lumpiness that appears on the finished fly. Added concentration and much patience will soon overcome the bad habit.

7. Tails on nymphs should be chosen for the action they have in the water and for appropriate color to copy the natural insect. Unfortunately, most are selected with little thought and probably more as a result of convenience or tradition.

8. There has developed in recent years a trend toward the use of a single type of material to the exclusion of all others. I fail to find the merit of such a practice and hope that the reverse will soon become the vogue, for we miss the great tradition of experimentation if we limit our approach to fly-tying in any way. Use all types of materials in the construction of your flies and let the final decision as to their worth rest with the adversary—the trout.

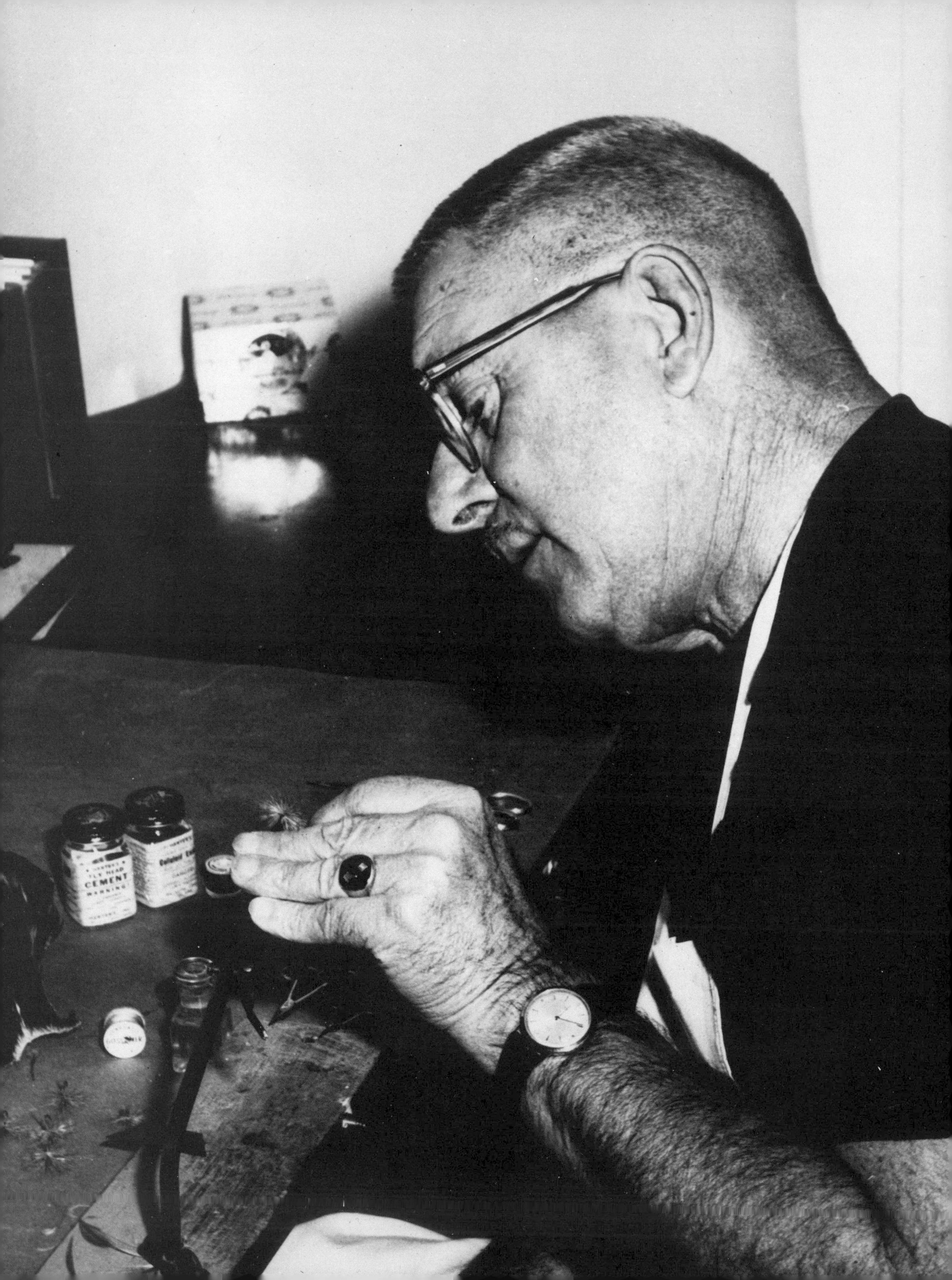
CEMENT
WARNING

# Art Flick

## THE DRY FLY

There are many ways of putting together a dry fly and I would be the last to intimate that my method is superior to other ways. However, I can say that flies constructed as I make them will catch more fish without coming apart than those tied by any other method I have found.

No one can argue that aside from its ability to catch trout, the chief requisite of a fly is that it will take fish after fish without requiring replacement. Nothing is more exasperating than being on a stream, with a good hatch in progress and fish feeding all over the place, when after catching two or three, your fly comes apart. You've got to stop and fuss through your fly box and then tie on a new one. The worst of it is, you are apt to be fishing with a fly that, when it comes apart, doesn't look at all the way it looked originally; the trout of course spot this immediately and leave it alone. Not only is it tough on the nerves, but it also raises hell with one's disposition. Valuable time is lost with fish in the mood!!!

Commercial tyers today are up against this problem. The cost of good hackles is almost prohibitive, if and when they can be found. It is the same with other materials, and the only way a tyer can come out on top, considering the comparatively low price flies sell for, is to tie them up as fast as possible. I mention this only because I certainly would not expect commercial tyers to take the pains in making a fly that I do in putting them together for my own use.

Photo by Terry Ireland

The method described will very likely take you three or four times as long, but it will more than pay off. Hackles and other materials cost too much today to let you throw away your flies because they are only half put together.

Note that no mention is made of a bobbin, which is used by most flytyers; I do not use one. Instead, I use a homemade gadget whereby the tying thread can be held under tension, the thread instead going through my fingers. I have better control of the thread using this method. Also, there is no need for waxing, as the thread is always under tension, and no half hitches are required while making the fly. For any who would like to try the threadholder I designed, it can be made very easily; if it were otherwise, I couldn't have figured it out.

This was dreamed up in the days before plastics, and although mine is made of brass (taken from a couple of old light fixtures), I feel certain that plastic or even well-polished hardwood would do as well. The dimensions given are of the one I made, but there is no fast rule as to size.

Select a piece of wood (to which the vise will be fastened) ¾ inch wide and 10½ inches long; bore two holes on front side ⅜ inch wide, large enough to insert a piece of brass that size, and ½ inch deep. The first hole should be drilled directly below where the mouth of your vise will be, the second, 2½ inches to the right. Bear in mind, these figures are for my vise, but may not be right for yours, so you will have to measure; you might need a slightly longer piece of board.

The material that will fit into the hole is cut ⅜ inch long and ⅜ inch wide; bore a hole in the center of this that will take a screw ⅛ inch wide and 1 inch long. Bevel the back end slightly to allow room for a small piece of spring that goes between the back end of the brass and the back end of the hole in the board. The spring will take care of the tension so that the amount needed may be adjusted according to the strength of the thread.

At the head, place a polished ⅜-inch brass washer; put in screw and tighten to whatever tension is wanted.

Obviously the head of whatever is used must be highly polished, otherwise the thread will fray when tension is applied.

You can tighten up the screw so that it will hold the thread when placed behind washer, but I prefer to have it just a hair looser and make two or three turns with the thread. I have found that when it is tightened enough to hold when just placed between the two metals the thread will often break.

Let's start with the Hendrickson, because it is probably the most popular early fly in the East. Except for a difference in body materials, the mechanics for building this pattern are substantially the same as for most dry flies.

Some may wonder at the vise shown in the illustration. It is the one I started with more than thirty-five years ago and is a far cry from those offered for sale today. However, it serves my purpose very well, for all I ask of a vise is that it hold the hook firmly without weakening the steel at the bend of the hook, causing it to break later. Talk to five different tyers about fly-tying vises and you are apt to get five different opinions. Almost any of them on the market will do the job, and I am not qualified to recommend one make over another. You "pays your money and takes your choice."

Start tying *not too close to the eye of the hook* (Figure 1). This seems to be one of the most common errors made by beginners; they begin tying so close to the eye that when they come to finish up, instead of having a nicely tapered head, they have a big humped up mess, with no room to bend on a leader.

Take a small portion (Figure 2) of the flank feather of a wood duck or mandarin duck (not the part with the black-and-white bars) and tie to hook, butt of feathers toward point (Figure 3), making three or four turns with thread; apply as much pressure as thread will stand. (I use Pearsall's Gossamer, which I find quite strong for its diameter.) Raise the wing material (Figure 4) and take a turn in front with thread. Divide the filaments into two equal amounts and, while divided, cross the thread to the left rear, which will hold the division; then come back with the thread around hook at rear of wing and again cross thread over the division going forward and right. Your wing is now divided and held in place (Figure 5). Next, loop the thread around the back side of the wing, going from left to right—through the division and back to the front and left, putting sufficient pressure on it to make the filaments stand up, forming the rear part of a "V" (Figure 6). Loop thread around front half of wing, going from left to right, and again cross the center of the "V," which brings the thread to the left rear of the back wing. Once more apply gentle pull to the thread, thereby forming the front half of the "V," and, by taking three turns around hook in back of it (the "V"), the wings are firmly locked in place (Figure 7). This may sound rather complicated, but it isn't. However, I would suggest you practice making this wing with some mallard feathers; practice making just the wing. Until you master this, you are very apt to spoil some material, and of course you don't want to do this with the more expensive and hard-to-find wood duck. Note: When making the loops around each portion of the "V," be sure the thread is as close to the hook shank as possible. If the thread is not down as far as it will go, when you tighten it to bring the material up, the wings will be pulled over.

1. Note how far back from the eye of the hook the line is tied in. (In this and in some of the other pictures, it may appear that the edges of the vise are jagged. Not so. This is a special paper that I cut to fit the jaws. It is so strong that I can put a bit more pressure on the hook without having to worry about "fracturing" the steel at the bend of the hook, causing it to break later.)

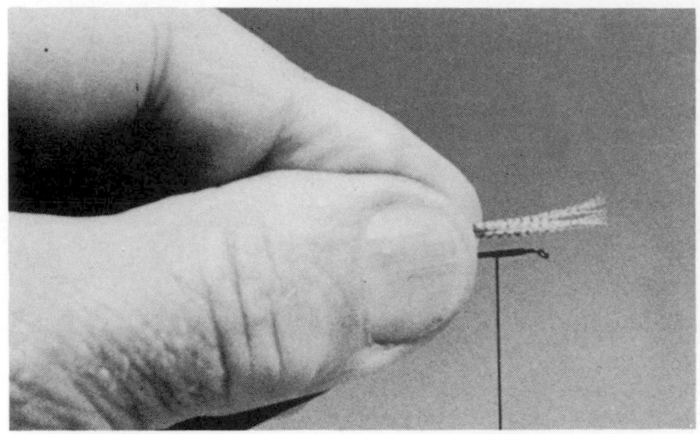
2. Tying in wing material.

3. This is the position of the wing material.

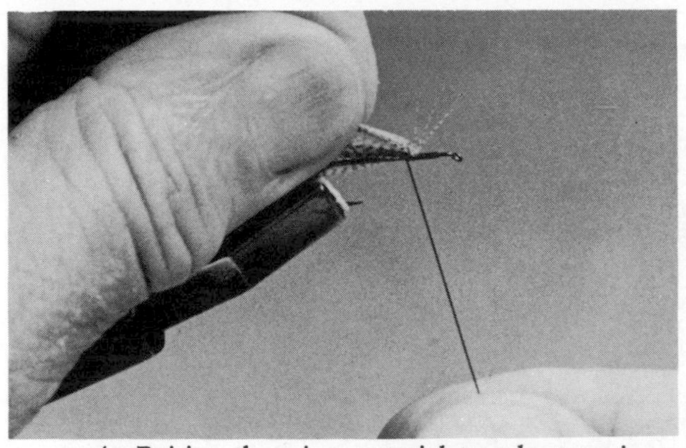
4. Raising the wing material to take turn in front.

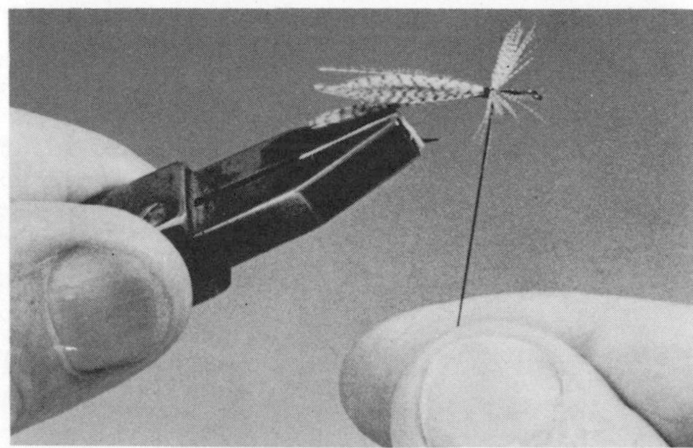
5. The wing after division.

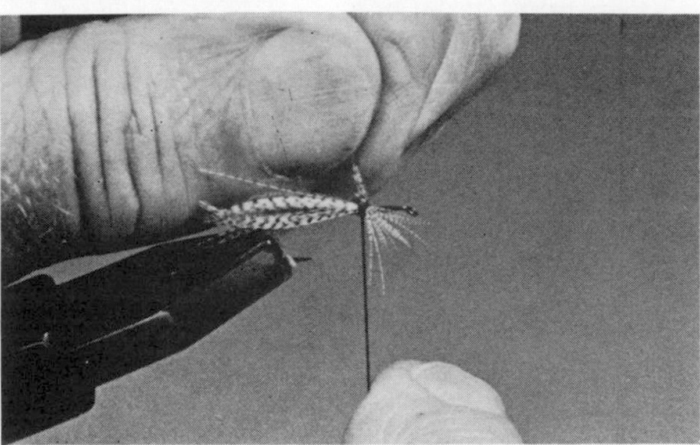
6. Making the rear "V."

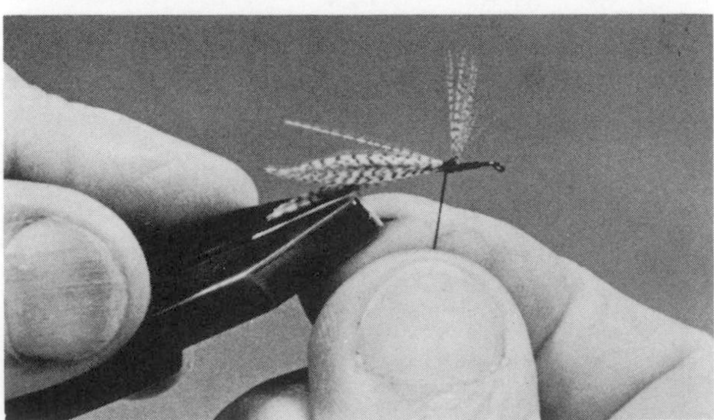
7. Securing the "V."

Next, with your dubbing needle, place a *very small* drop of head lacquer at base of "V" (Figure 8) and work it up into the filaments with thumb and forefinger. This will cement the filaments together (Figure 9) (be sure you keep the "V") so that when spinning your hackles you will not pick up some of the wing material. By using the same fingers, working them from the hook portion to the tips, the dried lacquer can easily be removed when the fly is finished, for it seldom sticks to the feathers, because of their natural oil. Should some of it adhere, use a dry dubbing needle and work through the filaments. This is a wing you will be proud of and one that will stay put. Cut excess material close to thread (Figure 10).

8. Applying a touch of lacquer at the base of the "V."

9. The wing after applying lacquer.

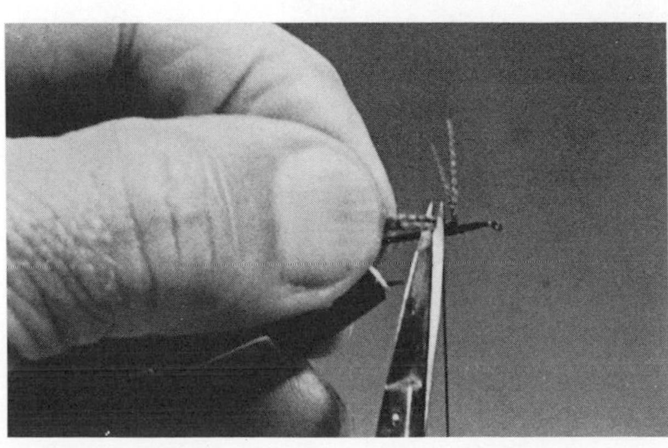

10. Cutting the base of the wing.

Next, place two hackles that were previously matched for filament size (Figure 11) in "V" (obviously, if they are not the same size, you will have a sloppy fly), butts toward point of hook, locking with several turns of thread at rear of "V." Move hackles to rear of wing so they will be out of your way (Figure 12). Cut off the butt of one hackle, just slightly past where wing butt was cut; cut the second one a bit farther back (Figures 13a and 13b). This will help the taper of your fly when body material is put on, heavier at the portion near the wing, to correspond to the thicker thorax of the natural insect.

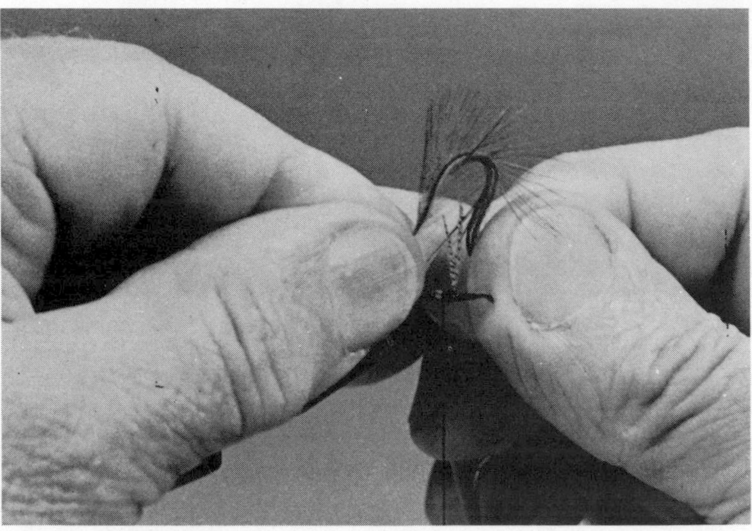

11. Matching hackles.

12. Here the hackles are moved behind the wing.

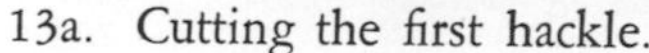

13a. Cutting the first hackle.

13b. Cutting the second hackle.

Next, tie in a few filaments of tail material (Figure 14) taken from either a spade or saddle hackle, tying it in at base of second hackle butt, which continues the taper. If you have cut hackle at about the right point, your tail material will start at about the middle of the hook, and by tying in the tail at this point, you can be reasonably certain it won't pull out on you, which happens quite frequently if not well enough tied in, so that for the want of a tail a fly is lost. Another word of caution: A very common mistake of beginners is to make the tails too heavy, too long, or both. Usually between six or eight filaments of a saddle hackle are sufficient (the diameters vary with different feathers); just be sure you do not put in too many (Figure 15). Bear in mind that there are only two or three tails on a natural insect, and that they are very fine. A fish that can see insects as small as and smaller than a size 28 fly can certainly spot a tail so phony that it resembles a shaving brush. Tails that are too long are a giveaway, and about the best rule of thumb that I know comes from Al Brewster, one of the very best commercial flytyers I know. His formula is:

> When I first met Rube Cross, he and I went round and round on his cocked tails. Rube could only tie dry flies. He took a couple of turns of silk in back of the tails which caused them to set up approximately 30 degrees of the hook shank. When the fly hit the water it would sink tail first. After a lot of discussion, I finally convinced him the tail should be tied parallel to the hook shank and extended beyond the bend, the same length as the hook shank. Hackles should be ⅛ to ¼ inch larger than the gape of the hook. When the fly hits the water the point of the hook acts as a keel and the fly will ride on the tail and hackle point with the keel just on the water. If the tail is too short the fly will sink tail first; if the wing is too far forward, the fly will land on the eye of the hook. If the wings are too long, it will lie on its side.

14. The amount of filament wanted for the tail.

One exception to normal tail length is in the case of tying an imitation of either a *Caenis* or *Tricorythodes.* These little stinkers, although imitated on sizes 26 and 28 hooks, have tails that are fully as long as a Green Drake's.

Now you are ready for the body. I always use fur for the Hendrickson, usually fox, preferring, when it can be found, the portion of the belly under the tail that may have been stained by urine, giving it a pinkish cast. Time can be saved by preparing the body material before doing any tying. In the case of fox fur, remove the guard hairs from a portion of the pelt and discard. Not only are they too wiry, they are almost always a darker color than the softer portions we want to use. Next, remove the softer hairs to be used and place on a piece of paper. After a fair-sized amount has been plucked, hold bits of the fur about an inch above paper and keep pulling apart, between your thumbs and the next two fingers. This will fluff up the fur and make it more workable; at the same time, guard hairs that have been missed will fall and can be removed. Place the good portion (blend first if so desired for color) in a small cellophane envelope. When tying a fly, it takes only a second to remove a sufficient portion to make your body. (Two synthetic materials, polypropylene and Mohlon, have been coming into use in recent years, especially by the pro tyers.)

To make the body, take a small amount of the previously prepared fur, place in the palm of your left hand (assuming you are right handed) and with the index finger of your right hand roll the fur until you form a tapered shape (Figure 16), so that when applied to hook it will correspond to the insect's body. With the point of your dubbing needle, place a *very small* amount of lacquer on thread (Figure 17), close to the hook, working it down the thread with the point of the needle. This will put just a bare trace of lacquer on thread. Lay the fur on the thread, placing the fine end between the hook and the thread. Make one turn with thread *(not fur)* to lock fur in and spin it around the thread with thumb and index finger from left to right (Figure 18). Care must be taken at this point not to spin fur and thread

15. Tying in the tail.

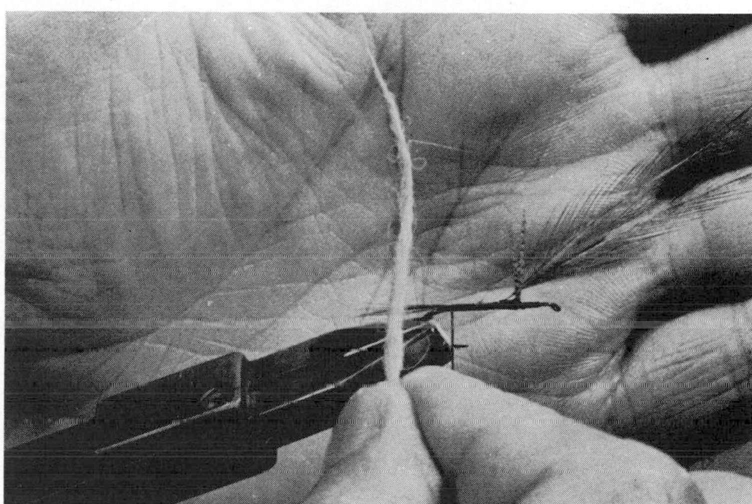

16. Here is the prepared tapered body.

17. Add a touch of lacquer to hold the body.

too much or the latter will break. Keeping the spun fur tight, wind neatly to the wings. If the body material becomes loose in the process, simply spin some more, so that when complete, your body is neatly tied. Lock in with a few turns of thread. With a little bit of practice, you will be able to estimate almost exactly the amount of fur you will need to make a well-tapered body of the proper size, without leaving a large amount of fur to be trimmed after locking in. After it is locked in, trim body and wind the thread toward the eye of the hook, to the front of the wing; allow sufficient room between wing and eye of hook for the hackles when spun.

18. Spinning fur to make the body.

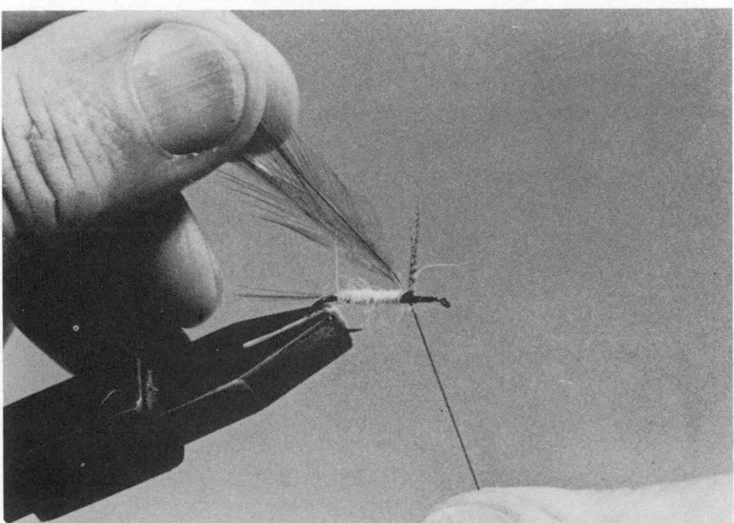

19. Ready to wind in the first hackle.

You are now ready for the hackles, a most important part of a good dry fly. Unfortunately, good quality feathers become more difficult to obtain all the time. Do not waste your time on those of poor quality, for a dry fly cannot be any better than the quality of the hackles it is tied with. Some day there may be good "synthetic" hackles, but at present we must struggle along with what we have. If you attempt to tie flies with "junk" you will be terribly disappointed.

Grasp the first hackle in your hackle pliers and take at least three turns in back of wing, working toward the eye of the hook; then go ahead of wing and make three or four turns there, keeping the hackles bunched together and as close to the wing as possible. Lock the tip of the hackle with at least three turns of thread and cut off the hackle tip (Figure 19). Follow the same procedure with the second hackle, winding it over the first one; then lock it in. Again cut off the hackle tip and take two or three additional turns of thread to make sure it is secured (Figures 20 and 21).

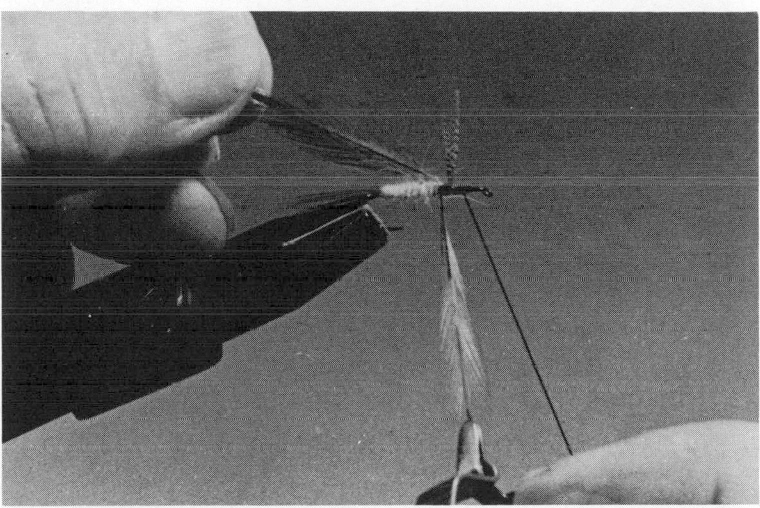

20. Winding in the first hackle while holding the second out of the way.

21. The second hackle secured.

Now you are ready for what I take the liberty of calling the "Flick Finishing-Off" knot (Figure 22). Actually, it is a simple method of tying the knot known as the "whip-finish," but no so-called "aids" are needed. I stumbled on this knot and believe it is much the easiest way to finish off your fly (Figure 23). To better illustrate it, I have done a separate series of pictures, rather than try to show the knot in conjunction with the fly.

22. Starting to finish off the knot.

23. The tying is now complete except for the trimming.

Grasp the thread in the thumb and index finger, forming a loop around your fourth finger (finger next to pinky). Hold the thread tight around fourth finger and lay thread left and right over piece held tight. The palm of your hand is toward the ceiling and the loop is to the right (Figure 1). Still holding this piece tight, transfer it to the thumb and index finger of your left hand, which will leave the other two pieces (with the loop on the right) over the tight piece (Figure 2). With thumb and next two fingers of the right hand (making sure loop is maintained) grasp the loose portion and force thread under the hook (Figure 3), making it fast with the thread in the left hand. Then wind the tight piece back toward

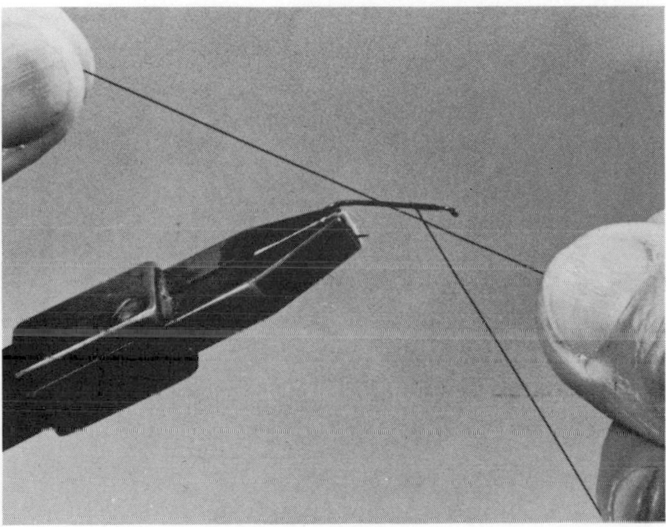

1. Start of the knot.

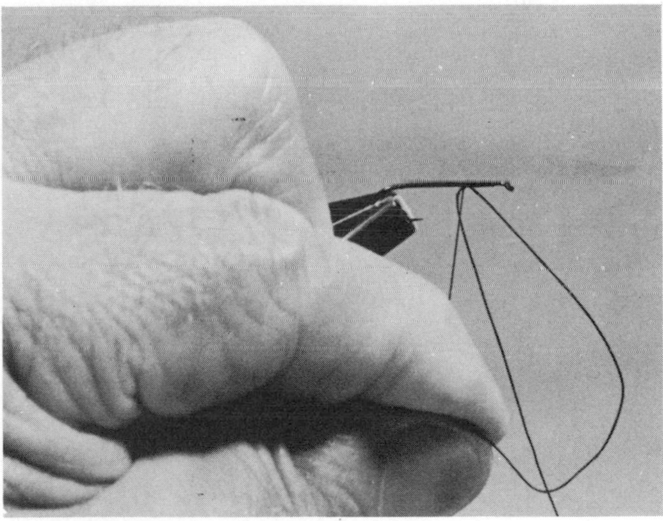

2. Locking in the thread.

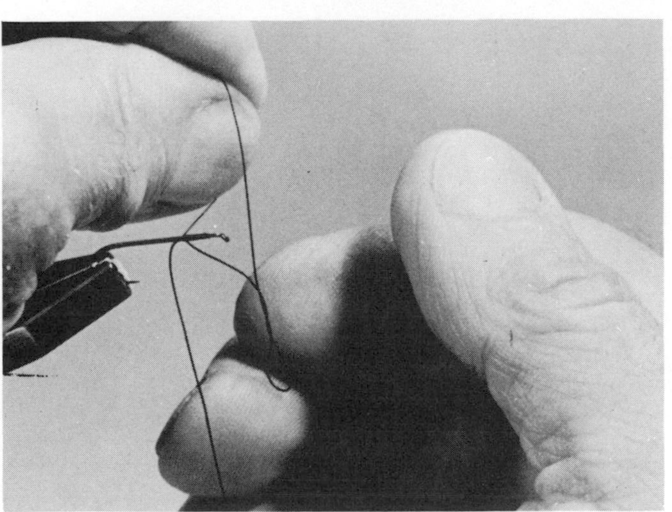

3. The thread is now locked in and ready to wind.

the point of the hook, making four turns; *make sure neither the loop nor the loose piece of thread turns with it.* As you can see, you are winding back over the loose piece of thread. Holding the loop tight, insert point of large pin (Figure 4) in loop and hold taut in right hand. With the left hand, pull on loose piece of thread slowly, closing the tightly held loop (Figure 5) and making the invisible knot final. Remove pin point and tighten. With a razor blade cut end. *Be sure* you have pulled thread tight before cutting, or you will cut the knot itself instead of the end of the thread.

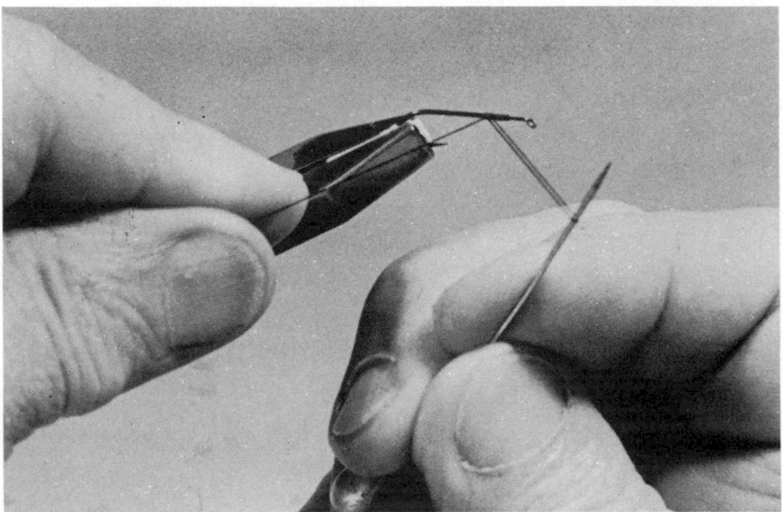

4. Holding the loop with a pin.

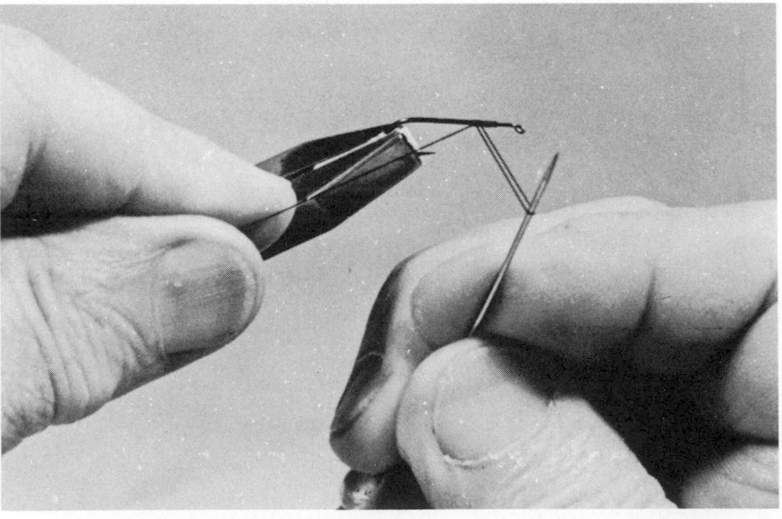

5. Pulling the knot snug.

This sounds like a complicated procedure, but when you see what the knot is all about, you will find it only slightly more difficult (but so much more satisfactory) than making a half hitch, and I feel certain you will agree it forms a much more attractive head for your fly. If your fly has been properly tied, you will have ample room for bending on your leader tippet. After cutting thread, remove fly from vise, cut hackle filaments that have "gone astray," and lacquer. At this point be extremely careful not to get lacquer in eye of hook. One of the most annoying things in fly fishing is to be on the stream and find the eye of a newly selected fly full of lacquer. Wasting good fishing time is criminal!

*Note:* The fly in the illustration was tied not on a hook of conventional size, which is usually a size 12 or smaller, but, hoping it might show up better, on a size 8. Also, when tying a Hendrickson to fish with, I always use Pearsall's Primrose silk thread; the one in the illustration was made with nylon size A black thread, to make the process more understandable.

## HACKLE-QUILL BODIES

This type quill was seldom if ever used for body material until I lucked onto the Red Quill, which was designed to imitate the male of *E. subvaria,* the female of which is known as the Hendrickson. I found it a better material for the Grey Fox Variant than the gold tinsel recommended by Preston Jennings, who originated it. It is impervious to water, holds up as well as or better than tinsel, is lighter and certainly looks more natural, although the latter is not apt to be much of a factor in a fly of the variant type. I also use this body for both the Dun and Cream Variants (different colors of course) and it also does well on a Ginger Quill and most other flies that call for a quill body. One notable exception is the Quill Gordon, which seems to work much better when tied with a body made of a stripped quill from a peacock quill, as explained at end of chapter.

Use the longest hackles from the end of a neck, feathers not suitable for anything else in making dry flies, and strip off filaments from the upper four inches, leaving about one half inch at the tip. Cut off balance (Figure 1). Soak well; this is *most*

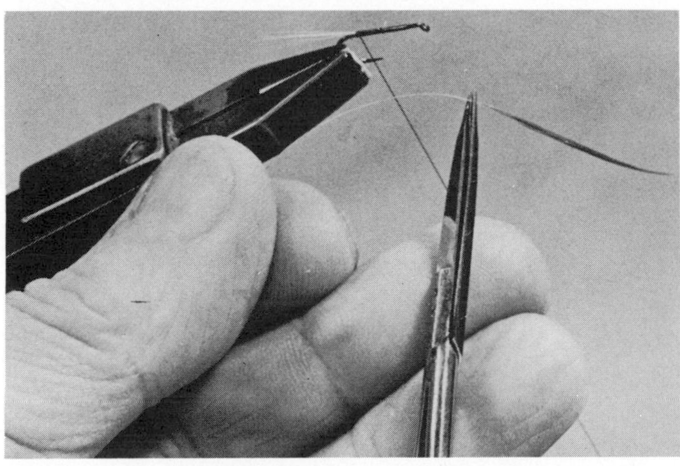

1. Cut off tip of quill ready to tie in.

*important*. If you are making a fly like the Red Quill, start the fly as described in making a Hendrickson, but instead of using fur for the body, take a *soaked* quill, cut off tip, and lock in by inserting tip between the hook and the thread (Figure 2) (tip is pointed toward the eye of the hook), and make three turns with thread to the right toward the eye of the hook. Using your hackle pliers, grasp the quill (Figure 3) and make three turns; lock in with one turn of the thread (Figure 4) and continue winding latter to the back of the wing, covering the butts of the tail feathers, hackles, and wing, giving you a smooth tapered body for winding the balance of the quill, which comes next. Be sure to wind the quill evenly, with no twisting, up to the wing; lock in with thread and cut as close as possible. After this is done wind over the cut portion to smooth it out. I find scissors do a better job here than a razor blade (Figure 5).

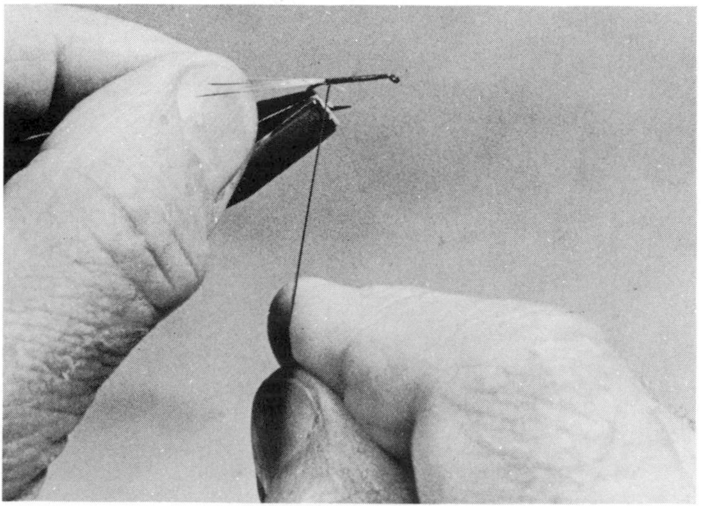

2. Starting to tie in the quill.

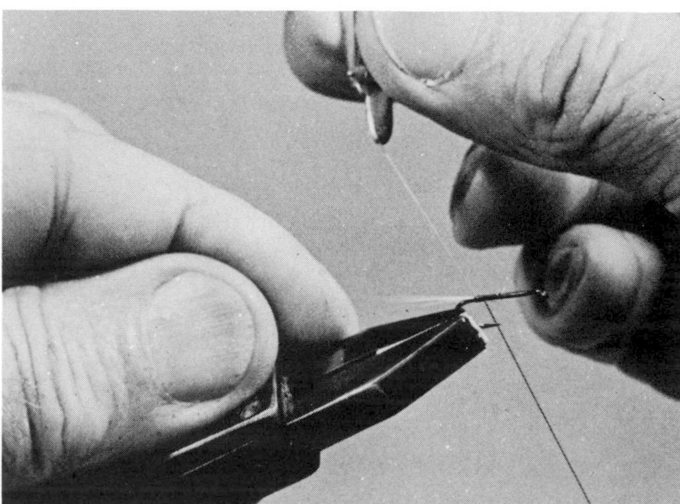

3. Start of quill body.

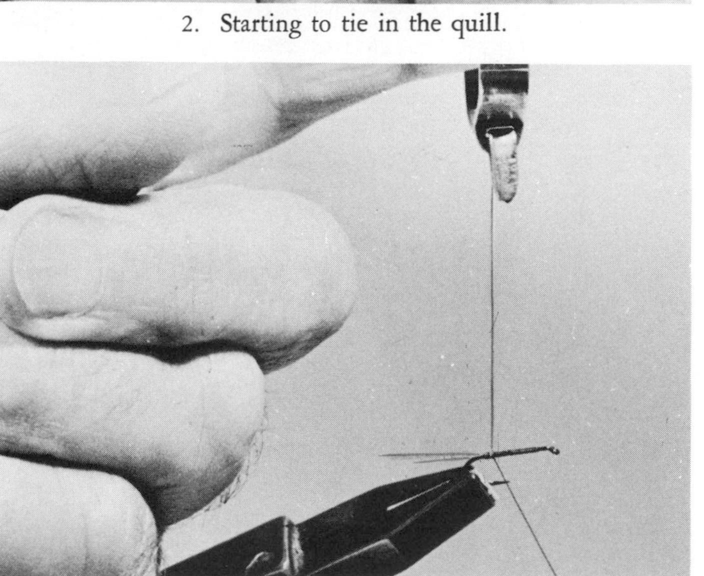

4. Where quill is locked in first.

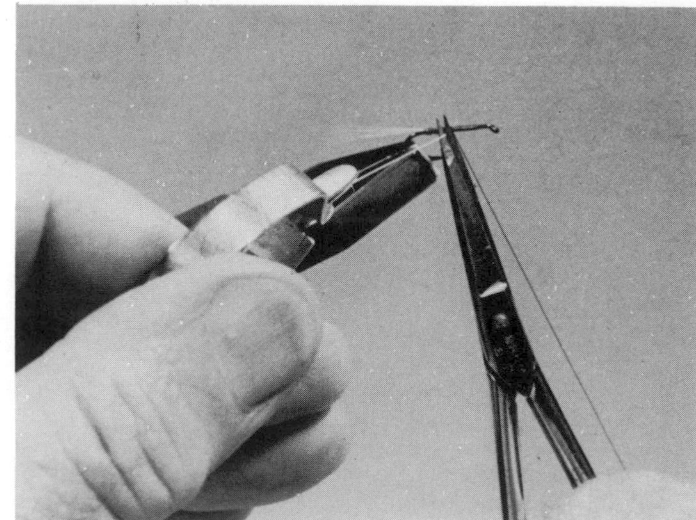

5. Cutting off the quill.

It is not absolutely necessary to undertake the extra operation of locking in the quill twice. You can wind the quill at the start right up to the wing, but it has been my experience that the extra precaution more than pays off, for sometimes the fine part of the quill will be cut by a trout's tooth. Should this happen, and the extra tie-in was accomplished, it is possible to take the fly off and make a minor repair at home, thereby saving the fly. If however, it has not been protected and tied right to the wing, your fly is pretty well shot, as it is difficult to tie in a complete body with wing and hackles in the way.

Feeling it would show the operation more clearly, the illustrations consist of only the quill being attached to the hook, without wings or hackles. And too, this will be the start of the type fly to follow.

*Note:* To make the quill body for the famous Quill Gordon, either dry or wet, a different technique is used. The most effective material seems to be the quill from a peacock eye. The best and easiest way to prepare this quill is to soak a complete eye in Clorox and leave immersed until the herl separates from the quill, leaving it bare. *Immediately* after the quill is free of herl, remove the eye and place it in a bowl containing water in which has been dissolved a tablespoon of baking soda, which will stop the action of the chemical. Then rinse in cold water. Caution: Be sure to watch this operation.

Do not be disappointed if on occasion you find that an individual eye will not take the bleach and might be brittle, for this will sometimes happen. Should you run into such an eye, discard it, for you will just have fits trying to wind it on, and these eyes are not expensive.

When tying a Quill Gordon, I always reinforce the body with fine gold wire, because the quills are quite fragile. Attach the wire to the hook before putting on the quill, and, after the latter is wound, put on the wire, winding it in the opposite direction from the one in which you wound the quill. Lacquer the body and wire when completely dry and you will have a fairly substantial body.

## THE GREY FOX VARIANT

If I were allowed only one pattern of fly over the entire season, I would not need to hesitate as to my choice—it would definitely be the Grey Fox Variant. The pattern was originally tied by Preston J. Jennings and described in his fine work, *A Book of Trout Flies.* He very kindly furnished me with some and I found them most effective. Over the seasons, I found that by varying his tying somewhat, I had a fly that worked even better. The original tying called for a gold tinsel body, for which I substitute the quill of a light-ginger hackle feather; his dressing calls for a ginger game cock, with grizzled cock hackle worked in as the front hackle. I have changed this to the three hackles mentioned later. There is no doubt in my mind that the combination of the three colors works much better than does the original dressing.

I make this fly in several sizes, from size 12 hooks down to size 18 hooks. However, in all cases the hackle sizes are much larger than they would be if tied on a conventional dry fly. For example, if I were making the Variant on a size 12 hook, the hackles would be about the size or larger than they would be if I were making a size 8 or 6 regular fly. A size 18 Variant would have hackles the size that one would use on about a size 14 fly. When properly made, this fly will catch many, many fish before coming apart; it floats as well as any flies that I know of, including the hair flies; and it is usually fairly easy to see. Although I use it more on fast water, it is amazing how often it will bring fish up in still pools. Often it is also a wonderful fish locater, as trout will frequently "splash rise" it when they really don't want it; one can then change to a conventional fly and sometimes take the fish after learning its location. Put it together as follows:

Start tying at about the center of the hook (Figure 1). Attach the tail material, the length of which will be considerably longer than in a conventional fly. This is more or less obvious because the hackle sizes are larger.

Proceed with a light-ginger quill that has been stripped and well soaked and make a quill body as previously described, but tying the quill only a short distance up the hook (Figures 2 & 3). Select three hackles that have been matched before for uniform size: one should be dark ginger, one grizzly, one light ginger. I hate to make a positive statement about it, but the fly always seems to work better if the hackles are put on in that order. Tie in, butts toward eye of hook, being careful not to have the filaments too close to the thread. You should be able to make about one half turn with hackle before the filaments come in contact with the hook. Try to place the hackles on the hook so the bright sides of the hackles face away from you, with the dark ginger first, grizzly second, and light ginger last. Cut off butts, but not all at the same time (Figure 4). Cut the first one, the second just a bit farther up, and the same with the third. Cutting them in this manner will give you a much neater fly, with less of a bunch at the point at which they are tied in. Here again a word of caution: *Do not tie in hackles too close to the eye*—leave yourself ample room so that when fly is completed you still have leader room (Figure 5).

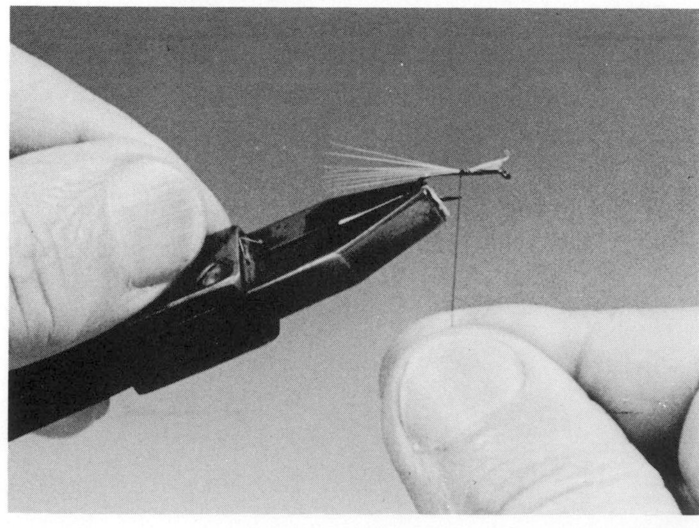

1. Beginning to tie the Grey Fox Variant.

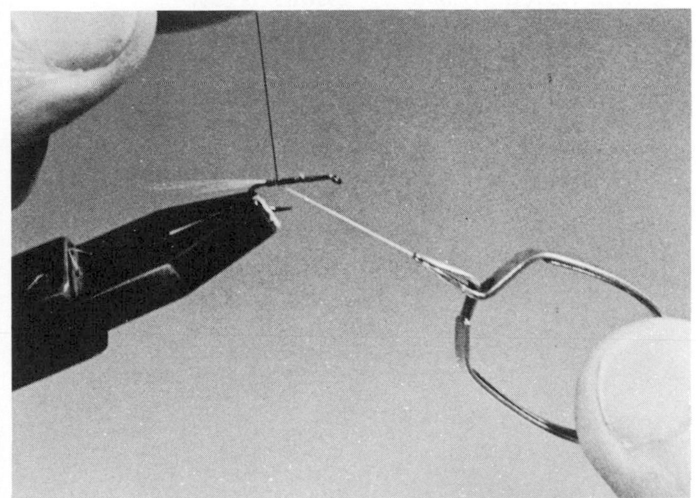
2. Where quill will be locked.

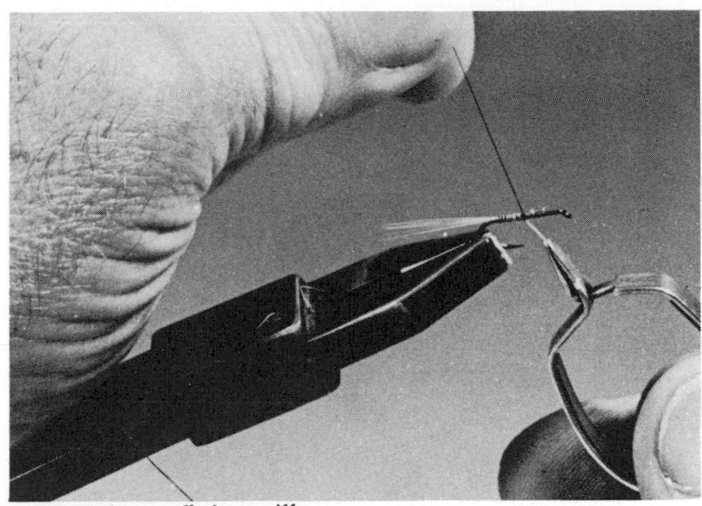
3. Locking off the quill.

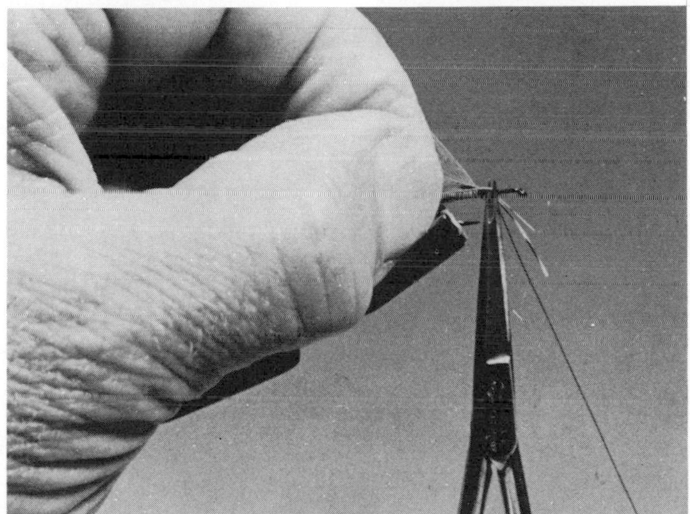
4. Cutting off the first hackle butt.

5. Hackle butts all tied in.

Spin the dark ginger, with bright side of hackle toward eye of hook, and make your turns just as close together as possible: *Do not spread hackle over a wide area of hook* (Figure 6). Lock in and do the same with the grizzly hackle, winding it over the ginger hackle. Yes, this will mess it up, but don't worry (Figure 7). Tie in, and wind light ginger hackle over the other two hackles (Figure 8). Strange as it may seem, winding the hackles over one another does not make a messy looking fly. Obviously some hackle filaments will be out of place, but only a very few; simply remove these. Using three feathers, there will be sufficient hackles to make a good floater. Be sure you use only good stiff hackles with a minimum of web. After the third hackle has been wound on, cut off the tip of quill and wind thread back (Figure 9), making sure the hackles are well locked in. Complete fly with the finishing-off knot previously described and lacquer head after trimming off surplus hackles (Figure 10). I like two coats of lacquer on body, but be sure quill has thoroughly dried before applying the first coat. *Do not attempt to make this fly winding the three hackles at the same time.*

6. The first hackle tied in.

7. The second hackle tied in.

8. The third hackle ready to wind.

9. Cutting the third hackle.

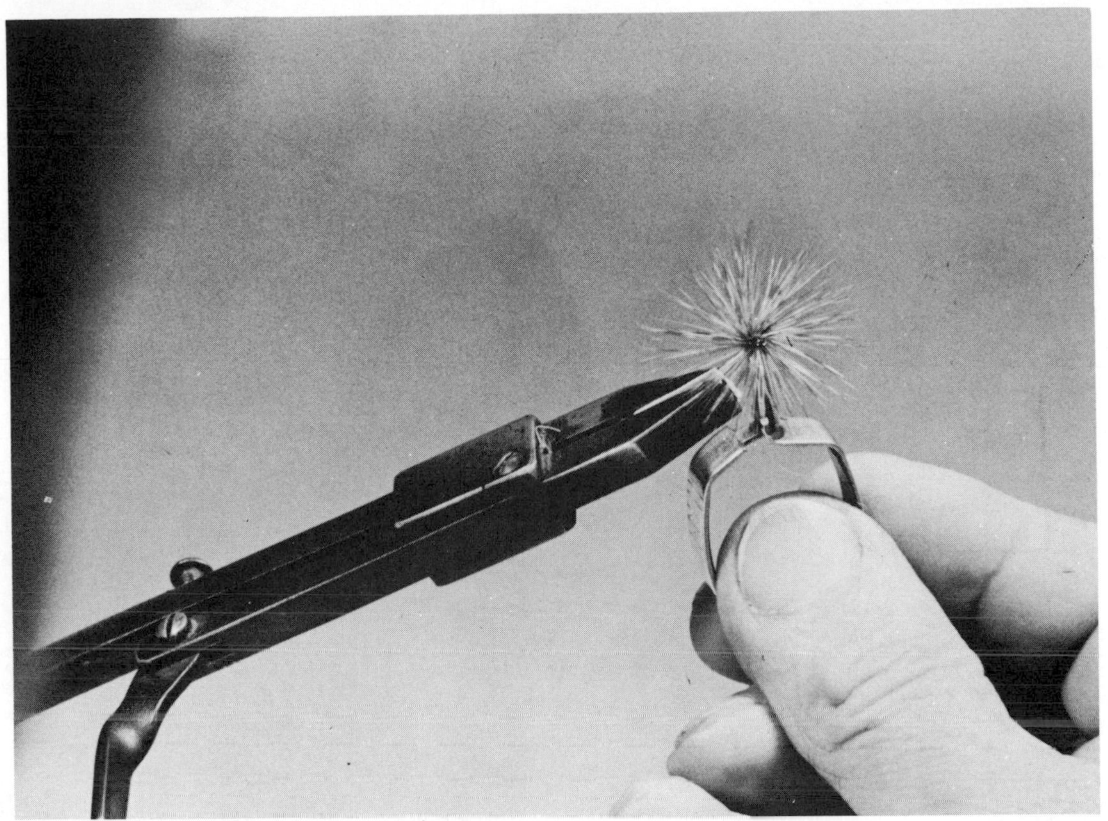

10. The finished fly. Note the uniformity of hackle lengths.

Three hackles should bc used on all variants tied on hook sizes down to size 16; two are sufficient in tying sizes 18 and 20, should you go that small. When only two hackles are used, tie in a medium ginger with the grizzly.

The Grey Fox Variant is an excellent fly, and well worth your learning to tie it.

# Doug Swisher and Carl Richards

## SWISHER-RICHARDS PATTERNS

Photographs and Drawings by the Authors

We originally developed these patterns because of our utter frustration with standard hackle flies. When faced with a large emergence of insects, mayflies in particular, the standards simply did not work with any degree of consistency. After many bitter experiences when trout were feeding heavily, we worked out a series of new patterns for these specific situations. It has been our experience that these patterns, when used at the correct time, outfish the so-called standards by a very wide margin.

For a while after developing these patterns, we continued to use the heavily hackled flies when no fish were seen working, in an attempt to "pound them up." During these dead periods, it has been well documented that the angler gets many false rises, flashes, or bumps. Fish come up to take a look but don't take the fly. Many times these attractor-type lures are known as fish finders. Once an active fish was located, a more realistic pattern would be presented in an attempt to get the fish to take it. It came as no great surprise, then, to find the No-Hackle Duns, Hen Spinners, and Hen Caddis extremely effective not only as fish locaters, but fish catchers, during these dull periods. After all, once you analyze the situation, it's only natural that a fish on the alert for something edible is most likely to take an artificial that closely resembles the naturals he is accustomed to feeding on every day. Why should he be more interested in a large bushy "thing" resembling a fuzzy dandelion seed than in a realistic-appearing, lifelike artificial?

We have seen and used many superrealistic imitations of aquatic insects tied by flytyers who are real artists, some even going so far as to paint markings on wings and bodies and bend individual legs at the correct angles. These patterns do work very well. However, it is doubtful if this type of fly will ever become generally accepted. They can never be available to nonflytyers at a reasonable price, and it takes even an expert tyer thirty to sixty minutes or more to create one. For any new idea in fly patterns to become popular, it must have two basic qualities: it must be effective, and it must be simple to tie. The patterns we will discuss really do work, and as you will be able to see, our flies are reduced to the bare minimum of materials.

This is not to give the impression they can be just thrown together. The proportions must be right to give a good outline, and certain steps must be taken so they balance and ride the water in a natural position. For the duns, this position would be upright but low and level with the surface; for the spinners, flush in the film; and for the caddis, either high off the water or low, depending on the stage.

We have become known as advocates of the no-hackle dry flies, and in many cases this is true. However, by no means do we eliminate hackle for all situations. Many times a high-riding fly is needed. With insects such as caddis, stone flies, and midges—which fly low over the water, sometimes dipping down to touch the surface during egg-laying swarms—the hackled fly keeps the body up off the water and resembles the rapidly beating blur of the wings. This is the reason the Adams is such a good pattern; it looks like a flying caddis. In imitating freshly hatched mayfly duns, which ride the water parallel and either close to or touching the surface, we advocate no hackle because it fuzzes up the delicate saillike outline and tilts the body at an unnatural angle. We also eliminate hackle from the spent spinner because this imitation, like the natural spinner, must lie flat in the film with both wings and body touching the water. The Hen Caddis, however, is heavily hackled, palmer style, and is one of our favorite attractor flies, especially on faster water. This pattern simulates the caddis that bounce over the riffles all day long on most rivers.

## NO-HACKLE DUNS

The first pattern we will discuss in detail is probably the best known of our flies, the No-Hackle Dun. It is designed to imitate the newly hatched dun, or subimago, of the mayfly. One curious fact became obvious to us early in our study: the smaller the natural to be imitated, the less effective a hackled fly became during a hatch. For us, imitations size 16 and smaller did not work with any reliability when trying to entice selective trout, so our initial no-hackle experimentation was directed at the smaller sizes. Until recently, we did not tie the No-Hackles in sizes larger than 12 or 14, as the weight of the larger hooks, even in 3X fine, was too much. By using a smaller hook and an extended body, the core of which is either nylon or polypropylene monofilament, a larger high-floating no-hackle can be constructed.

Tails on this hackleless pattern are split widely to act as balancing outriggers that help the fly to ride in an upright position. We developed a wing-mounting technique so that the wings, instead of protruding from the top of the body, actually radiate from the sides of the body, creating a wedge effect. Wings mounted in this manner add two more outriggers, which greatly improve stability. More importantly, this type of structure practically insures that the fly will land upright and will also be locked properly into the surface film.

Some other new developments include the use of polypropylene yarn and beaver-belly fur as body materials. Poly yarn has a specific gravity of less than water so it contributes greatly to the flotation of the fly; it is also waterproof and completely impervious to fish slime. Poly is also available in floss, and either form can be wrapped as it comes or cut up and dubbed as fur. Both methods work well and look very realistic.

White domestic rabbit fur was originally used as a body material on our No-Hackle Duns, mainly because of availability and the obvious dyeing advantages. Recently, however, we have found that beaver belly, if bleached and dyed properly, can be utilized to dub bodies of the highest quality. It displays two outstanding characteristics—fine texture and very few guard hairs—both of which greatly facilitate the formation of neat, well-tapered bodies. Excellent flotation is also produced by such a fine-grained structure. The finer the fur the more fiber "flats" and fiber "ends" that touch the water and correspondingly increase buoyant qualities.

The duck primary wing segments as originally used for the upright wings of the pattern presented the most realistic outline but were not very durable. By applying a thin layer of vinyl or polyurethane resin to the inside of the wings, we found that they held up under repeated use and landed many fish. Hen hackle tips, duck and goose shoulder feathers, and turkey body feathers can also be used to fashion durable wings, although it is a little more difficult to create the important wedge effect with these center-stemmed materials.

The following tying techniques are the ones we use personally. Professional tyers would differ in some respects for speed. For instance, if one were tying for production, tail fibers would all be tied in at the same time and then crisscrossed with tying thread to split them. We tie each on separately and use a ball of fur to keep them apart, thus locking them into position permanently. This, of course, is very important for balance. These methods may take a little longer, but the extra time assures a durable, well-balanced fly. In fact, these flies are so uncomplicated that we believe even professional tyers should use these techniques.

Colors of duns vary greatly, but here is a list of our favorite patterns in various sizes:

| | |
|---|---|
| Slate/Tan | sizes 12–22 |
| Slate/Olive | sizes 14–20 |
| Gray/Olive | sizes 16–24 |
| Gray/Yellow | sizes 16–22 |

*Slate/Tan No-Hackle**

Hook: Nos. 12–22, 3X fine (1X fine acceptable if polypropylene yarn is used)
Thread: dark-brown Nymo
Body: tan fur or poly yarn, either wrapped as floss or cut, mixed and spun as fur
Wings: dark-gray duck-quill segments
Tails: bronze blue-dun cock-hackle fibers, widely spread
Hackle: none

1. Wrap tying thread to bend of hook and spin a small amount of fur on tying thread.

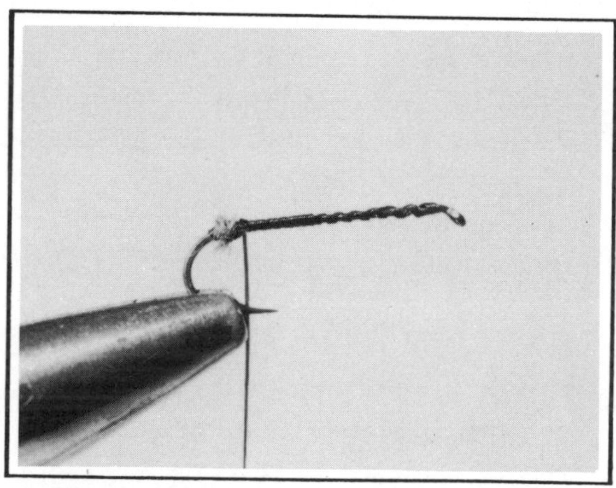

2. Wrap a tiny tuft of fur at bend of hook.

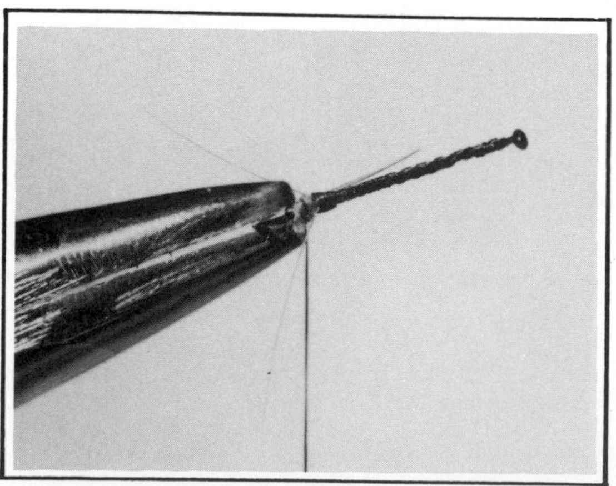

3. Tie in tail fibers on either side of tuft and crimp into fur so tails are widely spread. On small flies, use one fiber per side; on larger flies, use two or more fibers per side. Tails should lie in the same horizontal plane as the body.

* In our terminology, the first name is the color of the wing, the second is the color of the body, and the third is the type of fly, such as the Hen Spinner, Emerger, No-Hackle.

4. Spin more fur on tying thread and wrap body to wing position.

5. Tie on two perfectly matched sections of primary duck quill. These segments must be cut from opposite right and left feathers. The wings should be tied in such a fashion as to radiate from the sides of the body. (See six sketches for detailed mounting procedures.)

6. Spin more fur on tying thread, wrap thorax, and tie off. If desired, coat inside of wings with vinyl cement or polyurethane resin for durability.

## MOUNTING DUCK-QUILL-SEGMENT WINGS, SIDEWINDER STYLE

These sketches illustrate the method for mounting paired duck-quill segments so that they radiate from the sides of the body. Once the wings are put into position, this procedure is almost completely concealed from the view of the tyer by his left thumb and left forefinger. For simplicity of illustration, the fingers have not been sketched in. Body and tails have also been eliminated.

1. With tying thread at wing position, place wings, convex sides together, so that they straddle the hook and slant backward at approximately 60° to the shank. Hold in this position with left thumb and forefinger and make final adjustment for proper wing length, which should be equal to body length plus hook eye.

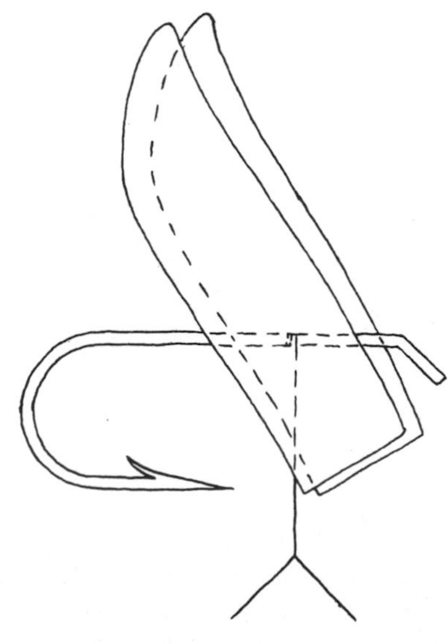

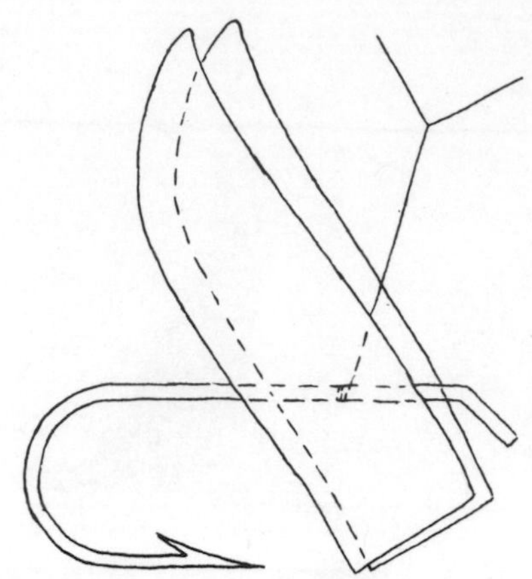

2. Slightly loosen pressure between left thumb and forefinger and bring tying thread up between wings. Tighten pressure between left thumb and forefinger.

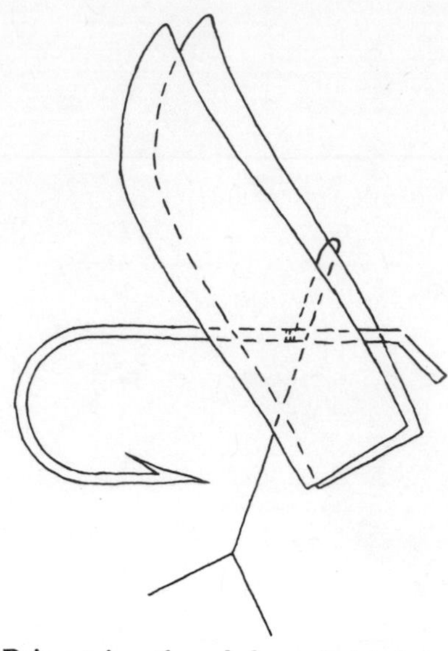

3. Bring tying thread down behind far wing, forming a loose loop. Slightly loosen pressure between left thumb and forefinger. Slide thread between forefinger and far wing. Retighten pressure between thumb and forefinger. Do not pull loop tight.

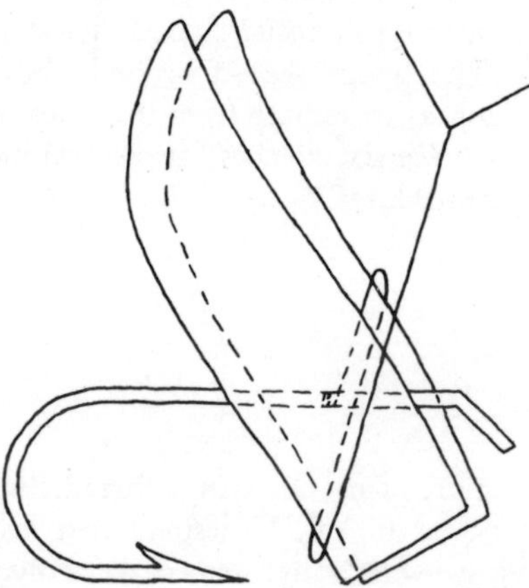

4. Bring tying thread up around near wing, forming another loose loop. Slightly loosen pressure between left thumb and forefinger. Slide thread between thumb and near wing. Retighten pressure between left thumb and forefinger. Again, *do not pull* loop tight.

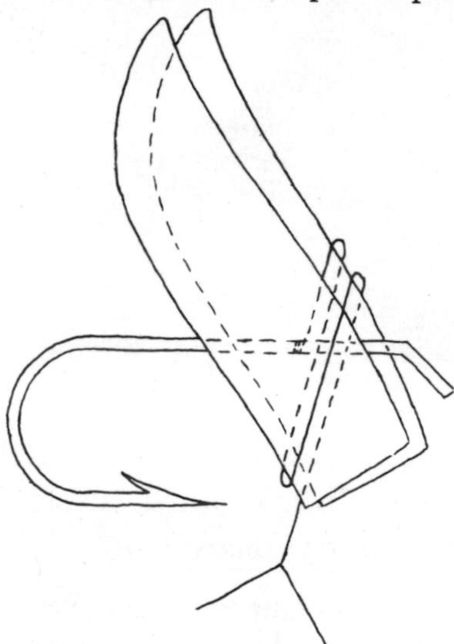

5. Bring tying thread down behind far wing, forming another loose loop. Slightly loosen pressure between left thumb and forefinger. Slide thread between forefinger and far wing. Retighten pressure between thumb and forefinger.

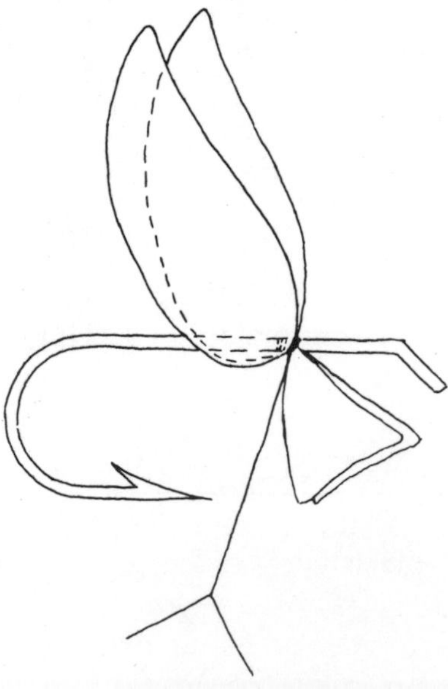

6. Slowly pull straight down on tying thread, keeping firm pressure between thumb and forefinger. After tightening all loops completely, add several more turns of tying thread. Wings should be secure and positioned properly at this point. The only step left (not illustrated) is to clip the butts.

*Slate/Olive, No-Hackle, Extended Body*

Hook: No. 14, 3X fine
Thread: brown Nymo
Body: olive-green fur or poly yarn
Wings: dark-gray goose primary sections
Tails: three condor fibers from short side of feather
Hackle: none

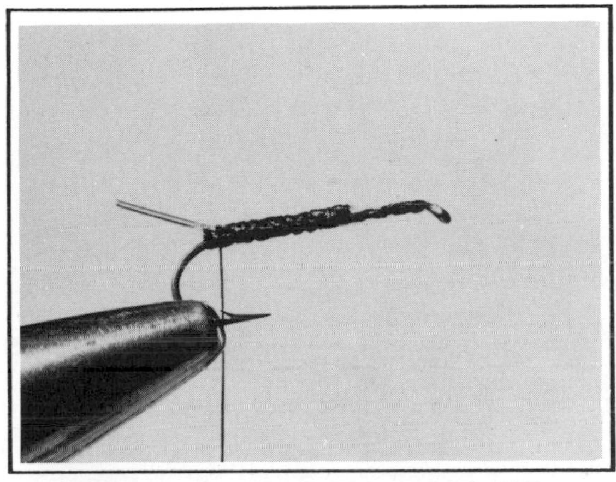

1. Wrap thread from bend of hook to eye. Tie in a piece of approximately 10-pound test nylon or polypropylene monofilament and attach securely to shank by wrapping thread back to bend of hook. Tie off and cement.

2. Tie in three tail fibers at bend of hook. Wrap thread around tails and extended part of monofilament to the desired length of the finished body. Bring thread back to hook. Put vinyl cement on split tails to hold them in position.

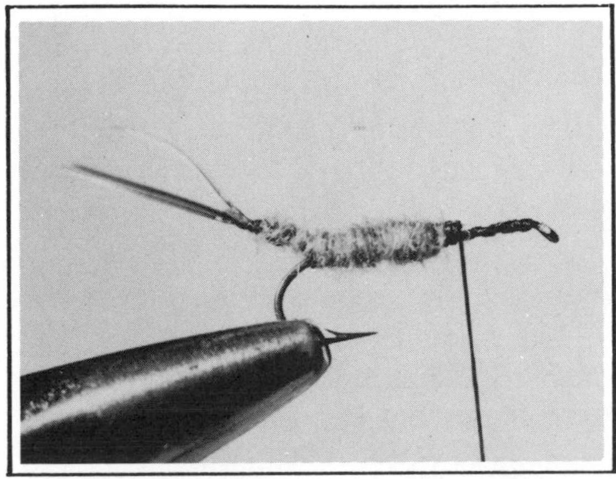

3. Spin fur or poly yarn on tying thread and wrap up to tail and back to wing position.

4. Tie in two dark-gray goose primary sections, sidewinder style.

5. Spin more fur on thread, wrap thorax, and finish.

6. A variation of this type would be to tie in one very high quality olive game-cock hackle, wrap, and then trim top and bottom, leaving only those fibers that radiate to the side and slightly downward. This is called the V-hackle Drake. By trimming hackle the fuzz effect is eliminated while the side fibers provide balance. This technique works well with large drake limitations.

### *Paraduns and Paradrakes*

Paraduns are used for the smaller, more delicate mayfly imitations, sizes 14 to 28; the Paradrakes are used to imitate the larger mayflies, commonly called drakes, from size 4 to 12. These patterns are characterized by clump-type wings with gamecock hackle wound around the clump for balance and support. Hen-hackle fibers form the clump on the smaller flies, and elk and deer hair are used on the larger drakes.

The effectiveness of these patterns is due to the unencumbered wing outline and the parachute hackle that allows the fly to ride low and level with the water. The body of the large Paradrake is extended beyond the bend of the hook and is constructed of hollow elk hair. Deer hair can be used also, but it is not as efficient and has a poorer appearance. Not all elk hair is hollow, however, so you must be sure to obtain hair that has this quality. The largest and longest hair is usually best.

*Gray/Olive Paradun*

Hook: Nos. 14–28, 3X fine
Thread: dark olive
Body: olive fur or polypropylene yarn
Wings: clump of gray hen hackle or hen body-feather fibers
Tails: olive cock-hackle fibers
Hackle: olive, parachute style

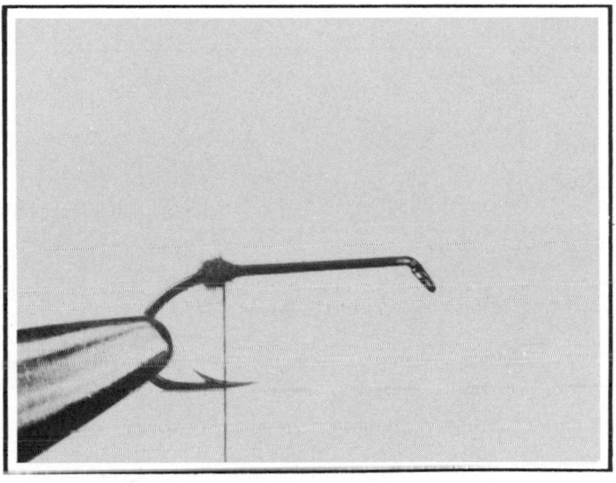

1. Attach tying thread at bend of hook and spin a small amount of fur on tying thread.

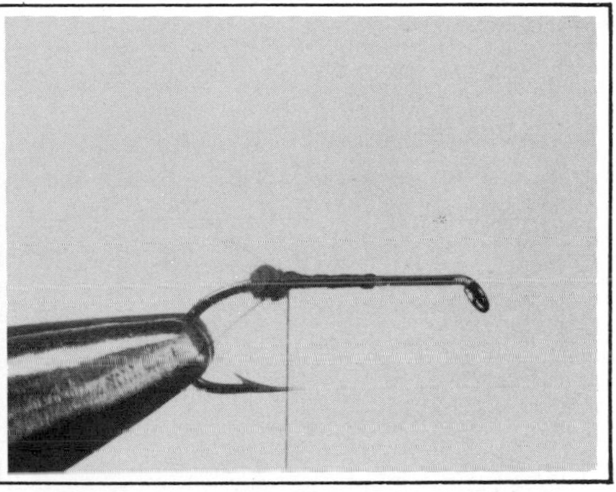

2. Wrap a tiny tuft of fur at bend of hook. Tie in tail fibers on either side of tuft and crimp into fur so tails are widely spread.

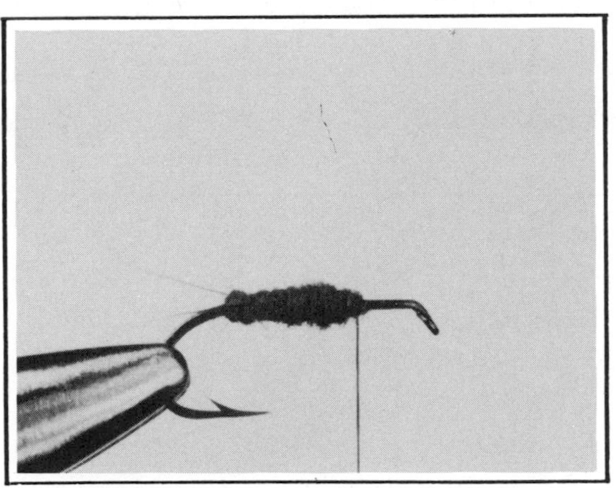

3. Spin more fur on tying thread and wrap body to wing position.

4. Tie in a clump of hen-hackle fibers for the wing. The best hackle for this purpose is all web, even at the tips of the fibers. Stand fibers upright with several turns behind clump; trim butts.

5. Attach a short-fibered cock hackle on top of hook at the base of the clump-wing. At this point, before winding the hackle, be sure to check the body for correct shape and fullness. Normally, a small amount of fur must be added in the thorax area for proper proportions.

6. Wind the hackle around the base of the clump-wing, parachute style, and tie off.

---

*Slate/Cream Paradrake*

| | |
|---|---|
| Hook: | Nos. 12–16, 3X fine |
| Thread: | cream Nymo |
| Body: | light tannish-cream elk hair, hollow and extended |
| Ribbing: | cream tying thread |
| Wings: | clump of dark-gray elk hair |
| Tails: | three gray condor fibers |
| Hackle: | cream, parachute style |

---

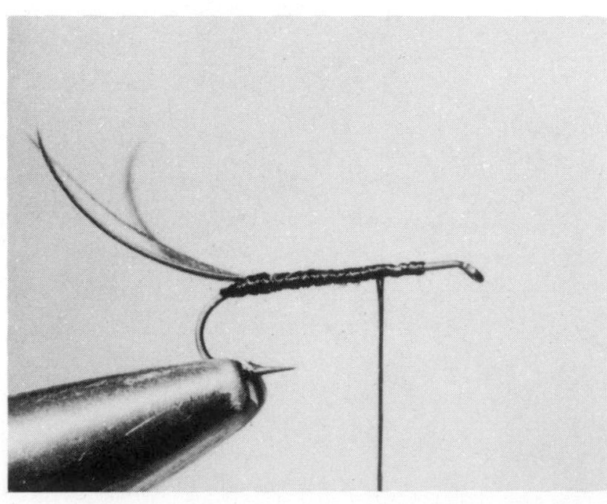

1. Attach the thread to hook and tie in three condor fibers (or mallard primary fibers on smaller sizes) longer than normal to allow for the extended body. Return thread to wing position and tie off.

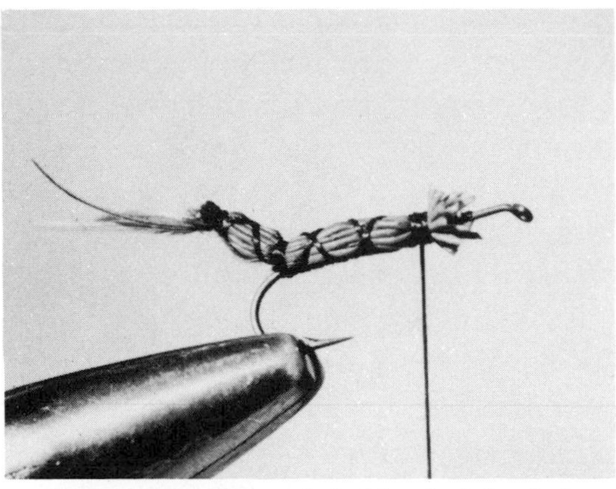

2. With butts forward, hold a bunch of the elk body-hair parallel to and surrounding the hook shank. Tie in with several turns, still holding the hair in proper position with thumb and forefinger. The tying thread is wrapped around the hair, like ribbing, past the bend of the hook to the desired body length. When the end of the body is reached, the thread is reversed back to the wing position, creating a criss-cross ribbing effect.

3. Clip off the flared butts and tips of hair. Tie in a clump-wing of dark-gray elk hair and trim butts. A top-quality gamecock hackle is tied in on top and close to wing.

4. Wind hackle around base of wing, tie off, and finish head.

The Paradrake is a good solution to the problem of realistically imitating large duns. The hollow elk hair allows the large flies to float well while keeping a realistic shape. A smaller, lighter hook may also be used for either of the parachute-style flies.

*Hen Spinner*

The Hen Spinner was originally designed for specific rise situations, namely those periods when the trout feed on fully spent imagos that are riding in the surface film. We have found them to be unequaled for this purpose. Normally they are tied with the wings radiating directly from either side of the body, or 180° apart, a feature that gives them an airplanelike appearance. We have also found them to be very effective when the wings are tied either half or partially spent. These positions imitate various stages from the time the natural spinner lands on the surface of the water until it is fully exhausted.

Further experimentation has proven the Hen Spinner to be an excellent attractor pattern, especially during the early-morning hours of midsummer and late summer. At these times, trout, often large ones, seem to be cruising in search of a good meal. Possibly they are looking for the previous evening's spinners that are occasionally released from backwaters and eddies. Whatever the reason, a fairly large Hen Spinner, size 14 or 16, is frequently just the right fly for "blind" morning fishing. This type of fishing can provide feverish activity even though a heavy hatch or spinner fall is not taking place. This is also relatively simple angling for the fly-fisherman. The Hen Spinner, with its large light-gray wings, is very easy to follow as it is drifted methodically over likely holding areas and known feeding stations.

Due to its uncomplicated design, the first impression of most flytyers is that the Hen Spinner is very easy to assemble. The pattern has such a clean-cut, unencumbered silhouette, and requires so few materials to create it, that many try to neglect the details of construction and even take short cuts. If the Hen Spinner is to accomplish effectively what it was designed to do, great care must be taken, especially in the selection, preparation, and mounting of the wings.

The unique wings of the pattern are normally made of hen-hackle tips. They are wide and webby and retain their shape when wet. Mayfly wings are wide, and the normal cock hackle is too narrow to simulate the natural. Hen hackle has been traditionally used for wet flies because it absorbs water and sinks. But when it is well dressed it absorbs the flotant, sheds water, and supports the fly while retaining the natural wing outline. Hen-body and breast feathers can also be used as wing material.

The Dun/Brown Hen-Spinner pattern, in various sizes, is almost a universal pattern for 90 percent of the naturals. Add a few Dun/Olive Hen Spinners in sizes 16 to 22 for western *Ephemerellas,* and some *Baetis,* and Dun/Cream Hen Spinners for eastern Green Drakes and *Stenonemas,* and you have all the colors needed across the country.

---

*Dun/Brown Hen Spinner*

Hook: Nos. 12–28, 3X fine
Thread: dark brown
Body: reddish-brown fur or poly yarn
Wings: light-gray hen-hackle tips
Tails: light-dun cock-hackle fibers
Hackle: none

---

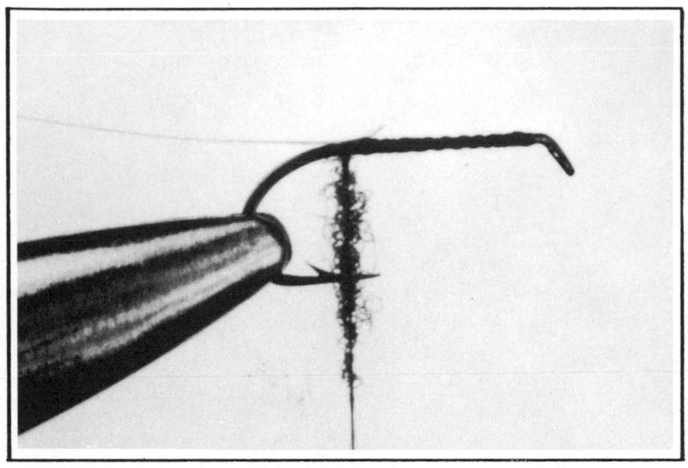

1. Attach the tying thread to the head of the hook and wrap back to bend. Tie in a single light-dun cock-hackle fiber. (For two-tailed spinner this step can be eliminated.) Spin a small amount of poly yarn on tying thread. Wrap a tiny tuft at bend of hook.

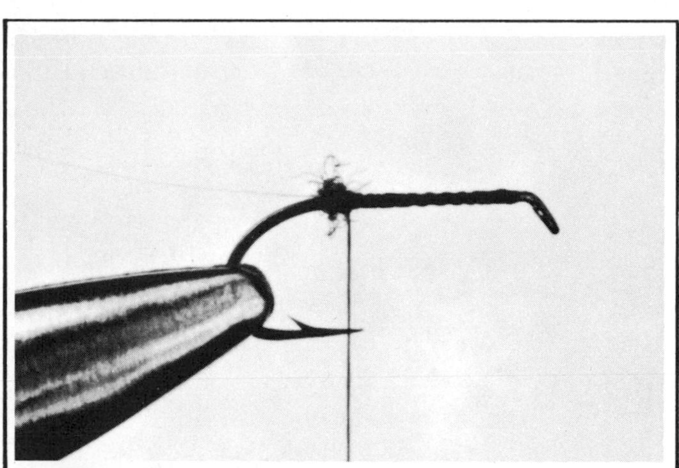

2. Tie in one tail fiber on each side of the tuft and crimp into poly yarn so they are widely spread. In this pattern, the split tails are really not needed for balance. The spent wings are more than adequate, but the split tails add considerably to the appearance and realism of the outline.

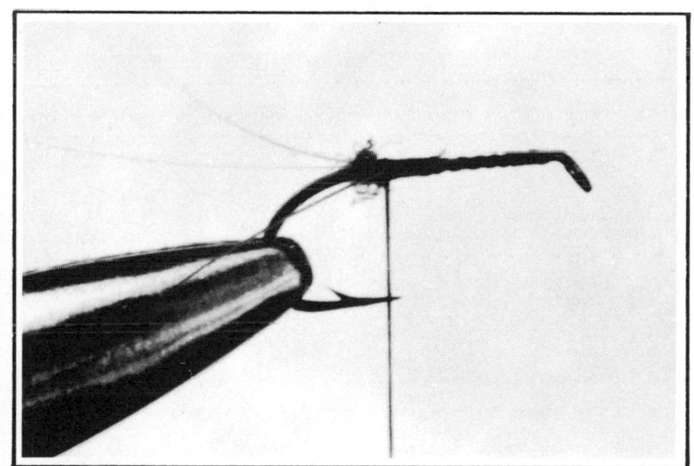

3. Spin fur on tying thread and wrap body to wing position.

4. Tie first hen-hackle tip-wing into spent position, convex side down. Butt should be clipped, not stripped, as this adds rigidity and strength to wings.

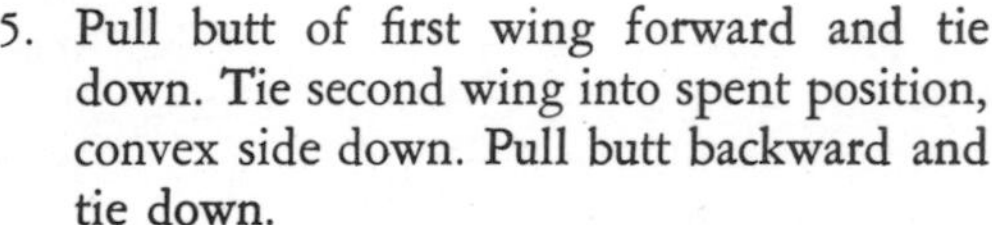

5. Pull butt of first wing forward and tie down. Tie second wing into spent position, convex side down. Pull butt backward and tie down.

6. Trim wing butts. Wrap more spun fur around base and in front of the wings and finish.

---

### *Hen Caddis and Spent Caddis*

Natural caddis flies are found on nearly all rivers and seem to be especially abundant on some with a dearth of mayfly hatches. They are sometimes profuse on waters below impoundments where the water level fluctuates drastically due to varying hydroelectric power requirements. Though they are second only in importance to the *Ephemerids*, too little time is spent on their simulations. A superabundance of species makes their recognition as individual species very difficult. We can simplify this greatly by stating that only three basic body colors, blackish-gray, tan, and green, in various sizes, will imitate almost all the naturals over the entire country. Wing colors are predominantly gray, tan, or cream. These flies are tied in two variations: a palmer-hackled fly to imitate a flying, buzzing insect, and a sparsely hackled "at rest" pattern to imitate the spent fly. These are the only dry flies you need to be successful on any stream or lake when caddis are on the water.

On most streams in the daylight hours a few adult caddis are dipping over the water, and fish seem to be on the lookout for them. Thus, the palmered-hackle hen caddis becomes a great attraction for searching the water. It is just right for realism, and it rides high and is pleasant for the angler to follow as it drifts through runs and riffles.

In the evening, when other species are fluttering over the water, the spent caddis is often devastating. This can be an extremely trying time for people who do not recognize a caddis fall as opposed to a mayfly spinner fall. In fact, on some of the great rich rivers such as Henry's Fork of the Snake in Idaho, it is possible to have spent caddis, spent *Ephemerids,* and mayfly duns all on the water simultaneously. The angler must be able to discover which stage of what insect the fish prefer, and the discovery must be made quickly as the rise does not last indefinitely. If you guess wrong too many times, the action is over.

*Dun/Tan Hen Caddis*

Hook: Nos. 14–22, 3X fine
Thread: brown Nymo
Body: tan fur
Wings: two light-gray hen-hackle tips
Tails: none
Hackle: light-bronze blue dun, tied palmer

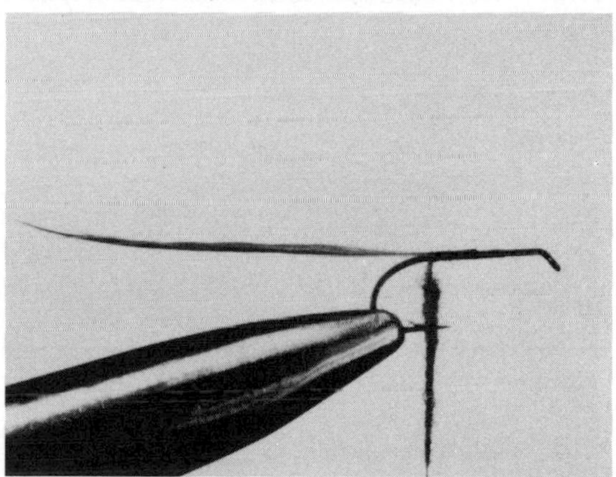

1. Attach thread to hook and wrap to bend. Tie in bronze-blue gamecock hackle of best quality. Spin fur on tying thread.

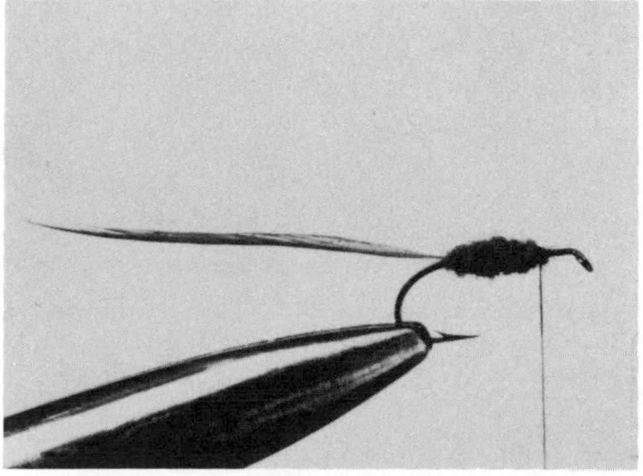

2. Wind a fat fur body to simulate body of natural, leaving room for the wings.

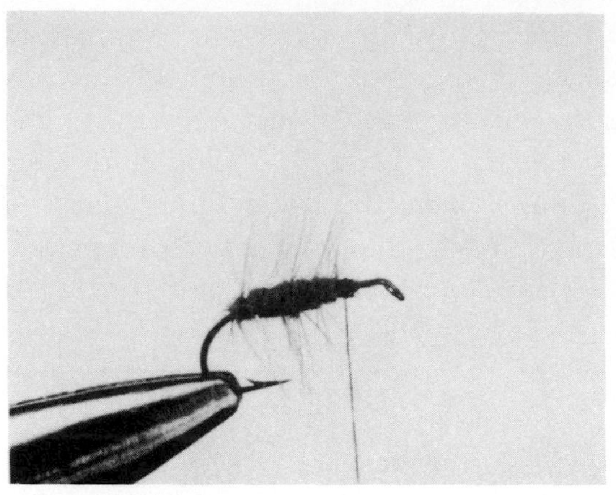

3. Wind the hackle from the bend of the hook to head, over the body, palmer style.

4. Tie off hackle, then tie in two light-gray hen-hackle tips flat over body to simulate downwing of caddis fly. Form head and tie off.

---

*Cream/Olive Caddis Spinner*

Hook: Nos. 14–18, 3X fine
Thread: cream Nymo
Body: yellow and light-green fur, mixed
Wings: cream duck-quill segments
Tails: none
Hackle: cream trimmed, top and bottom

---

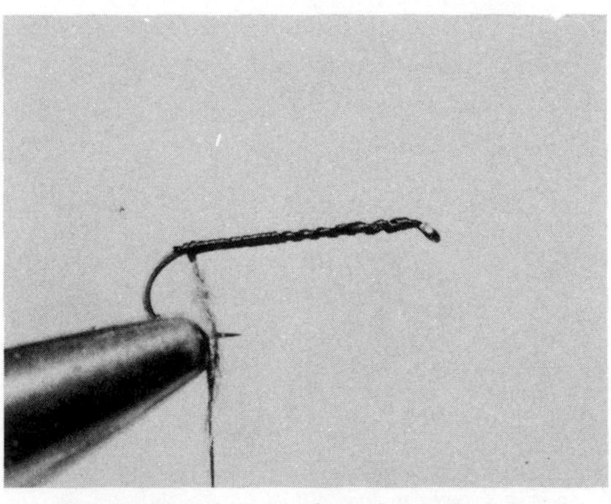

1. Attach thread to hook and wind to bend. Spin a blend of light-yellow and light-green fur on tying thread.

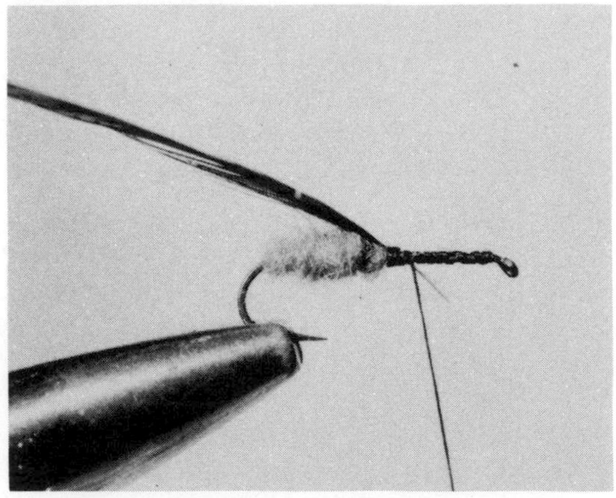

2. Wrap a fat body over two-thirds of shank length. Tie in a short-fibered cream gamecock hackle.

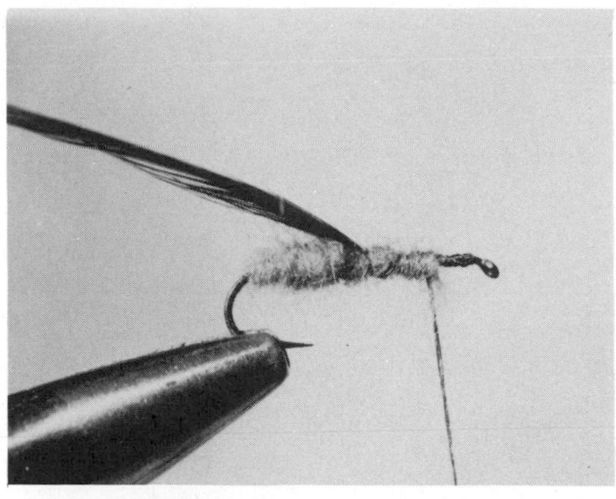

3. Wrap balance of body, much thinner, with tying thread only, leaving just enough room for the head. Wind hackle almost to the head and trim top and bottom.

4. Mount first cream duck-quill-segment wing flat over the body, with concave side down and point to the outside.

5. Mount second wing, with concave side down and point to the opposite side. Trim butts of both wings. Form head and tie off.

### *Caddis Pupa*

One of our favorite nymphal-type patterns is the Caddis Pupa. This artificial not only is a deadly hatch matcher, but it also works very well as an attractor. Such effectiveness undoubtedly is due to the fact that great numbers of caddis live in much of our trout water; in addition, the most important stage of many caddis species is the pupal stage. The reason that the pupa stage is so important is its availability to the trout. Unlike mayfly adults, which normally float for relatively long periods of time on the surface, caddis flies burst into the air immediately after emergence takes place. Thus the vulnerable stage for this insect is the rising and drifting pupa.

Until recently, few anglers knew exactly what a caddis pupa looked like. They are quite different from a mayfly nymph in both appearance and actions. The traditional imitation has the wing pads on the top, but this is not the way of the natural. The pads extend more from the side of the body and hang down in a low-slung position. The artificial should be tied accordingly. This more realistic imitation is fished dead drift on the surface, dead swing, or sunk deep and then raised with short twitches. These methods are deadly when used at the proper time. Like the adult caddis flies, the most common body colors are tan, blackish, and green. Some very large and some very small species are locally present and even abundant, but the average size over the country is size 14 to size 18.

---

*Tan Caddis Pupa*

Hook: Nos. 14–22, 1X fine or heavier depending on how deep you want fly to sink
Thread: brown Nymo
Body: tan fur
Wing Pads: dark-gray duck-shoulder feathers
Tails: none
Legs: Hungarian partridge fibers
Head: dark-gray fur or condor quill

---

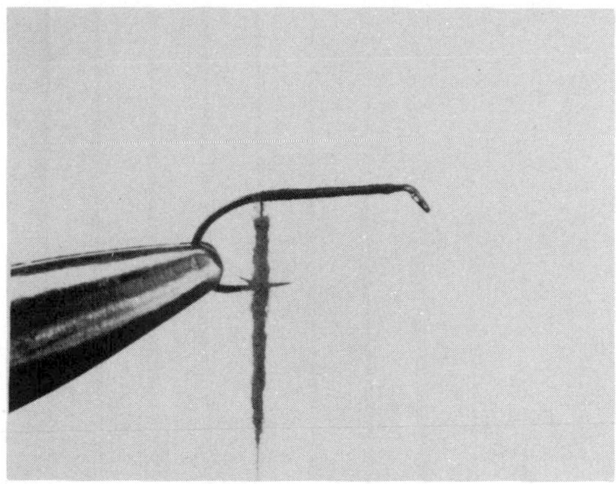

1. Attach thread to hook and wind to bend. Spin fur on tying thread. Wrap a fat fur body, leaving room for legs, wing pads, and fuzzy head.

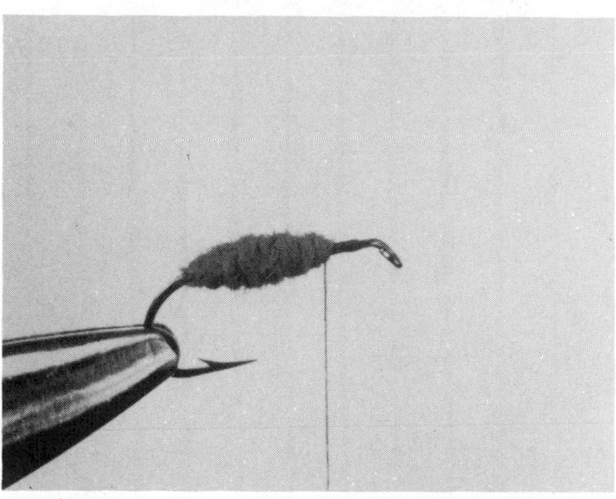

2. Tie in six Hungarian partridge fibers, beard style, extending past hook point.

3. Mount wing pads so that they hang low on sides. Spin a very small amount of dark-gray fur on tying thread.

4. Wrap fur to form a fuzzy, shaggy head, and then tie off.

5. Finished fly.

# Ed Koch

## TERRESTRIALS and MIDGES

Photographs by Norm Shires, Carlisle, Pennsylvania

The limestone waters of Pennsylvania have over the years produced an outstanding array of fly-fishermen and flytyers. Such names as Ed Shenk, Charlie Fox, Vince Marinaro, Ernie Schwiebert, C. K. Lively, Ed "Tony" Skilton, Barry Beck, and Ron Eichelberger are but a few who in one way or another met the challenge of the fabled streams and emerged victorious as contributors to a new dimension in the art of fly-tying and fly-fishing.

Their task was not necessarily to match a specific hatch, as had been the problem in the past. The limestone trout fed constantly all season long, hatch or no. The main object became to match an apparent hatch of "no see-ums," as they were called back in the early days. Some of what they tried to imitate were minutiae; others were not but were assumed to be so because a trout could be seen rising when no fly was on the water. As it turned out, they found the trout to be feeding on land-bred insects or terrestrials. Much has been written on the development of the terrestrials, so this chapter will deal with the tying of specific patterns—patterns that have proven themselves on trout waters the world over.

Terrestrials are fished differently from other flies. They are presented on or in the surface film. Generally the cast is upstream as with a dry fly, and the fly is fished with a drag-free float. Terrestrials are productive spring, summer, and fall—

more productive than most anglers realize. To select the best all-around pattern would be difficult if not impossible. At times the hopper is best; but at other times the ants are deadly. Often the trout go crazy over a size 14 cricket. Fished properly they all work well. The order in which they appear here does not necessarily imply the order of effectiveness.

### *Letort Cricket*

The Letort Cricket, originated by Ed Shenk of Carlisle, has been an outstanding trout taker for some fifteen or more years. Shenk fished the pattern long before the public was aware of it. In 1962 I took a 27½-inch, nine-pound brown from the Letort on a No. 12 cricket. Shortly thereafter, articles on the cricket appeared in *Outdoor Life*, *Sports Afield*, *Trout*, *The Pennsylvania Angler*, and in Charlie Fox's book, *This Wonderful World of Trout*. It wasn't long before the cricket had earned a well-deserved place on the list of great fly patterns.

You'll note that the material needed for the cricket is minimal. The deer hair for dyeing should be the white hair from the flank or belly because this hair takes the dye better without becoming brittle; the white hair is very porous and adds greatly to the ability of flaring the hair on the head of the fly.

| | |
|---:|---|
| Hook: | No. 12 or 14, 2X long |
| Thread: | black nymph thread |
| Body: | black spun fur |
| Underwing: | dyed black goose or duck quill |
| Overwing: | dyed black deer hair |
| Head: | dyed black deer hair, flared |

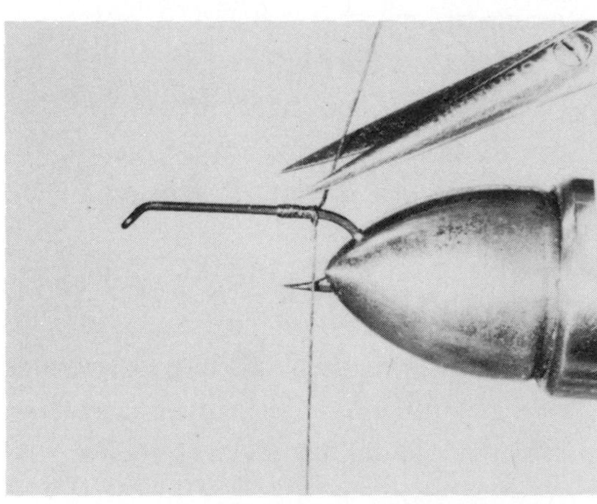

1. Attach tying silk directly above barb of hook by wrapping three or four turns forward to secure thread to shank. Wrap backward six or eight turns over thread just wrapped forward. This secures thread and prevents sliding. Half-hitch thread to secure.

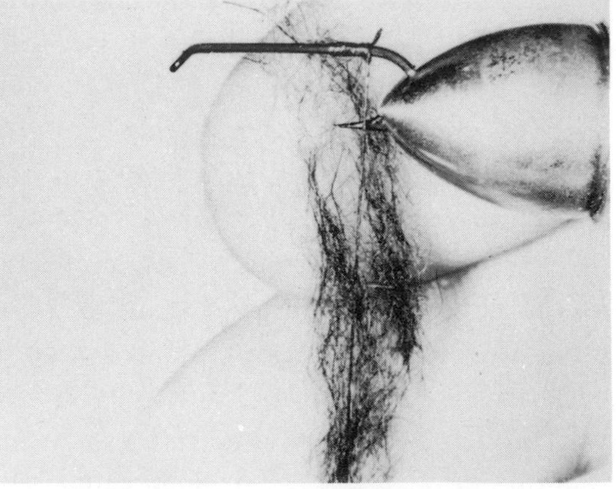

2. Pull small amount of spun fur from card. Spread fur out on first three fingers of right hand. Hold tying silk in left hand. Place fur on fingers against the underside of tying thread.

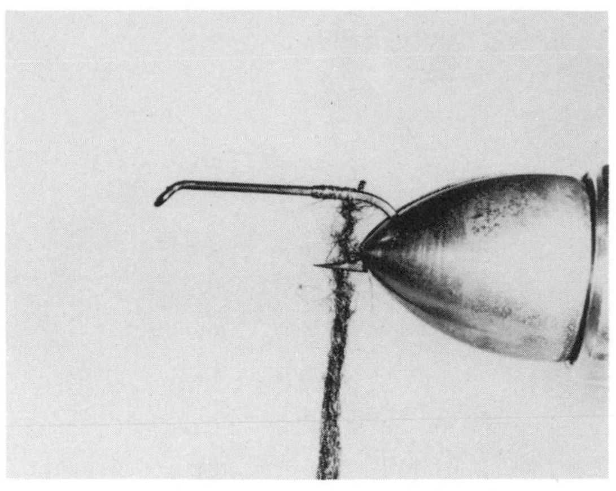

3. Press thumb against first finger and spin fur in counterclockwise motion while applying pressure with thumb and forefinger. This will spin the fur around the thread, making it impossible to pull off. Use only small amounts of fur to avoid a loose, bulky body.

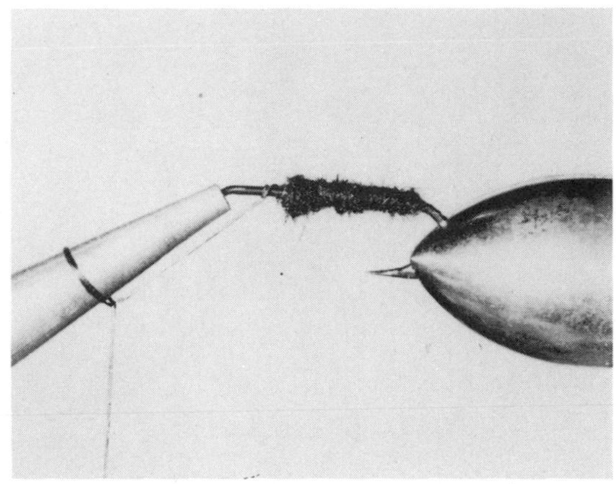

4. Wrap body of spun fur two-thirds forward on hook shank. Half-hitch to secure.

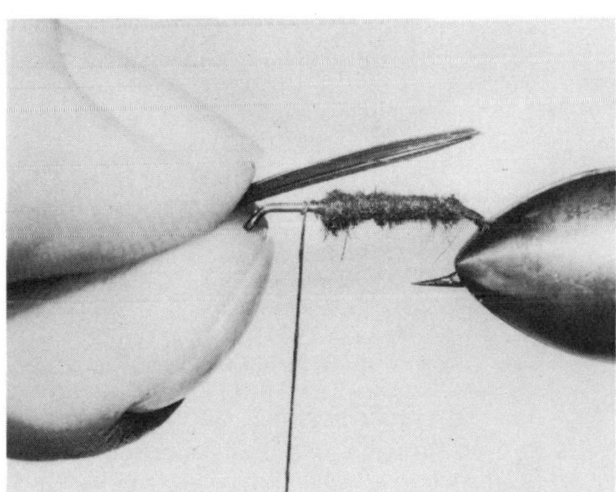

5. Cut section from black goose quill about ⅜ inch wide. Pull from quill and fold in half lengthwise. This double section of quill serves two purposes: added strength to keep it from splitting and a better silhouette when viewed from beneath.

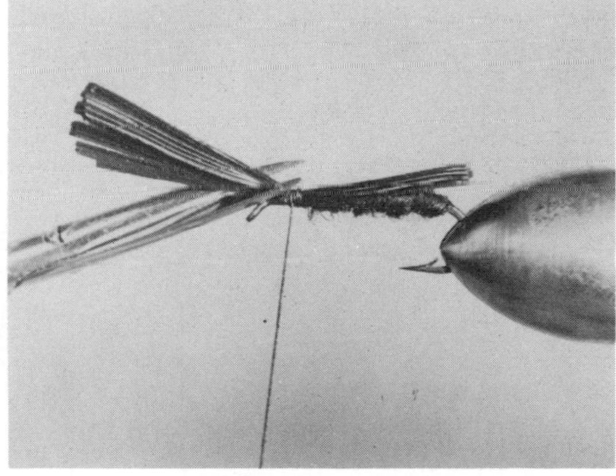

6. Place quill flat along tip of hook shank with left hand. Place thumb on top of quill, forefinger on bottom to hold it in place, and wrap remaining exposed section to eye of hook. Clip off excess and half-hitch several times.

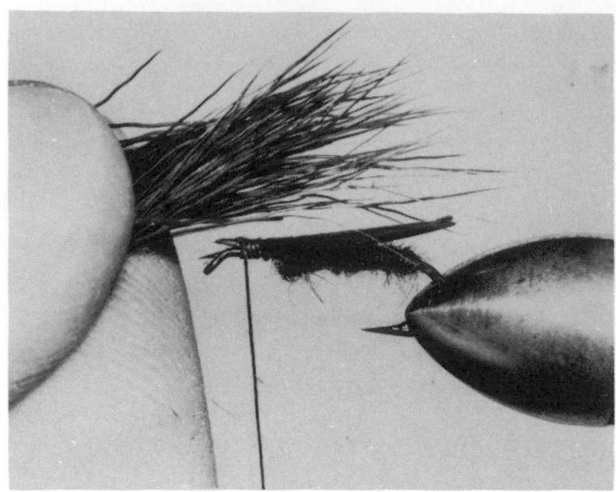

7. Cut clump of deer hair about ½ inch wide. Holding deer hair by butt ends, measure it along hook shank. The tips of deer hair should be even with the bend of hook.

8. Grip hair and slide it over hook shank, running through center of clump of deer hair. When tips of hair reach bend of hook, grasp deer hair, hook shank and all, between the thumb and forefinger of left hand just back of eye of hook. Pinch tightly to prevent slipping.

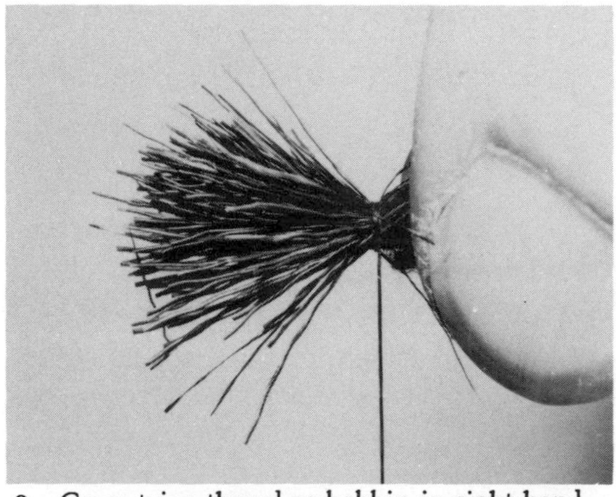

9. Grasp tying thread or bobbin in right hand and take two loose turns all the way around the hair in front of fingers of left hand holding hair. When two loose turns are in place, pull down on thread, easy at first. The deer hair sticking out over the eye will begin to flare out all around the eye of hook. Don't pull too tight or thread will break.

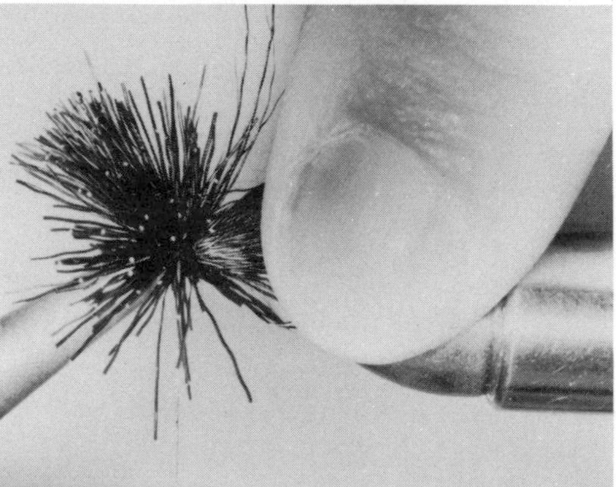

10. As soon as hair begins to flare, hold pressure on thread and take another turn forward through hair. After third turn is completed pull tight, causing additional flaring.

11. Continue to take three or four more turns of thread forward through the hair, pulling tying thread tight each time and flaring more hair with each turn of thread. If necessary use the thumb and forefinger of right hand or half-hitch tool to help flare hair during procedure by pushing hair toward rear of hook. Whip-finish head.

12. Clip hair of head to shape. Cut close to shank forming a small oval head of black deer hair. Clip excess hair from belly, sides, and top if necessary to finish fly.

### *Letort Hopper*

The Letort Hopper, another product of the limestone trouters, is as important as the cricket. Fished from late June through September, the hopper has enticed many a trophy brown from Pennsylvania waters. Since the hopper is tied exactly as the cricket is, all the flytyer need do is substitute yellow spun fur for the body, mottled brown turkey feather for the flat wing, and brown deer hair for the overwing and head. Use yellow nymph thread instead of black.

---

Hook: No. 12 or 14, 2X long
Thread: yellow nymph thread
Body: yellow spun fur
Underwing: mottled brown turkey feather
Overwing and head: brown deer hair

---

### *Black and Cinnamon Fur-Bodied Ants*

If I were asked to select the most consistent trout takers of the terrestrial patterns, the ants, black or cinnamon, would have to get the nod. As with the cricket or hopper, the ants are excellent all year long. A well-presented ant, size 22 or 24 on a 7X tippet, will fool even the wariest surface sipper. The ants, in smaller sizes, are often taken, I'm sure, for various minutiae of the same color spectrum. If a tan-colored midge is on the water, the tiny cinnamon ant will often fool feeding trout. The same is true for a small black ant.

Generally the ants are fished beneath overhanging trees or limbs. Fished near the stream's edge, a foot or so from the bank, the ant will often get more looks, rises, and takers than any other fly. Small sizes, 20 to 28, are best. Occasionally I have been confounded by trout who were surface-feeding regularly and refused time after time the tiniest well-placed ant; but minutes later, I'd present a monstrous size 14, and the trout took as if they hadn't eaten for a week.

A generous supply of the fur-bodied ants is strongly recommended for any fly box. The nice thing about them is that they are easy to tie. An evening's work will produce a more-than-ample supply for your next trip astream.

---

Black Fur Ant
Hook: Nos. 14 to 28
Thread: black nymph thread
Body: black spun fur
Hackle: dyed black

Cinnamon Fur Ant
Hook: Nos. 14 to 28
Thread: brown nymph thread
Body: cinnamon spun fur
Hackle: light brown or ginger

---

1. Attach tying thread at bend of shank as in step No. 2 for Cricket.

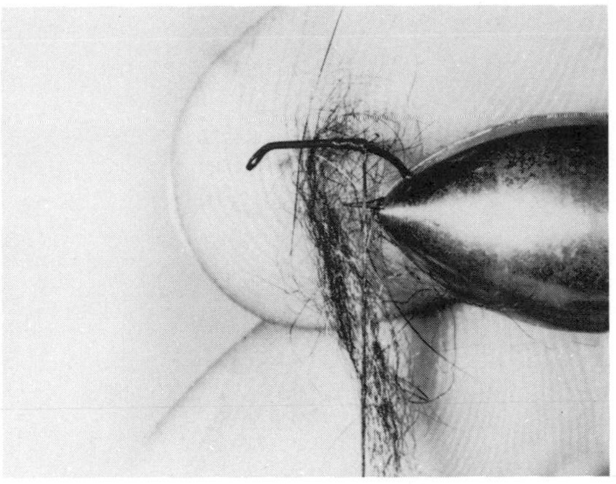

2. Pull small amount of spun fur from card. Spread fur out on first three fingers of right hand. Hold tying silk in left hand. Place dubbing fur on fingers against the underside of tying thread.

3. Press thumb against forefinger and spin fur in counterclockwise motion while applying pressure with thumb and forefinger. Again, use only a very small amount of fur. When you think you have enough, throw half of it away and you'll be safe. The problem with most tyers is that they try to dub or spin too much fur on the thread at one time. Remember, to build a hump or segment on a 24 ant doesn't require very much spun fur dubbed on thread.

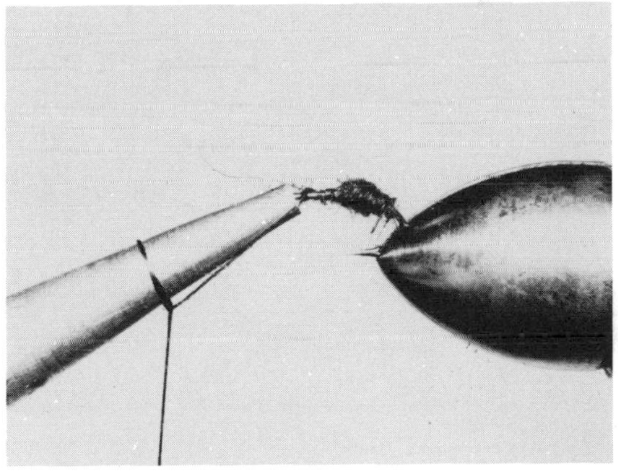

4. Starting at bend of hook, build a small but definite hump or segment of fur. Half-hitch in front of segment to secure thread.

5. Select proper size hackle. Remove soft fibers from butt end of hackle. Tie in hackle at butt.

6. Wrap two turns of hackle, tie off, and half-hitch. Clip off tip of hackle.

7. Repeat steps 3 and 4, building small hump or segment in front of hackle.

8. Wrap head of fly, whip-finish. Fly is complete.

## MIDGE DRIES

Twenty-five years ago it was rare to see an angler using dry flies under size 16. In those days small hooks size 18 or 20 were not only considered useless but were extremely difficult to find in tackle shops. A popular theory was that those tiny flies just couldn't hold a decent trout.

How things have changed! Today, during the so-called "dog days," or on super-selective trout, it's the midge fisherman who goes home successful after a day astream. Midges have come of age. Inevitably they will become as important a part of fly-fishing as wet flies, dry flies, streamers, and nymphs.

Tying the midge dries is not as difficult as many believe. If you can tie a standard dry-fly variant you can tie midges. All that is required to make the switch to the smaller flies is learning to proportion the tail, body, and hackle properly. The same rule of thumb applies for midges as for the standard sizes. The tail should be as long as the hook shank, and hackle should be one and a half times the size of the gap of the hook. Wings are not necessary on 90 percent of the midge dries; general size, shape, and color are more important on the small flies than on many of the larger mayfly imitations, where precise duplication is essential.

The greatest problem the midge tyer encounters is a good source of small hackles in sizes 18 to 28 for his dry flies.

Perhaps the most common midge the angler will encounter on any trout water is the *diptera*—the only true midge fly. This fly, which can vary in size from 18 to 24, is generally gray or a combination of black and dun in color. There are no specific emergence tables on the *diptera*—it hatches all year long. When the water temperature and light conditions are just right the flies will be on the water, whether it is April, June, September, December, or February. Standard patterns such as Cahills and Hendricksons just aren't found in size 22; midge patterns must be of midge flies.

The first true midge imitation I'd seen was on the Big Spring at Newville, Pennsylvania. I was fishing with Ed Shenk of Carlisle and, as usual, he was having a field day while I was almost fishless. Finally he showed me the little grizzly hackled, gray-bodied size 20 fly he was using.

"What is it?" I asked.

"Don't know, really, but they've used it here as long as I can remember. Guess you could call it the 'No-Name,' " Ed replied.

Thus was my introduction to one of the most fantastic little dry flies ever to come out of the Cumberland Valley limestone waters. Nothing since then has appeared for a better imitation of the *diptera*.

---

*No-Name Midge*

| | |
|---|---|
| Hook size: | Nos. 20 to 24 |
| Thread: | gray nymph thread |
| Tail: | grizzly hackle fibers |
| Body: | muskrat fur |
| Wing: | none |
| Hackle: | grizzly |

---

1. Attach tying thread directly above barb.

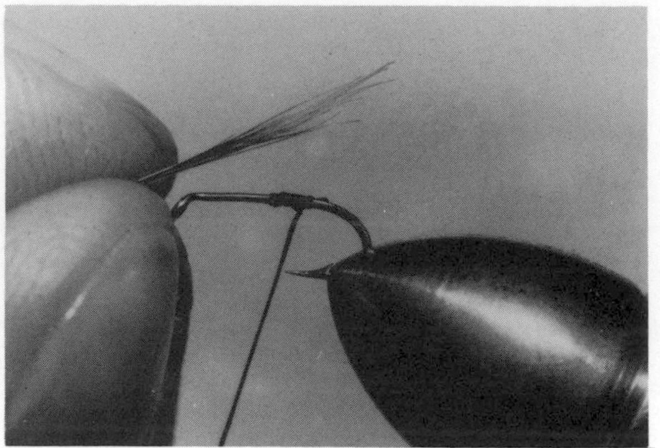

2. Select four grizzly hackle fibers for tail. Measure fibers along hook shank to determine proper length. Tail should be as long as hook shank.

3. Tie on tail; clip off excess fiber.

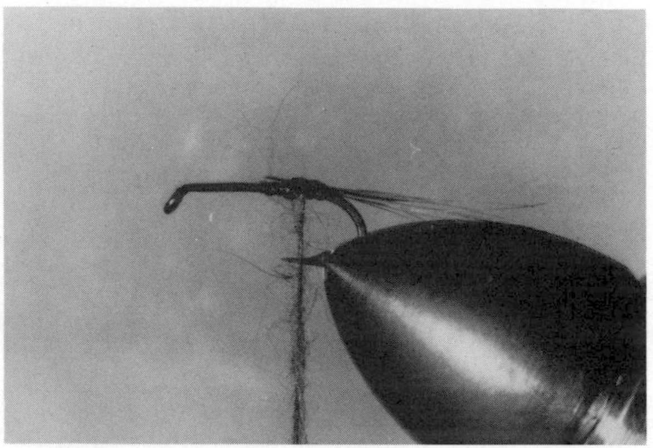

4. Dub small amount of muskrat underfur on thread.

5. Wrap tapered body three-quarters of way up hook shank.

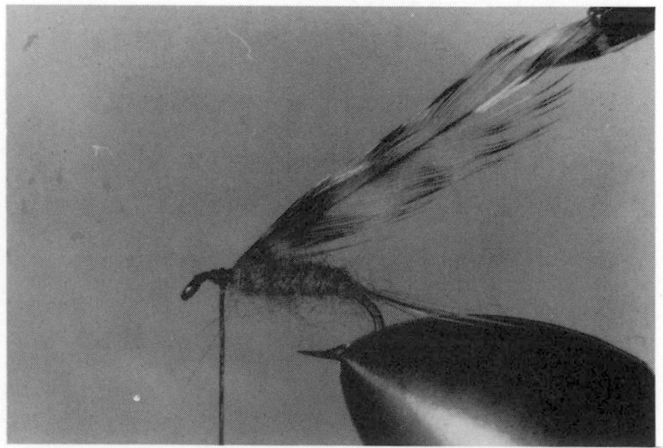

6. Select proper size grizzly hackle. Strip off soft fibers from butt end. Tie in hackle stem by butt.

7. Wrap two or three turns of hackle, tie off, and clip excess tip.

8. Wrap head of grey nymph thread, whip-finish, and fly is complete.

### *The Midge Nymph*

Three of the first real midge imitators—or attractors, as I later called them because they really suggested forms rather than imitated specific insects—were midge nymphs. They were called Sim-fectives—simple to tie, effective when fished.

The fly is literally what the name implies—simple. There is no tail, no whisks, no feelers, no legs, no wing cases—nothing but a dubbed fur body. The nymph is an attractor type rather than an imitator. It suggests by shape, size, and color more than half a dozen natural midge nymphs on which trout feed.

Three types of fur are used—muskrat, weasel, and fox. These give the basic colors used in most flies: gray for dark-colored flies in early season, brown for medium-colored flies during midseason, cream for light-colored flies during late season. Black or gray thread is used on muskrat nymphs, brown thread on weasel-fur nymphs, and brown or yellow thread on the fox-fur nymphs.

---

Gray Midge Nymph

Hook: Nos. 16 to 28
Thread: gray nymph thread
Body: muskrat fur
Head: gray thread

Brown Midge Nymph

Hook: Nos. 16 to 28
Thread: brown nymph thread
Body: weasel fur
Head: brown thread

Cream Midge Nymph

Hook: Nos. 16 to 28
Thread: yellow or brown nymph thread
Body: cream-colored fox fur, from belly of red fox

---

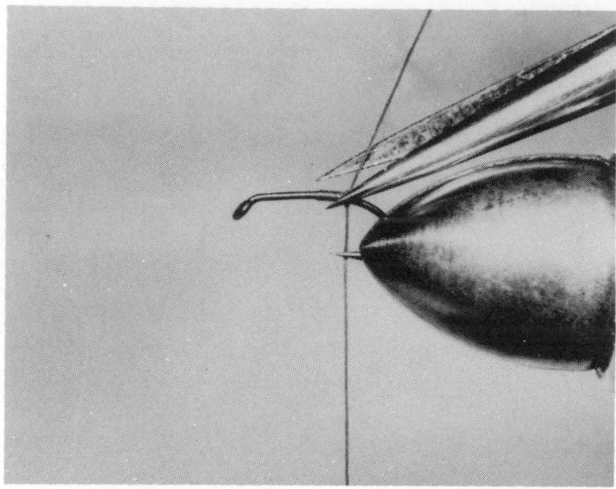

1. Tie on thread at rear of hook shank directly above barb of hook.

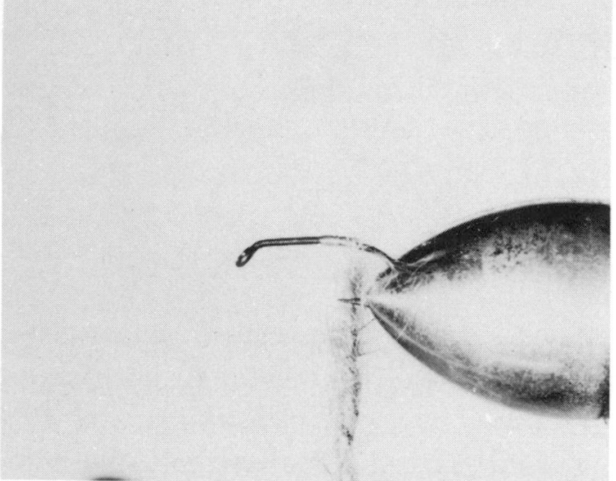

2. Dub on a small amount of fur, guard hairs and all. Use same method for dubbing as described in tying the ant bodies. Small amounts of fur are used so an even-tapered body can be formed.

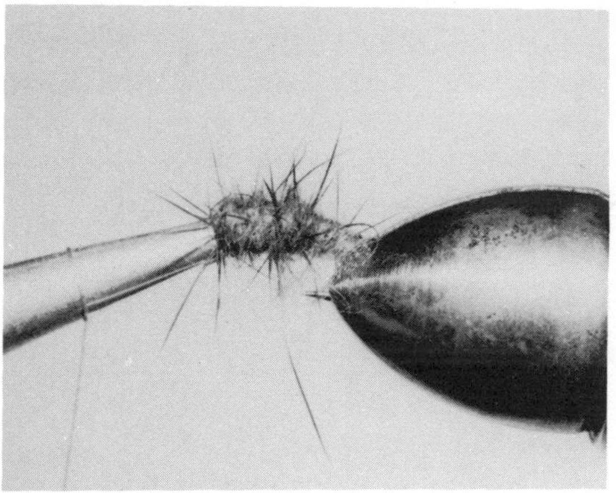

3. Taper body from bend of shank, forward to eye.

4. Build up head with tying thread, whip-finish, lacquer, and your nymph is finished. One additional step can be employed if desired, and that is to rib the small nymphs with three turns of fine wire, 33- or 35-gauge. This keeps the fur body from being chewed apart too easily. The ribbing does nothing to enhance the fish-catching qualities of the nymphs.

Effective? Yes, provided you are willing to observe and do a little practicing. Patience will produce dividends. First, check local streams for the type of insect life found there. Second, determine what size and color fly will come closest to imitating the general size, shape, and color of the real thing.

No hard fast rule as to how to fish a nymph can be set down for any particular stream or for any particular time of the season. Generally, begin by fishing the nymph deep, rolling it along the bottom. This is accomplished by using split shot or twist-on lead about ten inches ahead of the fly.

The second approach should be to fish the nymphs about halfway down. To get the fly in position remove small amounts of your weight at a time until the desired depth is reached. When fishing nymphs, cast directly upstream and allow the fly to drift toward you. The current should provide all the natural action needed.

The third method of nymph-fishing is in the surface film. Fish the nymph just as though it were a dry fly. No weight of any kind is used. The small nymph will soak up just enough water to keep it in the surface film, maybe an inch or so beneath the surface. Make short casts covering every inch of water as you move up or down stream. Maximum casts should be thirty or forty feet. Hold the rod tip high and keep the line between the tip of the rod and the spot where your line enters the water as straight as possible. Watch this spot at all times for a telltale twitch, an indication that a trout has picked up the fly. Strike fast!

For every strike you see or feel, you can be assured that the nymph has been picked up and spit out at least a dozen times without your knowing it. This is where patience pays off.

TROUT

# Dave Whitlock

## WESTERN FLY PATTERNS

Photographs by Nelson Renick and Associates, Saint Louis, Missouri

The phrase "western flies" is not as self-explanatory as other fly-design terms such as dry flies, salmon flies, or nymphs. Western patterns are usually tied for trout found on both slopes of the Rockies; they also see limited service on bass, panfish, and salmon west of the Mississippi. Styles include dry flies, wet flies, nymphs, and streamers—and each type has been in some way modified to accommodate the conditions in the Stetson-and-boot country.

These modifications came about because western waters generally were graced with lots of runoff from winter snow and huge springs. Added to this was a very sparse population of people and a high population of adult trout that provided some fantastic wildernesslike fishing. Streams and lakes carried trout averaging from two to six pounds, and these big fish had to thrive on something more than tiny mayfly hatches to grow to such magnificent proportions. An abundance of minnows, whitefish, sculpin, very large aquatic insects, shrimp, and unlimited terrestrial insect populations abounded in the clean water, land, and atmosphere.

Western trout dine freely on these large food forms wherever man has not destroyed them. Thus, when fly-fishing came to the West, the patterns that began to evolve were large and suggestive rather than the sparse imitative styles associated with eastern waters and those of England. Western fly-fishermen and flytyers were also the same stock that was settling this wild land, and their minds were not locked with Old Country tradition. Their flies took on some new forms that still receive scoffs from certain pockets of the blue-dun fraternity.

Most of the western fly-fishing has been developed in the last thirty to forty years, and only in the last twenty has there been much standardization of tackle and flies for the area. In the last ten years the popularity of western fishing has increased dramatically, with multitudes of anglers attacking from both coasts. The result has been a reduction in the size and number of the western trout. Some alteration of stream flows for irrigation and dam building has cut deep wounds in the quality of fishing. Food sources for the western trout are dwindling because of these water alterations and man's pollution with chemical and insecticide wastes.

What significance has this in a fly-tying manual? This evolution of conditions is altering the western fishing scene each season. Increased angling pressure for fewer and smaller fish is producing more selective trout. Although western waters are considered fantastic when compared to many once great eastern streams that have fallen into the put-and-take syndrome, these waters are on the wane. Natural reproduction and food supply provide wild fish, but these jet-age rainbows, browns, cutthroats, and brooks are becoming much more selective than their ancestors. Western patterns are undergoing a degree of refinement to keep pace with this growing selectivity. This situation is not unique to the West: the same is taking place in South America, Canada, and New Zealand. The eastern United States saw the evolution early in this century.

The flies I've selected are all new-generation western patterns. They have been evolved by those of us who have watched these magnificent waters yield to a growing demand on their rich treasures. Most of us now measure our fish in inches before releasing them; once a trout's size was spoken of only in pounds. These patterns have been chosen to offer the tyer the basic food forms that are most significant in taking western trout and bass.

I have excluded one very effective type, the standard emerged aquatic insect, which is very well described in the chapters by Art Flick and Doug Swisher and Carl Richards. More and more the smaller floaters are growing in significance with the reduction of fish size and the superpopularity of Spring Creek fishing. You will find that most standard dries and the new No-Hackle designs will work perfectly on match-the-hatch situations. However, when heavy water is encountered or huge stone, caddis, or mayflies are out over the riffles, some modification of floaters is necessary to ride out the rough foamy flows common in most fast-falling rock streams. Visibility and flotation must be considered as prime properties for a successful fly in such conditions. Hairwing patterns such as the popular Wulffs are perfectly suited for this fishing.

Basically, the western dry fly would be tied on a standard dry-fly hook with 1X fine wire such as the model 94840 Mustad. Sizes 6 through 14 are most effective, size 12 being the most popular. Deer hair and hackle are the two prime materials for supporting the hook above the surface. Most western dry flies have two or three cock-neck hackles or long saddle hackle to provide ample surface support for the thicker bodies and hair tails and wings. The Irresistible, Goofus Bug, and Humpy are effective rough-water designs because of the added bulk and buoyancy of their hollow deer-hair bodies. Even when these patterns are drowned by a riffle wave or sucked under in white-water eddies, they struggle back to the surface to continue their downstream float. Western trout in fast water take them equally well on hackle tiptoes or wet to the waist.

Few exotic color schemes are popular with western floaters. Shades of dun, brown, and grizzly are the popular hackle colors, and bodies are usually tied in tans, grays, or yellows. A few stone-fly and caddis patterns require orange, red, or olive wool, fur, or floss. Wings are almost always tied with hair, especially bucktail, calf tail, or deer hair. Natural colors are most popular. Some tyers, however, use a lot of white or fluorescent shades to enhance visibility. This makes following a rough-water float much easier and doesn't seem to hinder the trout's preference in taking the brightly doffed floater.

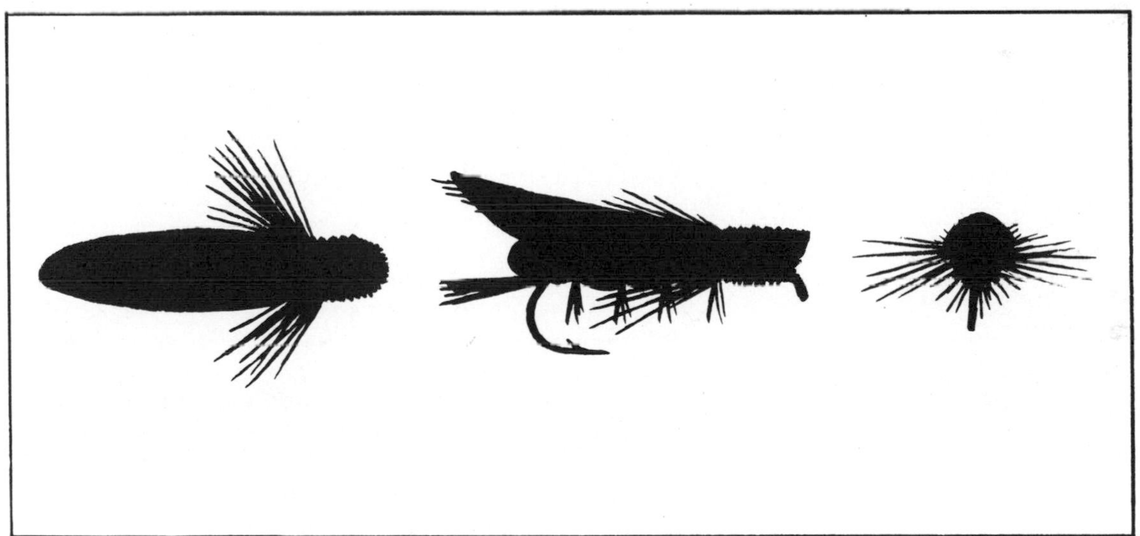

Dave's Hopper—top, side, and front views

### *Dave's Hopper*

This floater is a hybrid grasshopper imitation that I designed out of a dissatisfaction with the older standard hopper patterns. Their silhouettes, durability, and effectiveness needed improvement. I used what I liked about each pattern, added my own ideas, and came up with this pattern. It casts well, floats in all types of water when dressed with a flotant, and has wonderful fish appeal for trout, bass (especially smallmouth), and panfish. In fact, it outfishes all other hopper patterns I've seen used. Although it is a terrestrial imitation, it is also extremely effective when adult stone flies or caddis flies are over the water. Some deviation of the basic color scheme, wing shape, and head shape makes it a more realistic stone-fly floater than most of the popular patterns on the market. So when you learn to tie this pattern it will provide an excellent imitation for three of the most important insects in western fishing.

| | |
|---:|---|
| Hook: | TDE 2xL regular wire Mustad No. 9671, sizes 6, 8, 10, 12, 14 |
| Thread: | Herb Howard waxed nylon, brown |
| Glue: | clear head cement and rod varnish |
| Tail: | natural dun-brown deer hair, dyed red |
| Body: | yellow Orlon wool |
| Rib: | one medium-brown cock-neck hackle |
| Underwing: | pale-yellow deer hair |
| Wing: | shaped section from a speckled turkey secondary wing quill |
| Collar: | well-marked natural dun-brown deer hair |
| Head: | dun-brown deer hair |

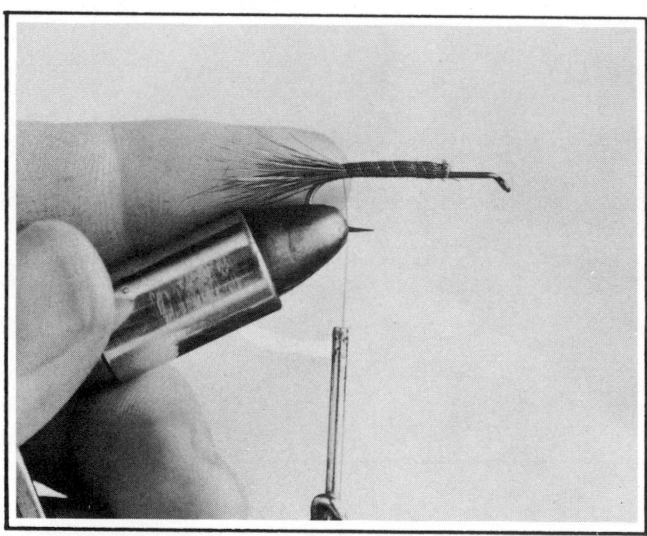

*TAIL*

1a. Place hook firmly in vise (do not cover barb and hook point with vise jaws; damage will often occur to this critical tempered area if clamped hard by vise jaws). Wrap thread on the rear two-thirds of hook shank. Cover shank well, as thread must provide a firm base for tail and body materials. Bring thread to front portion of wrap area.

1b. Take about 15 to 30 red deer hairs from which you have removed the under fuzz. Align tips fairly well, then lay trimmed-even butts down over top of hook shank, butt ends even with front thread-wrap.

1c. Catch ends with thread and carefully bind down hair with thread, not tightly but snugly. Work thread to bend of hook. Do not allow deer hair to separate or roll beneath the shank. Index finger should provide stability to prevent rolling if thread isn't too tight.

1d. A light coat of clear head cement will assure a tight durable tail and body foundation.

*BODY AND RIB*

2a. Choose a neck or saddle hackle long enough to rib two-thirds of hook shank over the thick body. Hackle should have minimum of web; flue length is not important as rib will be trimmed later. Attach hackle butt to back side of hook shank with bright side facing you, if righthanded. Reverse wrap is then used for rib.

2b. Take a strand of yellow Orlon wool and untwist it. Attach it in the exact manner as for the deer-hair tail in Figure 1. Be careful to keep it on top of the hook and not pull thread too tight each wrap.

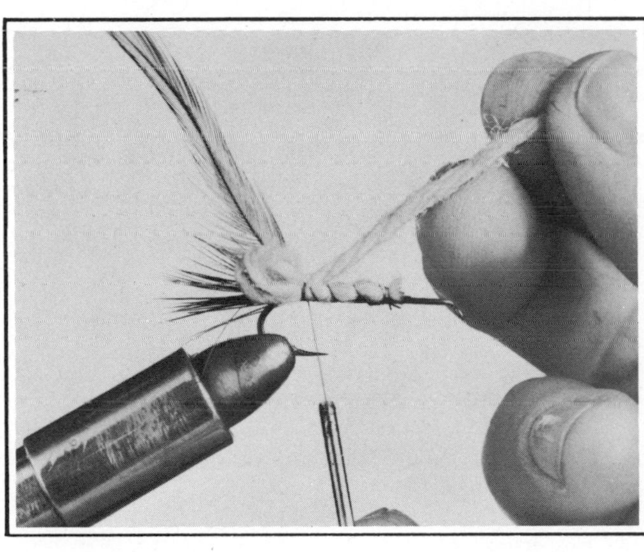

3. After wool is secured to bend of hook with thread, make a small vertical loop with the wool and wrap thread to hold it in place. This loop forms the extended butt of hopper. Apply a light coat of thin head cement over underbody.

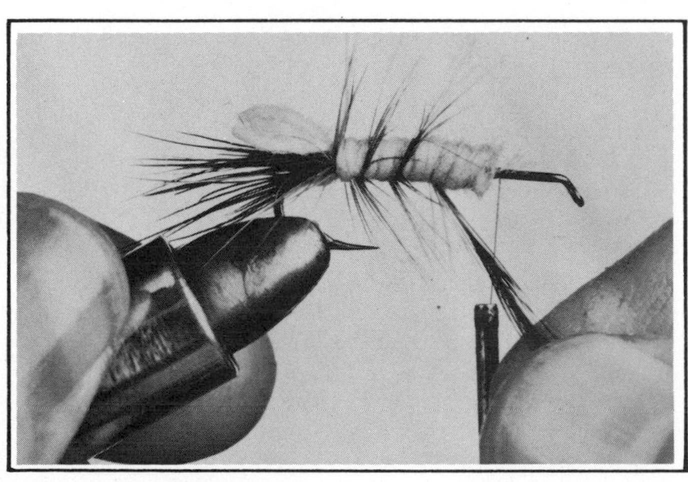

4a. Wrap wool clockwise around underbody to form a segmented-effect body. End wrap at exact forward position of underbody (two-thirds of shank). Front third must remain bare for proper tying of hopper head.

4b. Wrap the brown hackle tightly clockwise with a spiral to match grooves between wool wraps.

4c. Tie off at front of body and trim off excess hackle tip.

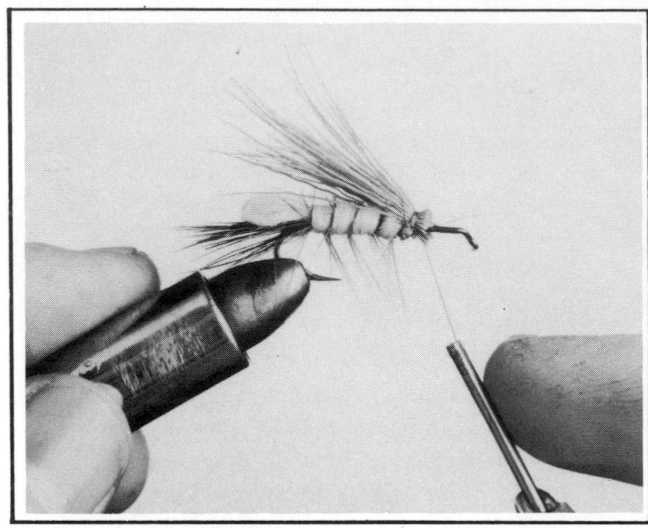

*UNDERWING*

5a. Take twenty to thirty strands of soft yellow deer hair and trim even the butts with scissors.

5b. Place butts exactly even with anterior portion of body.

5c. Hold hair snugly and take three or four wraps of thread around this butt-base area. Do not draw thread down tightly or deer hair will flare too much and also roll off top of body. Deer-hair tips should extend approximately the same distance back past bend as tail does.

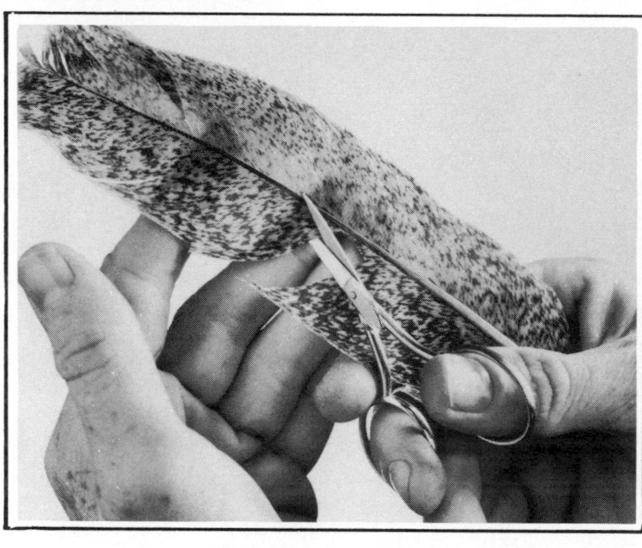

*WING FEATHER*

6a. Choose a wide well-mottled turkey quill (right or left side) and spray it with a clear acrylic enamel. I use Krylon, but there are many similar spray lacquers available. Two or three light coats on each side of the quill will dry quickly and weld the flue fibers without causing excessive wrinkling.

6b. After feather is dry, cut with scissors or razor blade a section from quill. You can cut enough at one time to form six to twelve wings.

*WING FORM*

7. Flue section will vary in width according to hook size. Size 6 will be approximately ½ inch wide, size 8 approximately ¹⁄₁₆ to ⅛ inch smaller, and so on down. Length should be enough to extend to or just beyond underwing if measured from front end of body. Trim length with scissors, rounding the tip to shape of hopper's wing. A little experimenting will quickly give you the right look on wing. Square off base of flue at right angle to the fibers.

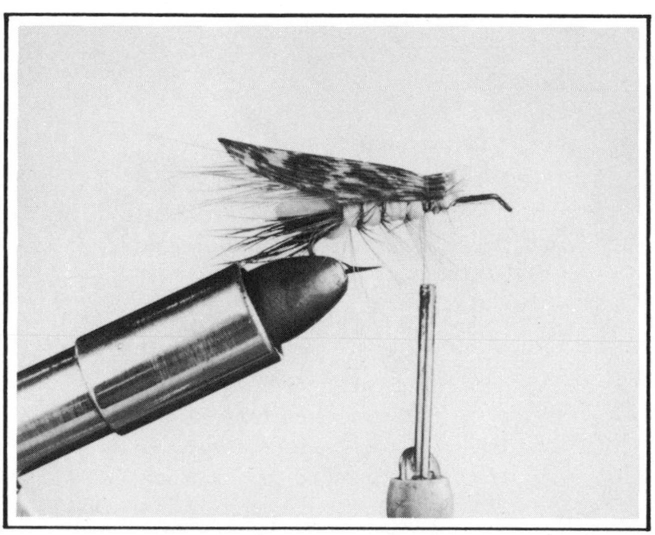

*WING*

8a. Apply a light coat of clear head cement to front of body and underwing tie-down.

8b. Lay the formed wing over the top, matching butt even with front on body and underwing.

8c. Carefully roll wing over body top and wrap with a few snug but not tight turns of tying thread. Tight wraps distort whole wing and underwing; snug wraps and cement provide adequate holding of wing. The wing should extend tentlike over body and cover underwing, forming basic hopper wing and body silhouette.

*COLLAR*

9a. Advance thread to front third of shank now and wrap six or eight turns directly in front of body.

9b. Select a small bunch of natural dun-brown deer hair and remove all under fuzz and short hair.

9c. Align tips and trim butts even.

9d. Lay deer-hair tips to the rear, parallel to hook shank. Take two loose turns with thread around the bunch of hair; then draw tight slowly, allowing hair to spin around bare shank while flaring.

9e. Three or four more very snug turns must be taken after hair has flared and been spun evenly around shank. Tips should extend just backward and length be about half that of total wing length.

9f. Bring thread forward of hair for three or four turns, then push this hair collar up against body with thumb and index finger or with a ball-point-pen barrel.

*HEAD*

10a. Take another moderate bunch of deer hair and clean fuzz out with bodkin needle or toothbrush.

10b. Follow Figure 9 procedure to flare and spin hair just in front of collar. If shank isn't yet filled add another bunch until it is. Allow enough room to tie off head with thread.

10c. Whip-finish at eye.

10d. The head must be shaped with either scissors or a sharp cutting blade. I prefer a quality curved-blade scissor. Keeping the blades parallel to the hook, carefully trim the flared deer hair into the shape of a hopper's head. The bottom should be a little shorter and flat to insure good floating balance.

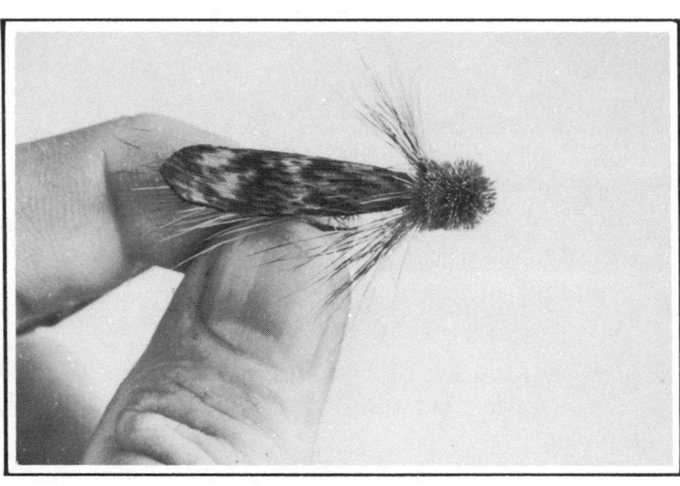

11a. Leave a few of the collar hair tips extending out on either side; this helps the flat float and simulates legs.

11b. Top and bottom are fairly well trimmed in order to improve the silhouette and balance.

11c. Trim brown hackle-rib short, allowing fibers to stick out just past body.

11d. After the hopper is through with his haircut, apply one thin coat of spar or rod varnish to back of wing and to the base of wing and collar—also a bit on the thread head. Varnish assures an extremely durable wing and head; it dries slowly and this assures deep penetration of materials it is applied to, though it remains flexible in use.

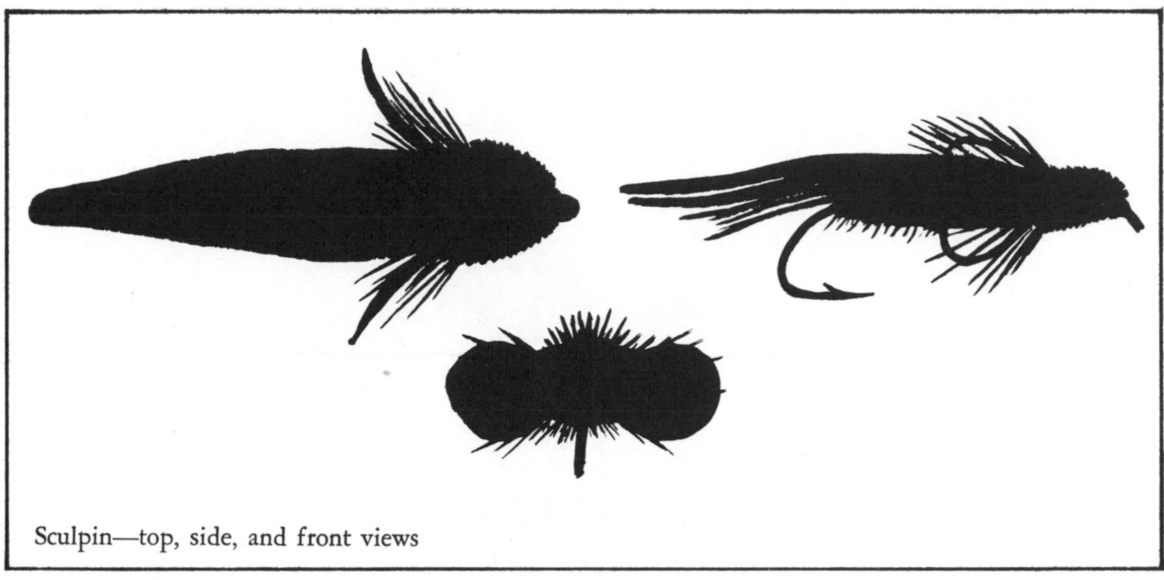

Sculpin—top, side, and front views

*Whitlock Sculpin*

The sculpin minnow is certainly the most important baitfish to western anglers when large trout aren't working on insects. Browns, rainbows, and brook trout exhibit a strong preference for this bottom-dwelling, rock-hiding character. It is also a terrific bass and striper fly. The sculpin's shape, color, and habits are centered on the fact that it lives on the stream bottom. Any good sculpin imitation must display these characteristics in its design or you won't take many sculpin-eaters for your effort. Keep in mind while studying this pattern that each step included must be followed rigidly or the finished fly will not look or fish properly.

| | |
|---|---|
| Hook: | TDE 3xL 2X stout; Mustad 9672 or 38941 or Buz's special 2x stout; Sizes 1/O through 8 |
| Weight: | lead wire |
| Thread: | Nymo 1560 (light orange) |
| Body: | fur-dubbing blend of light amber seal, yellow seal, tan fox, and white rabbit; tint should be a rich yellowish cream |
| Glues: | head cement and rod varnish |
| Rib: | gold oval tinsel |
| Underwing: | red fox squirrel tail |
| Wing: | two dark well-marked soft webby cree-neck hackles, tinted golden brown or golden olive |
| Gill: | red wool dubbing |
| Pectoral Fins: | two fanlike breast feathers from body of hen mallard, prairie chicken, or hen pheasant |
| Collar: | deer hair—natural light dun-brown, tinted yellow, golden brown, or golden olive, and black or very dark brown |
| Head: | same as collar |

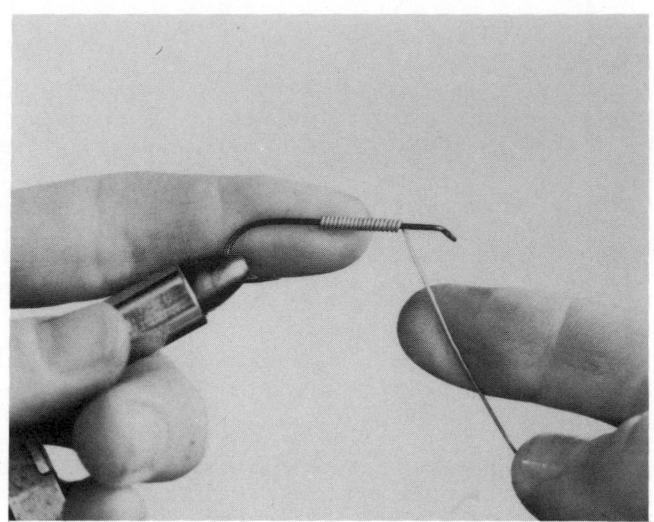

*HOOK AND LEAD*

1. Place hook in vise and lightly wrap lead wire clockwise around shank. Wire should be approximately the diameter of hook wire. Fifteen to twenty turns. Leave the *front quarter of hook bare.*

*BODY*

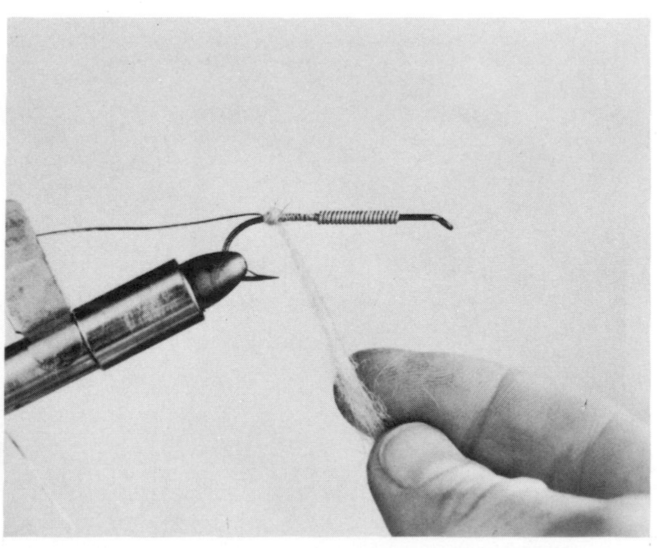

2a. Attach tying thread behind lead and tie on piece of gold oval tinsel. Size 12 for largest hooks; size 14 for size 4, 6, and 8 hooks.

2b. Coat lead and tinsel tie-down with thick, clear head cement.

2c. Begin to spin dubbed-fur body material on thread. Dub hook shank with fur, using a clockwise wrap if right handed. As you wrap dubbing, taper body.

2d. Stop directly behind last two or three lead wraps. Body should appear thick and fuzzy.

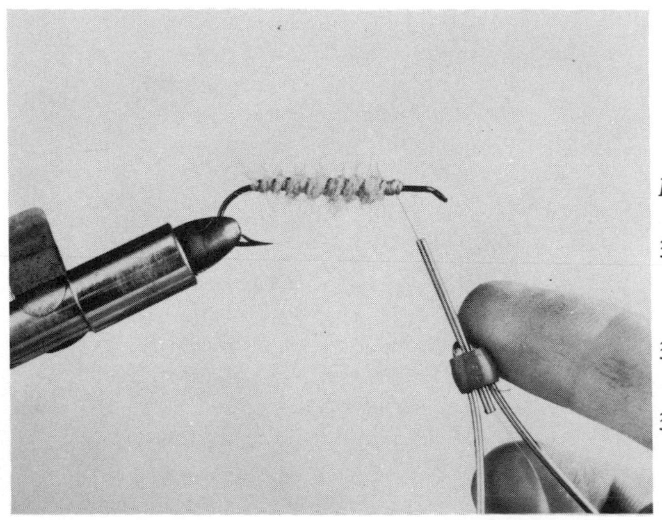

*RIB*

3a. Wrap gold tinsel clockwise toward hook eye also, increasing wrap distance as you progress. Tinsel should be very snug.

3b. Tie down and trim off excess at the same position the dubbing was ended.

3c. Add a drop of thick head cement to tie-off area, and half-hitch if bobbin is not used.

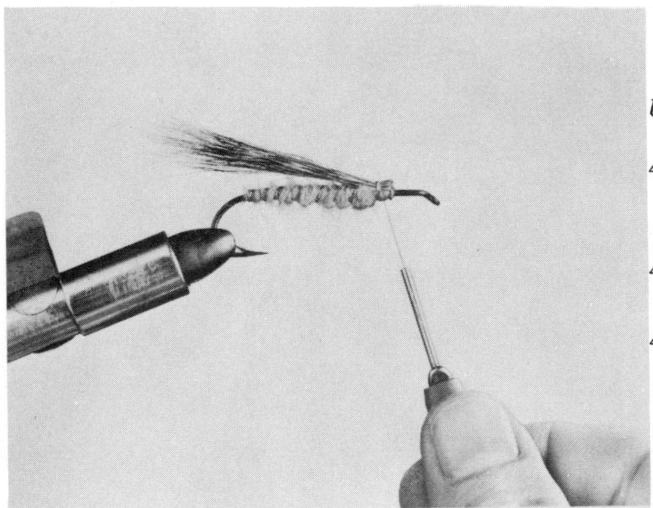

*UNDERWING*

4a. Cut a bunch of thirty to forty hairs from the side or top of a well-barred red-fox squirrel tail.

4b. Make sure butts are trimmed square and even.

4c. Place hair butts over last three or four lead wraps and tie down. Do not allow hair to roll or spin. It *must* be on top of shank. (This hair serves as a base for wing and also helps prevent wing from twisting under hook bend while casting.)

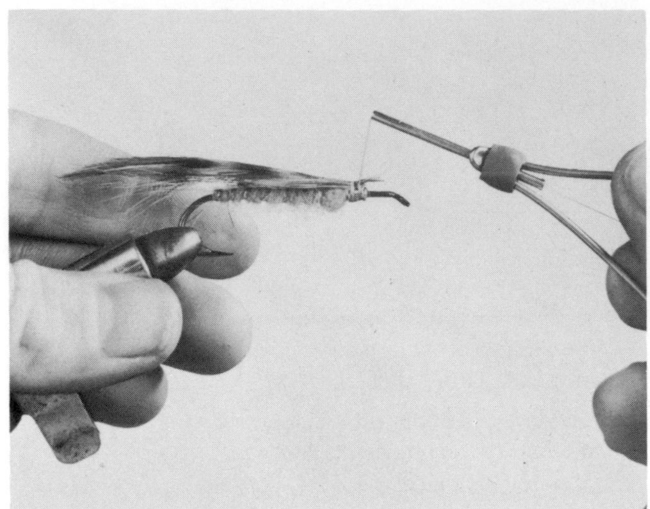

*WING*

5a. Select two wide, soft, webby cock-neck hackles with good markings. (I sometimes substitute grizzly hackle for cree.) It must be tinted dark golden brown, or dark golden olive like the cree if a more natural sculpin color is obtained.

5b. Size them to extend from lead tie-down area just past the underwing hair.

5c. With bright sides up, lay both together on top of underwing and width of feather flat horizontal with body. Conventional streamer wing is always vertical flat with body. Tie butts down snugly but not extremely tight as they *must not* flare up.

*PECTORAL FINS*

6a. Choose two matched fanlike breast feathers that have a light barring.

6b. Place each on right and left side of lead tie-down area with bright sides facing body, thus causing each to flare out away from body.

6c. Tie each on snugly. (These simulate the oversize walking fins that are so prominent on all sculpins.)

6d. Soak this important tie-down area with several drops of thin clear head cement.

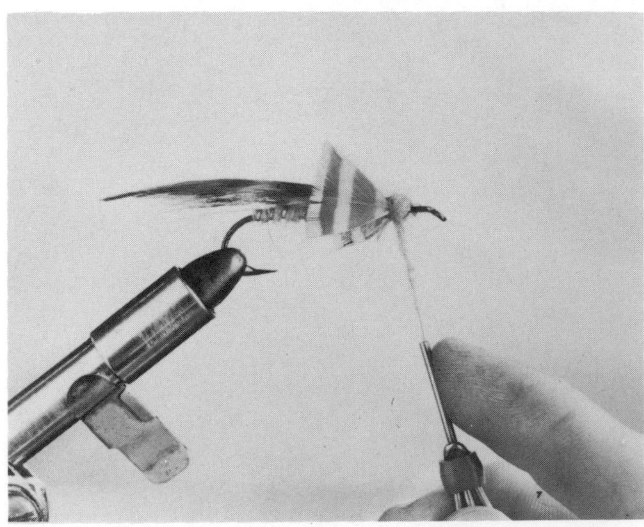

*GILLS*

7a. In order to cover up tie-down area, dub picked red wool yarn on thread and wrap over this area to hide butts and create a gill effect after head is finished in front.

7b. Now *for the first time* advance tying thread to the *front quarter of shank,* which *must remain bare* until beginning the next step.

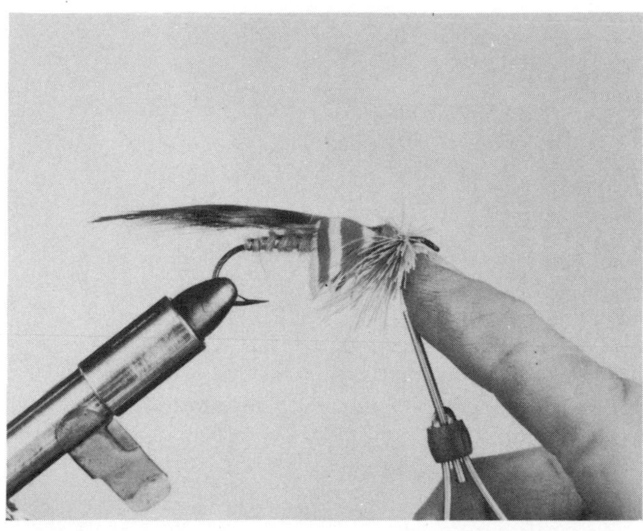

*COLLAR*

8a. The collar serves two functions: first, to simulate the dorsal fin and gill plates and, second, to unite the head with the body wing area. Without it the streamer silhoutte is ruined.

Take a small bunch of light-yellow deer hair and attach it to hook with two or three loose turns of thread. Tips must point toward bend of hook.

8b. Tighten very slowly. As hair begins to flare, allow it to roll under the shank.

8c. Hold it there and wrap another two or three turns of thread tightly. This is the first step in "stacking" the deer hair to accomplish a head and collar that are light color on bottom, dark on top.

*HEAD*

9a. Take a bunch of golden-brown deer hair and hold it *directly* over the top of the shank; wrap it loosely but hold it in fingers so that it will not move.

9b. Tighten wraps, flaring it too. Tips of deer hair and yellow should not extend past tips of the pectoral fin feathers.

9c. Then, *directly* over brown add a small bunch of slightly longer black or darkest-brown deer hair. Follow same procedure and do not allow it to mix with brown or yellow. If done properly, this "stacked" hair will give a perfect color scheme.

9d. Advance tying thread to shank in front of hair.

9e. With index finger and thumb, push the deer hair back against body hard.

9f. Secure with several tight wraps of thread against this base.

9g. Repeat the procedure of "stacking" the yellow, brown, and black deer hair.

9h. After this is accomplished, push it hard against the collar to pack the hair for a dense tight durable head.

9i. Whip-finish thread at eye of hook and trim the excess. Take care always to wrap the hook-eye bend with thread so that the sharp edge of wire is covered and will not cut leader while being fished.

*TRIMMING THE HEAD*

10a. With a pair of curved-blade scissors carefully trim the deer hair, always keeping blades at a near-horizontal angle to the body.

10b. Trim bottom flat and wide, leaving a few hair tips extending back to body, but allow red wool to show through.

10c. Trim sides, shaping head like a toad's—rather flat, wide, and oval. Also leave brown hair tips extending back to fins.

10d. Top of head is also cut short and the collar black hair-tips extend back to simulate dorsal fin.

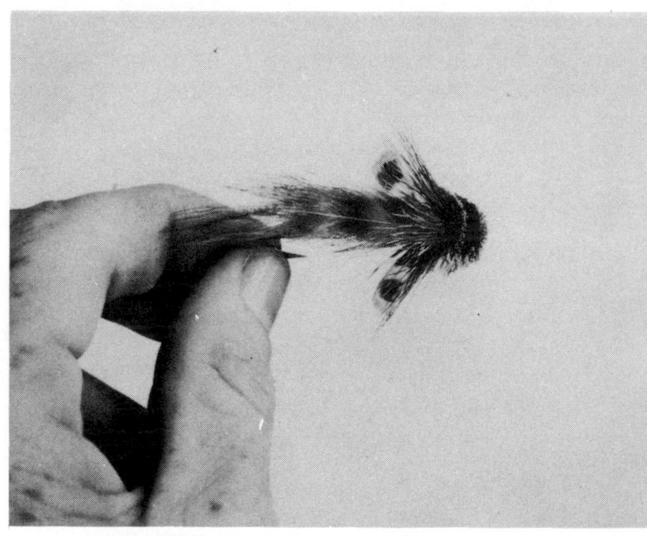

*FINISHING FLY*

11a. After trimming is complete, varnish underside of head with *thin* rod varnish.

11b. Also apply a little to top of head and over thread wrap at eye. Varnish makes the head very durable and helps assure you that shape is retained during fishing use.

NOTE: Sculpins vary in color depending on the stream-bed color. Usually a brown or olive shade, with darker banding, is most common. However, some are light tannish, cream, or grayish, or even dark black. So feel free to alter the basic colors given here if you find sculpins in the area different.

*Woolyworm*

The Woolyworm is one of the oldest and most effective of all western patterns. Before the Muddler Minnow became popular, the "woolie" was the most popular big-fish pattern in the Rocky Mountain lakes and streams.

It is an extremely simple but suggestive fly that simulates all sorts of food from nymphs to leeches, though it is doubtful that it is very often ever actually mistaken for its namesake, the woolyworm or caterpillar. The fly is fished wet and deep, and commonly with a swimming or darting action more like a minnow or dragonfly nymph; wherever trout are not selective it will take its share of fish any given day.

Woolyworms are tied in literally dozens of color combinations and sizes. This plus the fact that it is so suggestive of what food it simulates makes it hard to fish wrong. It is terrific for beginners and a great favorite with some of the West's most experienced flycasters. Bass and panfish also take the woolyworm readily; I have even had terrific luck catching large channel catfish with them while bumping the bottom of smallmouth streams. Big bluegill love a fuzzy size 12 woolie, and crappie strike them in light color patterns.

The following woolyworm pattern is the design I've found most effective. Since the color combination is only one of many effective combinations, I am listing others so that you can have a better range of effective patterns. I also encourage you to take the basic design and experiment with your own color ideas.

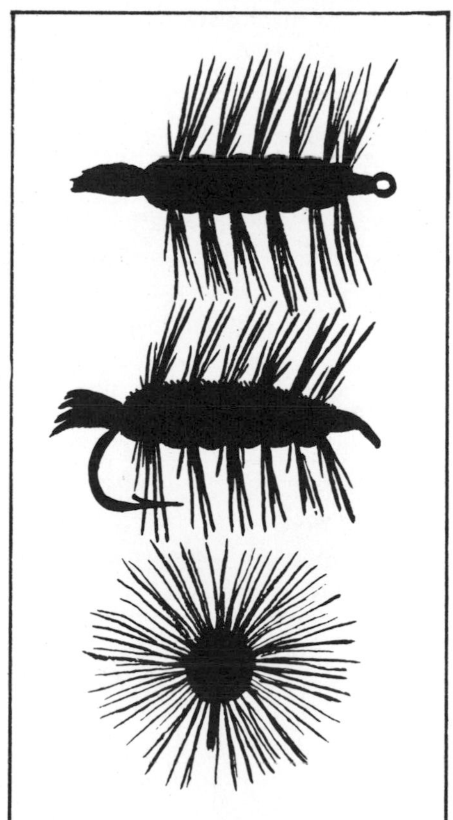

Woolyworm—top, side, and front views

| | |
|---|---|
| Hook: | TDE 3xL Mustad 9672, sizes 4–12 |
| Weight: | lead wire |
| Thread: | black Nymo |
| Tail: | red wool or none |
| Body: | golden-olive chenille or yellow, black, brown, dark olive, or tan |
| Back: | peacock herl |
| Rib: | none or flat gold or silver tinsel |
| Hackle: | grizzly saddle hackle or brown, black, olive saddle hackle |
| Head: | black |

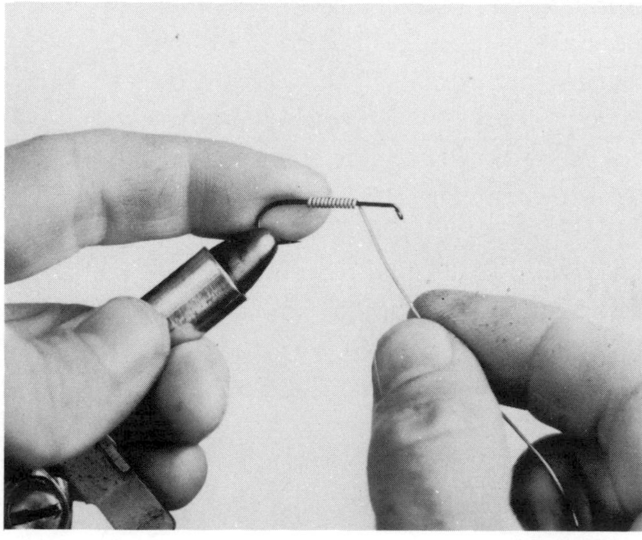

*HOOK AND LEAD*

1. Secure hook in vise and wrap middle area of shank with six to twelve turns of lead wire approximately the same diameter as the hook wire.

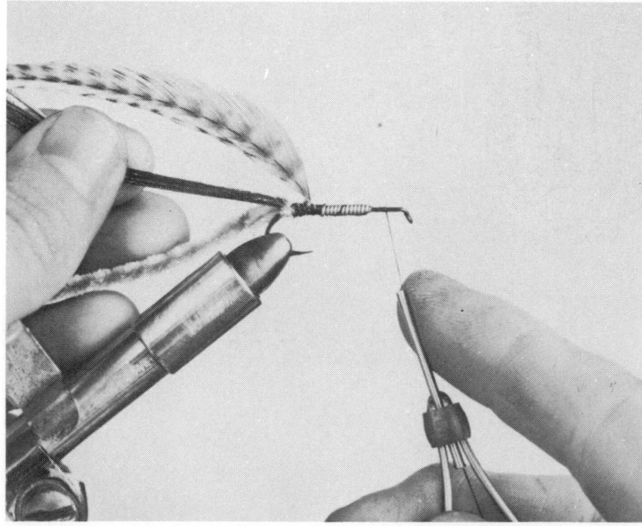

2a. Secure tying thread at rear of lead. Cut a short piece of red wool and tie it on at hook bend. It should extend only a short distance beyond bend.

2b. Attach a length of chenille at tail tie-down. Chenille should be size to accommodate hook without being too thin or bulky.

2c. Next attach six or eight peacock herls to top of hook, right above the chenille tiedown.

2d. Select a long grizzly saddle hackle that has little or no taper. Tie it to shank just behind the lead, not at bend. (If you intend to use the fly in calm water such as lakes, wider hackle is best; in swift water a narrow hackle will fish best.)

2e. Coat entire shank with thick clear cement after thread is brought forward to hook-eye area.

## HELEN SHAW/STREAMER, BUCKTAIL, AND BASS FLY

Ambrose Bucktail Streamer

Golden Furnace Streamer

Bubble Pup—Bass Fly

## ART FLICK/DRY FLIES

Hendrickson

Red Quill

Grey Fox Variant

Atherton Medium

Badger and Peacock

Catskill Coiler—Dark

Niemeyer Caddis

Grey/Olive No-Hackle on water. Note the "wedge effect"

White/Black Hen Spinner

A natural mayfly dun, its standard imitation, and the corresponding No-Hackle pattern on the water

Grey/Brown No-Hackle

Letort Cricket

Fur Ant

Letort Hopper

No-Name Midge

Midge Nymph

'hitlock Sculpin—three views

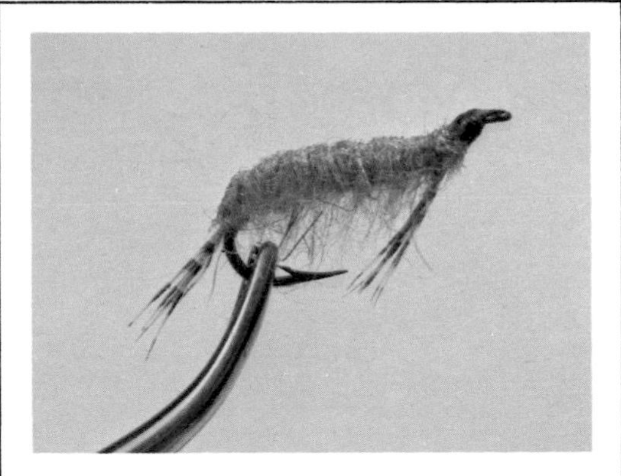

Dave's Shrimp

Stone-fly Nymph

Dave's Hopper

Woolyworm

arabou Muddler

Muddler Minnow

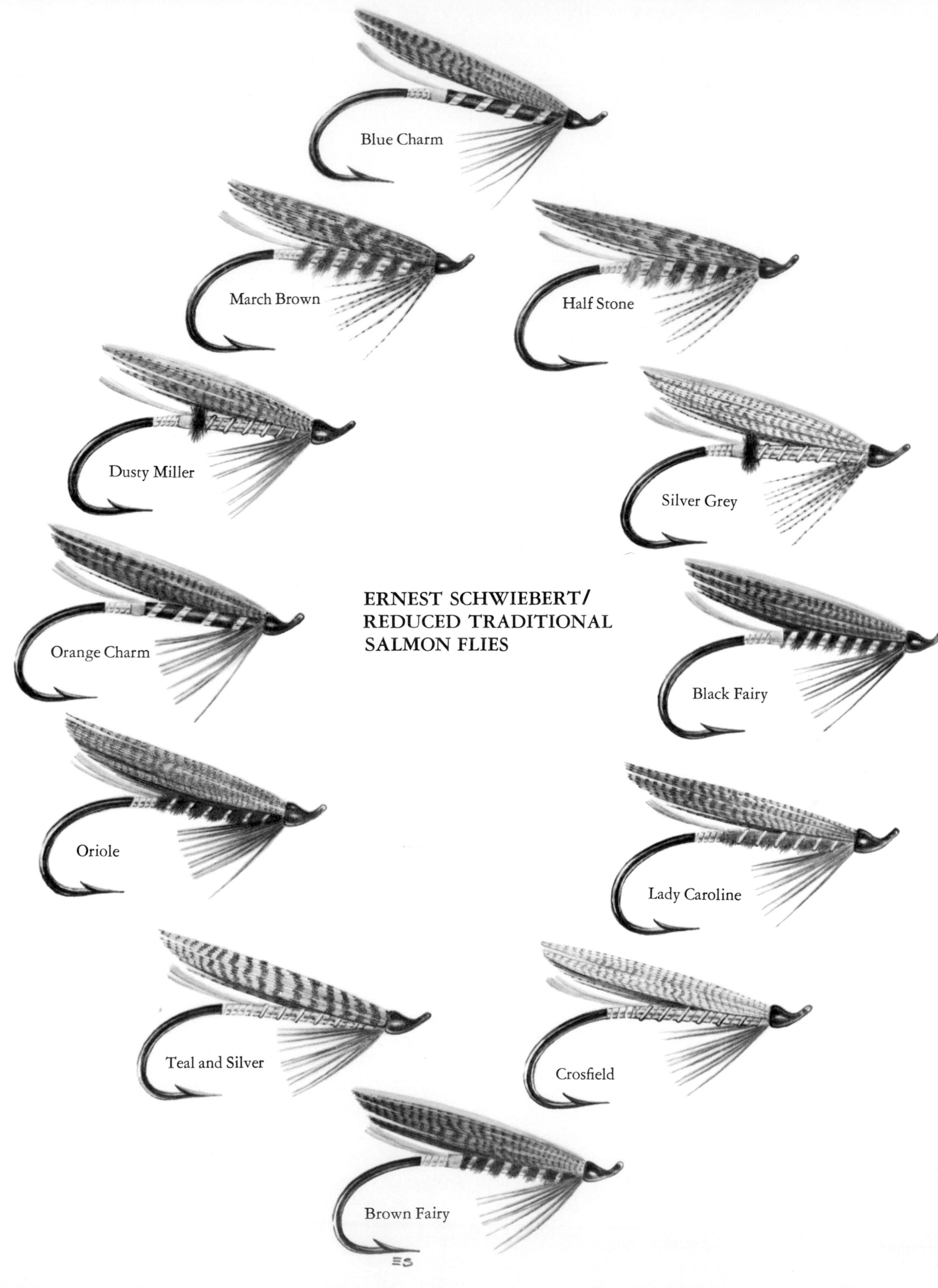
Blue Charm
March Brown
Half Stone
Dusty Miller
Silver Grey
ERNEST SCHWIEBERT/
REDUCED TRADITIONAL
SALMON FLIES
Orange Charm
Black Fairy
Oriole
Lady Caroline
Teal and Silver
Crosfield
Brown Fairy
ES

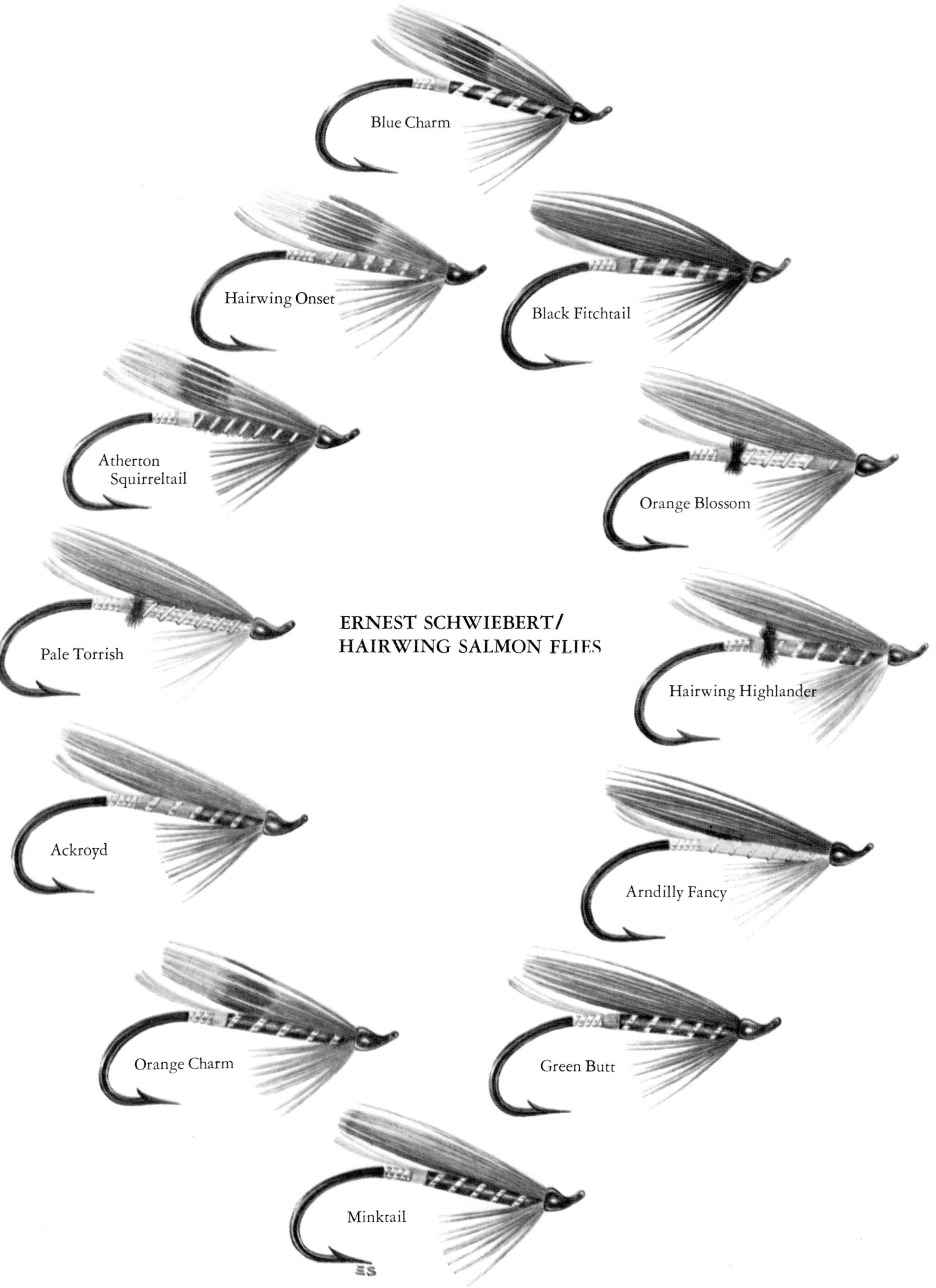
Blue Charm
Hairwing Onset
Black Fitchtail
Atherton Squirreltail
Orange Blossom
Pale Torrish
ERNEST SCHWIEBERT/
HAIRWING SALMON FLIES
Hairwing Highlander
Ackroyd
Arndilly Fancy
Orange Charm
Green Butt
Minktail
ES

Monofilament Fly—Glass Minnow

Lefty's Deceiver—three sizes, two patter

Joe Brooks's Blondes

Tarpon Flies—cockroach pattern

Keel Hook Fly

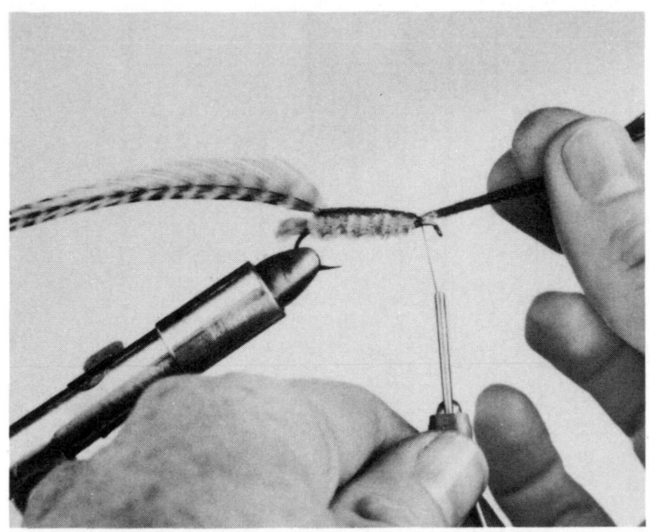

*BODY*

3a. Wrap the chenille clockwise over the shank, stopping just about one-fifth the shank distance from hook eye. Tie down with tying thread and trim excess.

3b. Pull herl forward and down tight over top of chenille body. Tie down ahead of chenille and trim off excess.

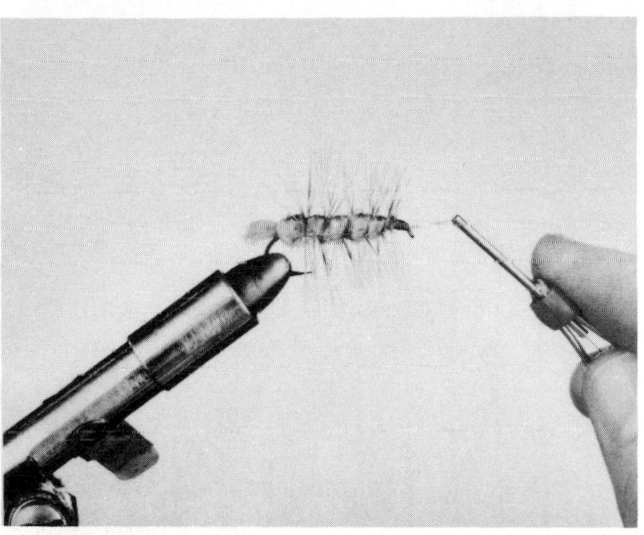

*HACKLE*

4a. Wrap saddle hackle clockwise over body in a spiral or rib pattern to the front of hook. Try to bury hackle stem between chenille wraps in order to prevent its being cut by wear or fish teeth. I prefer a reverse wrap that causes the hackle fibers to angle slightly forward and give the fly more action.

4b. Build up head with thread to protect the tie-down of materials and effect a closed protected hook eye.

4c. Whip-finish and varnish head.

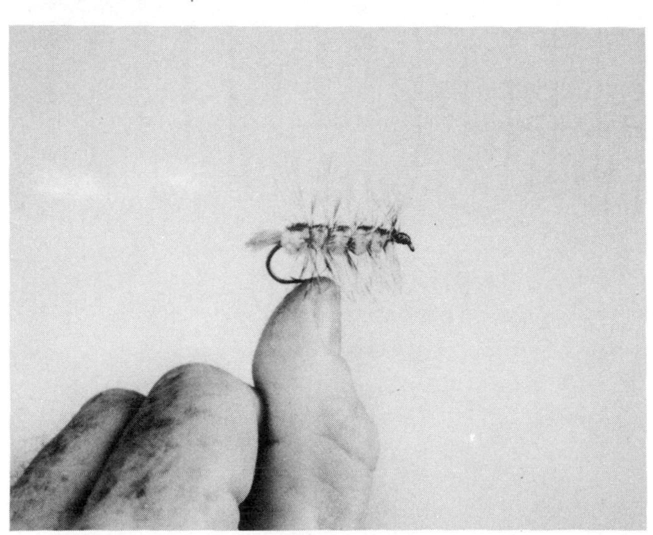

5. Finished woolyworm should have a long buggy silhouette; hackle can either be very long, sized to hook, or clipped short.

*Dave's Shrimp*

There is hardly a spring creek, stream, river, or lake in the West that doesn't have an abundant population of freshwater shrimp. In some, as in Henry's Lake in Idaho, they are so plentiful that the water almost seems half shrimp. Trout and other game fish love this rich crustacean and find it a twelve-month staple of their diet. They are easy to catch and digest and are extremely high in food value.

Imitating the shrimp or scud is not difficult. The pattern is also quite easy to fish since its erratic action of crawling, swimming, and drifting offers a fly-fisher a variety of retrieve methods. There appears to be a size-range fitting well between hooks 8 through 14. Most shrimp I've seen are one of three general tints—gray, tan, or light olive. After they die all turn a pinkish orange that is often mistaken for a true "shrimp" color.

The design of my shrimp provides a realistic shape and allows the fly to be fished deep without snagging on vegetation or stones.

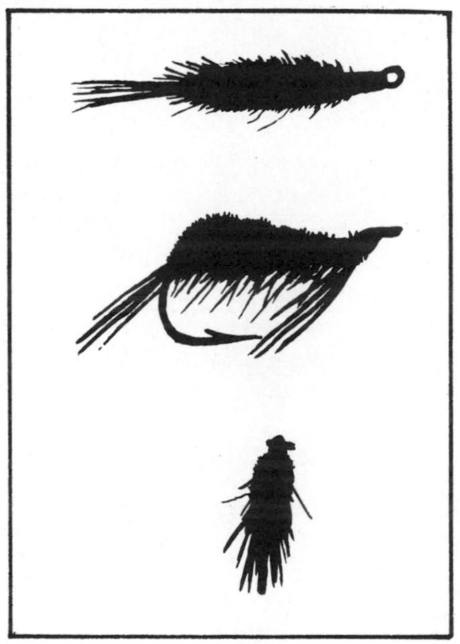

Dave's Shrimp—top, side, and front views

---

Hook: TDE 1x stout regular length; Mustad 7957BX size 8–14
Weight: lead wire
Thread: Herb Howard 8/O olive
Tail: barred wood duck flank feather
Body: fur-dubbing blend of amber seal fur, olive seal fur, bleached beaver belly, and natural gray muskrat belly—approximately equal portions of each
Throat: barred wood duck flank feather
Head: olive tying thread
Glue: clear head cement

---

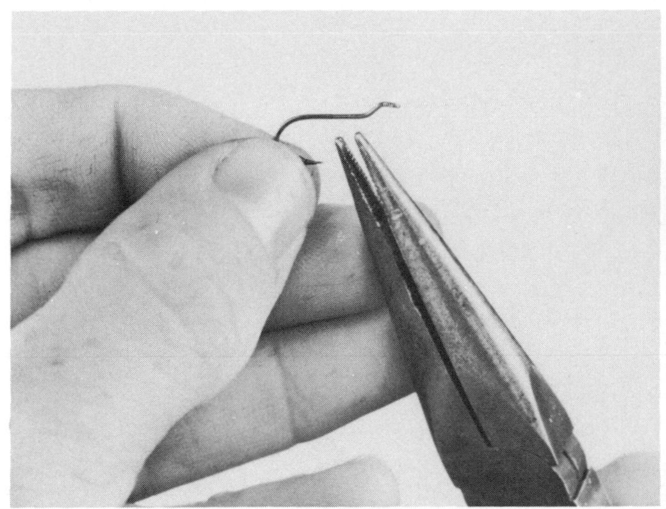

*HOOK*

1. With a pair of needle-nose pliers bend hook shank up about one-quarter length behind eye. Bend should not be sharp, but rounded. Eye should be parallel with hook shank.

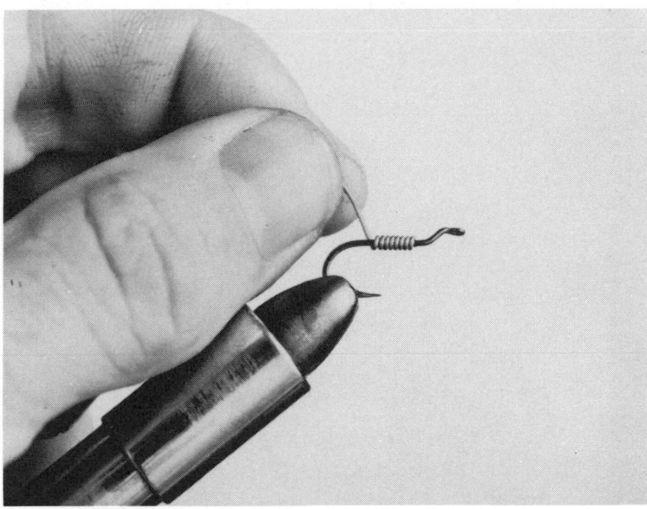

*WEIGHT*

2. Secure hook in vise and wrap lead on shank. Six to ten turns with lead wire approximately the same diameter as hook wire.

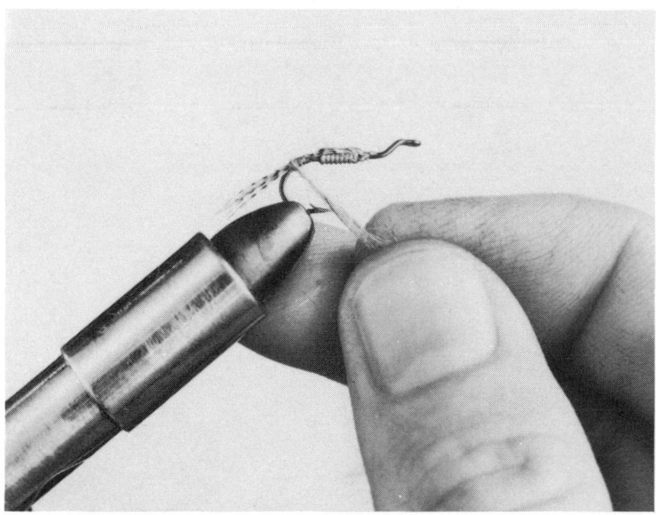

*TAIL*

3a. Attach tying thread to hook shank.

3b. Cut five to ten barred fibers from wood-duck flank and tie on at bend of hook. Fibers should be approximately three-quarters length of shank and point slightly downward.

3c. Coat hook shank with thick clear head cement.

3d. Spin dubbing on hook and start wrapping on hook shank just past bend of hook. Use a clockwise wrap.

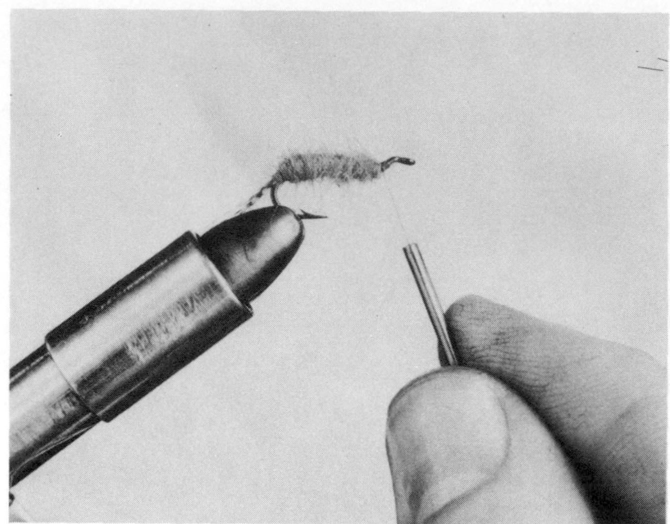

*BODY*

4. Continue wrapping the dubbing, building up the rear portion thicker on rear of shank. Gradually taper it toward neck bend on hook shank. A half-hitch is put over shank at this point.

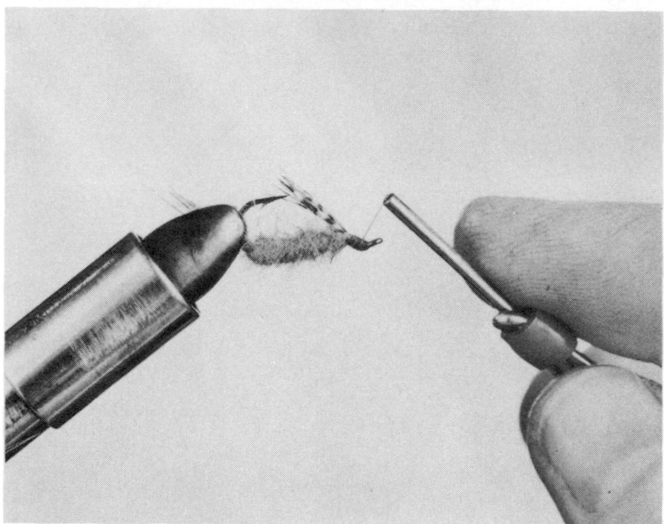

*BEARD AND HEAD*

5a. Remove the hook from vise and replace it upside down in vise.

5b. Take five to ten wood-duck fibers and tie on hook neck so that tips extend at that angle just past hook point.

5c. Add one or two turns of dubbing ahead of beard.

5d. Form head with tying thread and whip-finish.

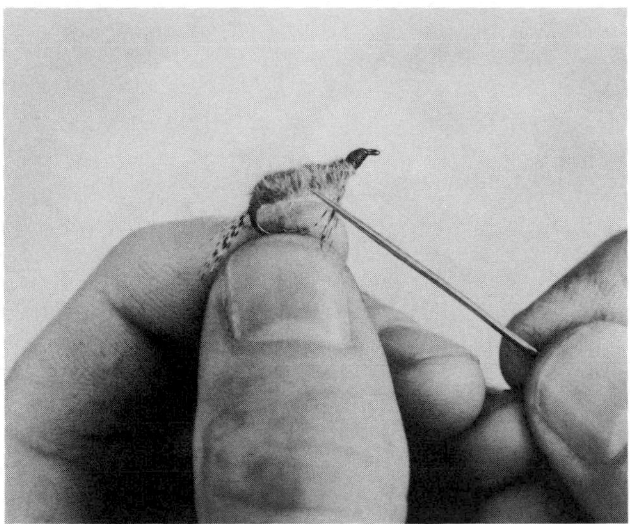

*SHAPING*

6a. Remove fly from vise and closely crop the back of fly with tying scissors.

6b. Next take dubbing needle or bodkin and pick out a number of hairs from underside of fly.

6c. Apply a coat of clear head cement to head and over back.

*FINISHING*

7. Completed shrimp should have a curved body shape with tail and beard at approximately same angle. Dubbing picked out, tail and head plus offset hook make this fly practically snagproof.

*Marabou Muddler*

This is a unique new western streamer pattern with fantastic versatility and fish appeal. The shaped deer-hair head, long marabou wings, and flashy body are a combination impossible to beat for "turn-on action" in any water. All trout, all bass, and popular panfish love the Marabou Muddler. It is fished top, shallow, or deep with action or dead-drift. It will invariably bring strikes if the game fish you are after are feeding on minnows. I tie it in several colors, but white is most universal in appeal. You might also try marabou wings dyed black, brown, gray, and yellow—and a gold mylar body is also a good second choice.

For bass that feed on shiners or shad I tie this pattern with the capacity to float. It simulates extremely well a crippled minnow struggling at the surface. This variation is included in the tying information along with the standard pattern.

Marabou Muddler—top, side, and front views

| | |
|---:|---|
| Hook: | TDE 3xL size 1/O through 10, Mustad 9672 or Mustad 38941 |
| Thread: | white Nymo and fluorescent orange Herb Howard nylon |
| Tail: | none |
| Underbody: | 1) peacock tail quill or 2) curon and lead |
| Body: | silver mylar piping |
| Underwing: | white kip or bucktail |
| Wing: | two white marabou plumes and peacock tail herl |
| Collar: | natural dun-brown northern white-tailed deer body-hair |
| Head: | same as collar |
| Cement: | clear flyhead cement |

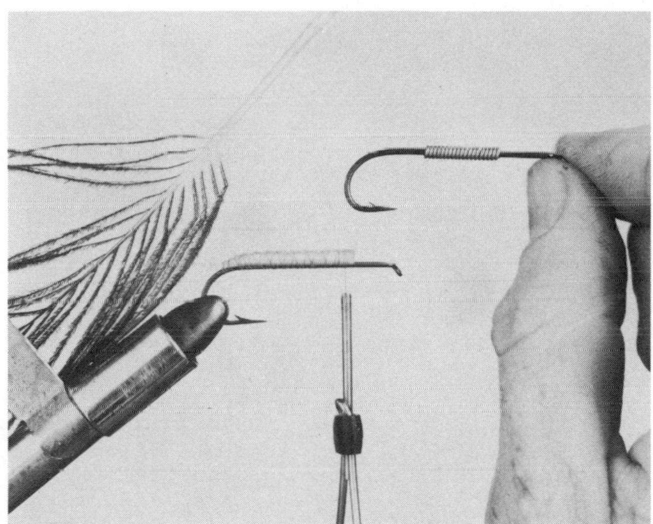

*FLOATING BODY*

1a-1. Secure hook in vise and wrap tying thread on rear two-thirds of shank.

1b-1. Strip the herl from a peacock tail quill, either sword or eyed quill.

1c-1. Cut a section from quill stem of the exact length you have wrapped hook shank.

1d-1. Lay soft side of quill section next to top of hook shank; firm side remains on top. Bind to shank with a number of turns of tying thread. Two half-hitches and cut thread.

1e-1. Coat quill and hook shank with clear head cement and set aside to dry. (Figure 3 will continue this body-building procedure.)

*SINKING BODY*

1a-2. Secure hook in vise and wrap ten to fifteen turns of lead on hook shank; wraps should be about in center third of shank.

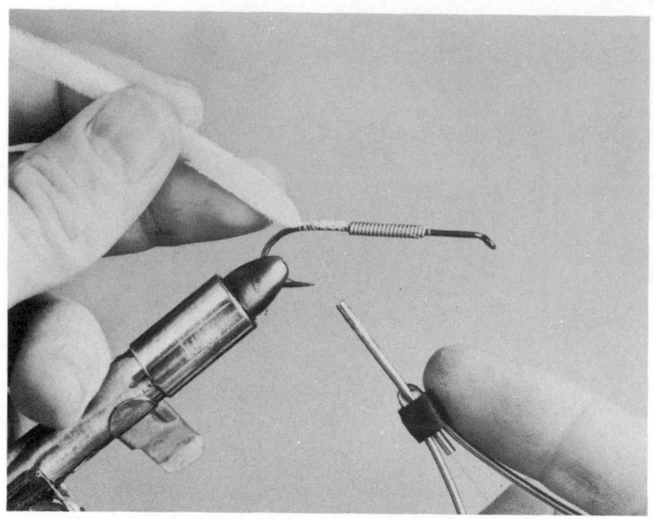

2a-2. Cut a strip of white curon approximately ¼ inch in diameter and three or four inches long.

2b-2. Attach curon strip behind lead wraps with tying thread.

2c-2. Coat shank and lead with a thick coat of clear head cement and bring thread forward of lead.

2d-2. Now wrap curon clockwise around shank, tapering it by stretching with tension as you wrap.

2e-2. Tie off curon leaving the front quarter of shank bare. Half-hitch two times or whip-finish and cut thread.

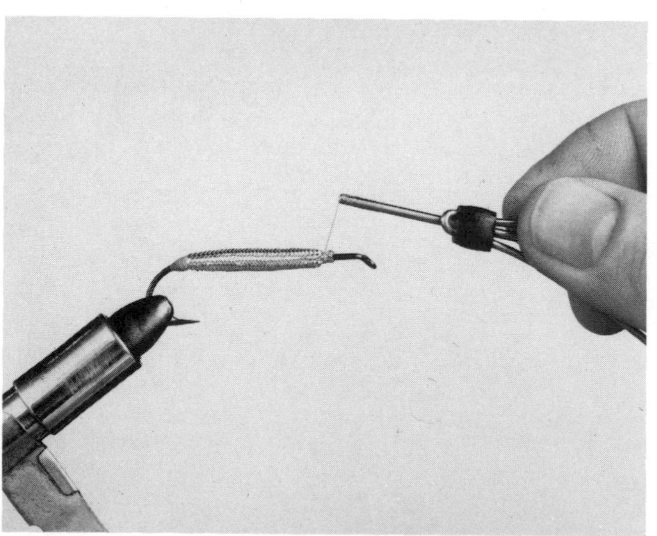

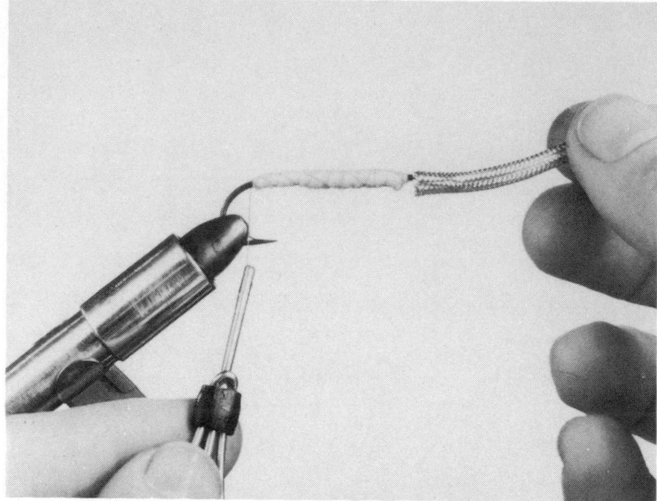

*MYLAR BODY*

3a. Attach fluorescent orange or red thread at hook bend of either quill or curon-formed underbody. (The same procedure is followed for both bodies from this point.)

3b. Cut a section of silver mylar piping an equal length of the underbody. Remove cotton center and discard.

3c. Carefully slip the mylar piping or tubing over the hook's eye and down hook shank covering underbody. If underbody isn't too large this is done easily; if too small, it will fit loosely.

4a. Catch the very end of piping with the tying thread and bind it down just at hook's bend. Be careful to keep this even and neat.

4b. Whip-finish and cut excess thread off.

4c. Attach tying thread to front of shank and repeat the tying down of piping's front portion.

4d. Be careful to leave the front quarter of shank bare and then half-hitch or whip-finish this tie-down area and cut thread.

4e. A covering of several thin coats of clear head cement over mylar insures a durable body. Allow to dry at least one hour. (More bodies can be made while waiting.)

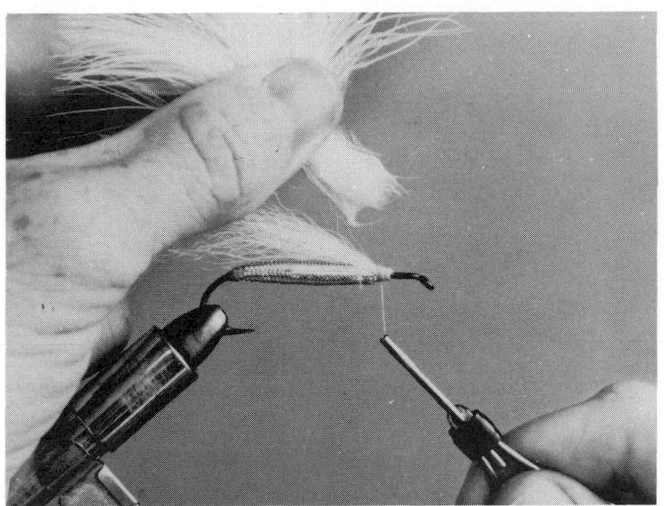

*WINGS*

5a. Secure mylar body in vise and attach white tying thread just ahead of the fluorescent orange or red wrap at front of shank.

5b. Cut a small bunch of white kip or buck tail about one-third longer than streamer's body. Pick out excess under fuzz and even butts with scissors.

5c. Tie it on top of hook shank just in front of body. It should not flare but lie almost parallel to top edge of mylar body.

5d. Match two white marabou feathers. Choose ones of similar texture, stem, and size whenever possible. Length should be be about one-half again as long as streamer's body.

5e. With feathers back to back (each flaring to its right or left side) tie directly over the hair underwing.

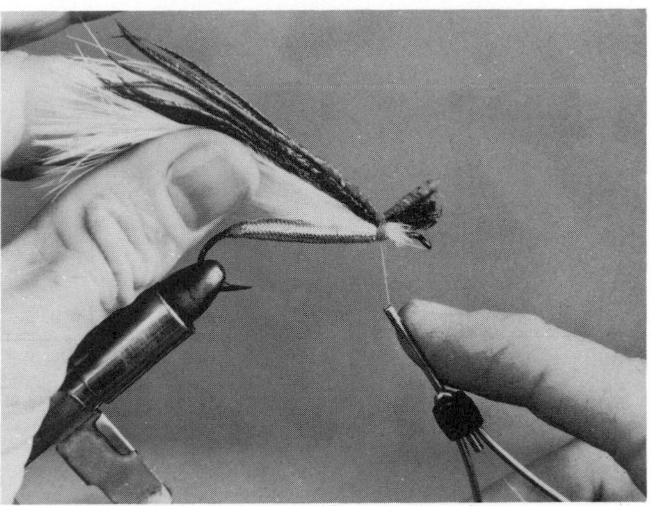

*OVERWING*

6a. Cut six or eight herls from an eyed peacock tail feather. Trim butts even with scissors.

6b. Directly over the marabou tie these on. Their length should be approximately the same as marabou.

6c. Trim excess butts of hair, marabou, and herl, then advance thread to bare portion of shank behind eye.

*COLLAR*

7a. From a well-marked piece of natural dun-brown northern deer hide, cut a moderate bunch of hair. Remove all excess fuzz and short hair.

7b. Place hair tips down in a small metallic container with a flat bottom. Tap container gently from bottom. This straightens and aligns tips.

7c. Remove carefully from container and trim butts even also. Hold deer hair tips with thumb and index finger, facing rear of streamer horizontally over shank.

7d. Wrap two turns of tying thread around center of bunch. Tips should extend about half the distance back to hook point.

7e. While still holding hair firmly, begin to draw thread wraps tight. As hair begins to flare, release your thumb and finger-hold; hair will then quickly spin around hook shank to form collar.

7f. Take three or four more tight turns in same place with thread after deer hair has been flared and spun evenly around shank.

7g. Advance thread in front of collar hair and push collar back against the body and wing base very snugly. Several thread turns against this hair will secure the position.

7h. Add one or two more bunches of deer hair to front of collar, flaring as for collar. Whip-finish at hook eye and cut thread excess.

*HEAD*

8. Remove the streamer from your vise and shape head by trimming deer hair with curved-blade scissors. Always remember to keep the blades near the same plane as head or parallel with shank plane, to effect a smooth cutting job. Trim most of head but leave most or all of the collar tips uncut; these are important in the action and silhouette of the fly.

*SHAPING, FINISHING*

9. Head is shaped bulletlike and small on the sinking model, much more bulky on the floater. The large bulky head will assist the floating and create more surface disturbance, which is so effective for bass and stripers. Mucilin or silicon are great aids in maintaining a floating minnow action. Grease *just* the *deer hair head,* not the body or wings.

*Stone-fly Nymph*

Because of its size and abundance, the western stone fly has been recognized as an important food for trout in many of the country's most famous streams. Since the adult fly hatches only a few days each year the nymph becomes the major food stage for trout. There are several genera of western stone flies that provide a wide range of sizes and colors, however, the two most significant large nymphs are commonly called giant dark stone (salmon fly) and golden stone. These two nymphs range commonly from ¾ inch to 2½ inches in length, depending on age and individual stream.

Since most western stone-fly nymphs are shaped very like one another, I shall describe only one basic pattern, but am including an alternate color in the material data so that you will have the two effective patterns.

Stone-fly nymphs do not emerge like caddis or mayfly nymphs, but usually crawl out on the bank or a surface-protruding stone or tree limb and shed their case; therefore they are seldom taken by trout any place but on or near the bottom. Your fly must sink quickly, stay deep, and have materials that provide good silhouette and action.

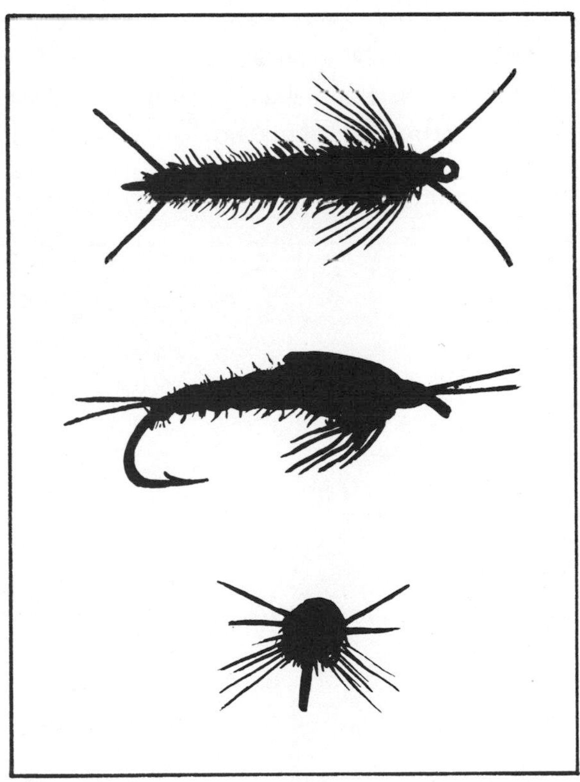

Stone Fly Nymph—top, side, and front views

| | |
|---|---|
| Hook: | TDE 3xL; Mustad 38941 or Buz's Special 3xL, sizes 4 through 8 |
| Thread: | 1) Herb Howard's orange nylon (prewaxed) 2) Herb Howard's yellow nylon (prewaxed) |
| Underbody: | 1) brown curon 2) gold curon |
| Weight: | lead wire |
| Tail: | 1) dark-brown or black horsetail hair 2) light-brown horsetail hair |
| Body: | 1) fur-dubbing blend of ½ dark-brown seal, ¼ seal-brown rabbit, ⅛ burnt-orange seal, and ⅛ dark natural amber seal |
| Abdomen: | 2) fur-dubbing blend of ¼ dark-amber seal, ¼ light-amber seal, ⅜ yellow seal, and ⅛ golden rabbit or bleached beaver belly |
| Rib: | gold silk or nylon buttonhole twist |
| Wing Case: | 1) dark-brown turkey secondary 2) golden-brown turkey secondary |
| Thorax: | 1) fur-dubbing blend of ¼ dark-brown seal, ¼ burnt-orange seal, ¼ dark-amber seal, and ¼ golden-brown rabbit or beaver belly 2) same as abdomen no. 2 |
| Legs: | 1) grizzly neck hackle dyed light-seal brown 2) light variegated cree or grizzly dyed gold |
| Head: | 1) dirty orange and dark brown 2) yellow and golden brown |
| Antenna: | 1) dark-brown or black horsetail hair 2) light-brown horsetail hair |
| Cement: | clear head cement, rod varnish |

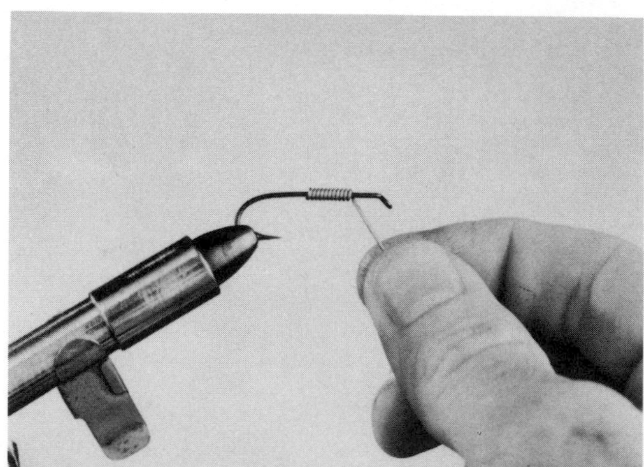

*HOOK AND WEIGHTING*

1a. Secure hook in vise.

1b. Wrap hook shank with six to twelve turns lead wire approximate diameter of hook's wire. Wraps should be in middle third of hook shank or slightly forward.

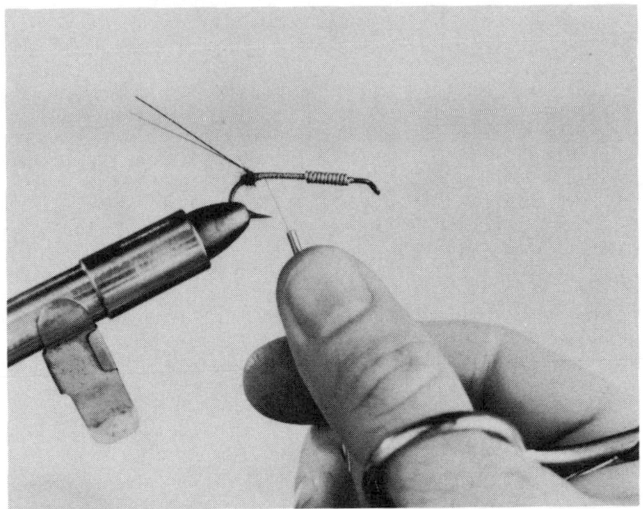

*TAIL*

2a. Attach thread to rear of shank behind lead wraps.

2b. Dub a small ball of fur blend just at hook's bend.

2c. Take a 3-inch piece of horsetail hair and double it.

2d. Place ends' point to rear and tie hair on just in front of fur dubbing.

2e. Separate hair so that each end angles to right and left side of hook shank. Tying thread can be used to help bind them apart.

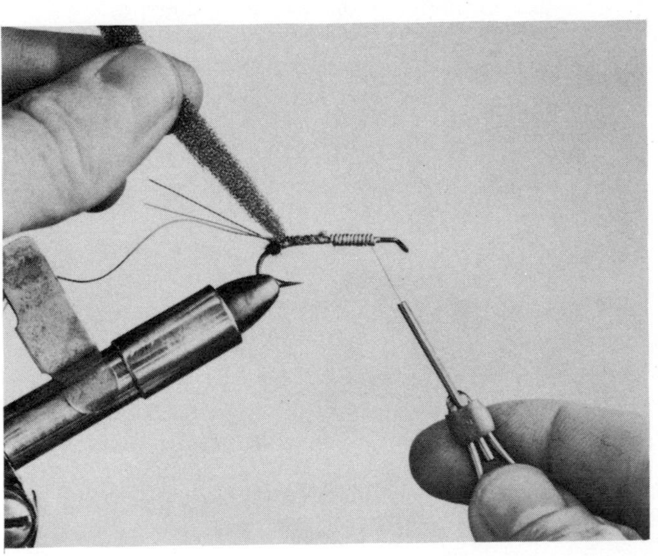

*UNDERBODY AND RIB*

3a. Tie on a 6-inch length of gold ribbing thread at base of tail.

3b. Cut a strip of curon and attach it just ahead of tail.

3c. Advance tying thread to front of lead wraps.

3d. Coat hook shank and lead wraps with clear head cement.

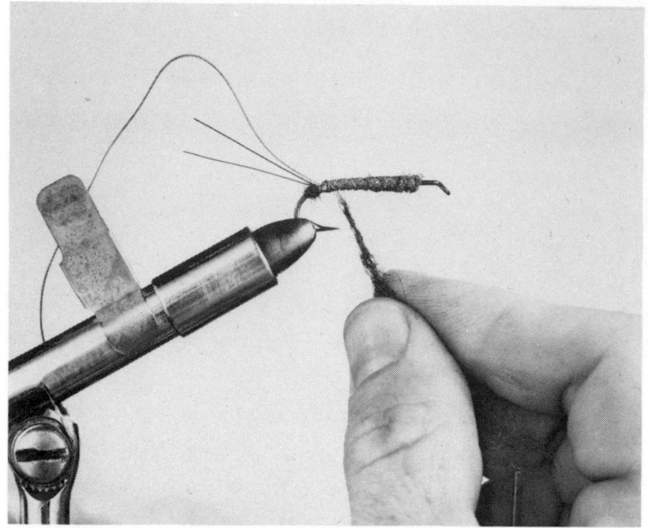

*UNDERBODY AND ABDOMEN*

4a. Wrap curon strip over shank forming a neat tapered underbody.

4b. Tie and trim off excess just in front of lead wraps.

4c. Return tying thread to base of tail.

4d. Begin to dub abdomen fur blend on thread to form abdomen.

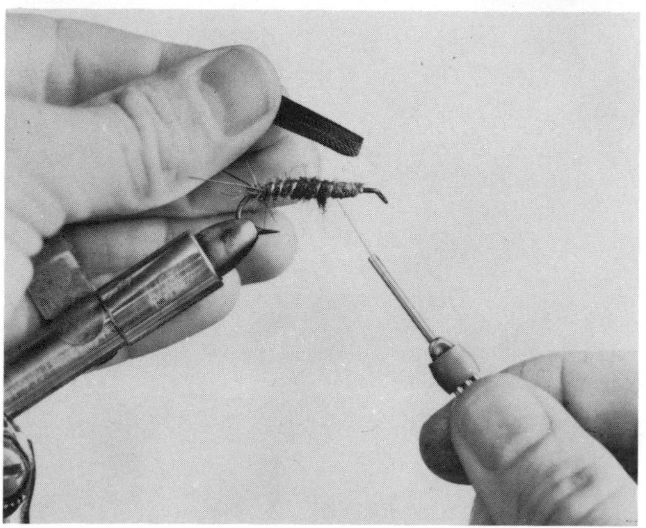

*ABDOMEN AND RIB*

5a. Wrap dubbing clockwise up the shank. Take care to taper abdomen.

5b. Stop abdomen dubbing midway of lead wraps.

5c. Now rib abdomen with gold ribbing thread. Increase segment width each wrap toward front.

5d. Tie down rib thread just in front of fur abdomen, trim excess away.

5e. Select a section of dark-brown turkey quill and tie it on top of lead wraps and just overlapping the abdomen dubbing. Section should be a fraction wider than abdomen.

5f. Coat wing-case tie-down and thorax area with clear head cement.

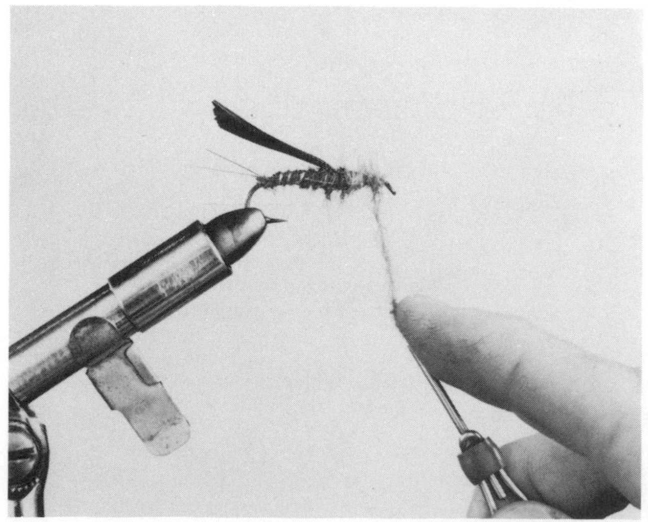

*THORAX*

6a. Spin thorax dubbing blend on thread.

6b. Wrap thorax area clockwise with dubbing. Make sure it covers abdomen junction and extends just past front of underbody.

6c. Check to see that thorax is at least as thick as or thicker than base of thorax; if not, add more dubbing to it.

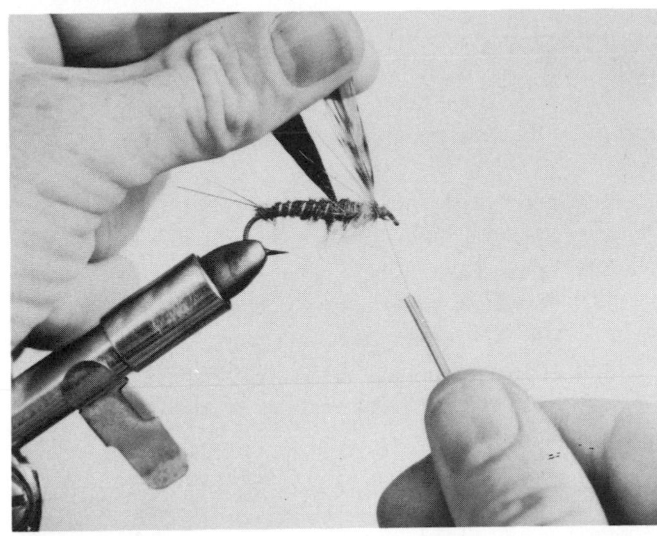

*LEGS*

7a. Select a hackle which should be soft and webby to fit hook size.

7b. Attach it with tying thread just in front of dubbed thorax. Make sure dull side faces fly body to insure proper hackle angle.

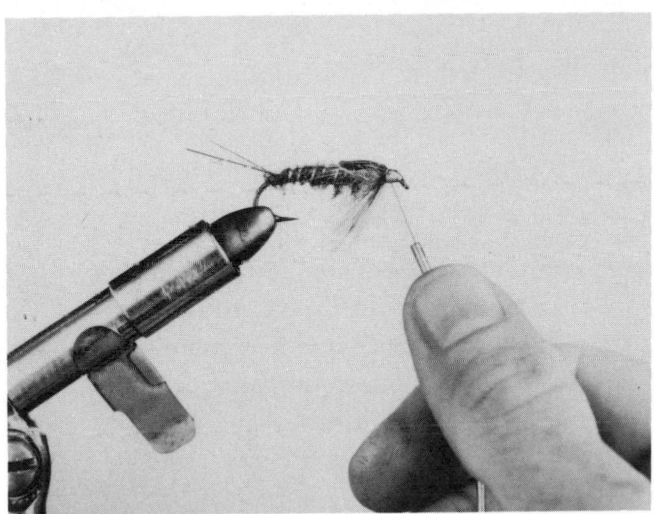

*LEGS AND WING CASE*

8a. Wrap hackle one or two complete turns as close to thorax fur dubbing as possible.

8b. Tie down excess hackle tip and trim off. Also trim off those fibers that are at top of shank.

8c. Pull wing-case forward and down over thorax snugly.

8d. Bind down just ahead of hackle legs with tying thread.

8e. Trim with scissors excess wing case that extends beyond hook eye.

8f. Bulk of wing-case tie-down aids in forming large tapered head.

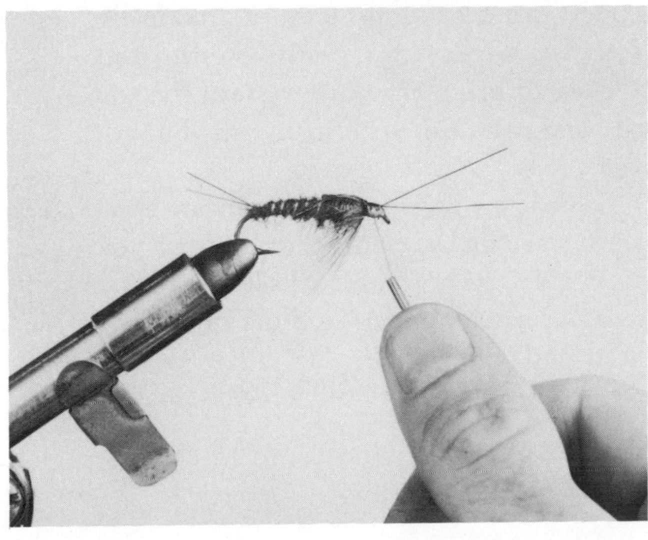

*ANTENNA AND HEAD*

9a. Place a doubled 3-inch piece of horsetail hair over top of head. Ends point to the front.

9b. Bind down with thread. Make sure hair is positioned to sides of head as you bind it down.

9c. Continue to shape head with tying thread.

9d. Whip-finish the head and cut thread excess.

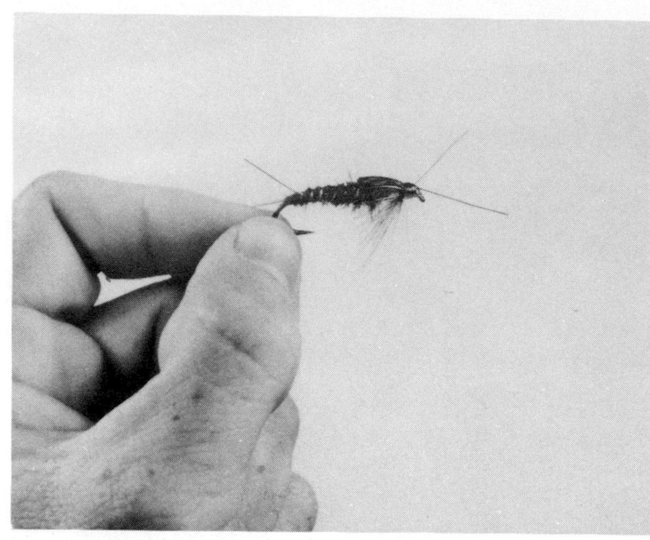

*FINISHING*

10a. Trim both tails and antenna with scissors. Make tail somewhat shorter than antenna.

10b. Both pairs should spread to right and left of nymph.

10c. Trim hackle legs from bottom of thorax; leave six or eight fibers on each side of nymph.

10d. Pick out dubbing with needle point to create a fuzzy look at sides of abdomen and thorax.

10e. Paint top of head with dark-brown dope or enamel. Varnish head after paint dries.

### *Muddler Minnow*

No western fly selection could be considered complete without including the muddler. Though the fly was designed by Don Gapen for Canadian brook trout, it has spread over the fly-fishing world like the English sparrow over our continent. My hat off and a deep bow to Don's wonderful creation—and one more bow to Dan Bailey for adapting the original a bit to suit western conditions. Dan and Joe Brooks have made the muddler a household word wherever waters carry trout.

The muddler is a fantastic pattern, with the most unusual suggestive appeal of any pattern I've ever tied or used. Its range of imitations includes the sculpins, chubs, little trout, crayfish, mice, grasshoppers, stone or caddis flies—a practically endless list of what it might suggest to game fish. Given a wide range of sizes and several fishing methods, it comes extremely close to being the only western fly you need. And besides trout, it is a terrific bass fly and rates top with many smallmouth enthusiasts. Saltwater fish and salmon love it, too.

The Muddler Minnow here is the Bailey version, which I prefer over the original Gapen model or other variations. However, by varying the color scheme a little you can further extend the pattern's usefulness. It has a great action and silhouette and should not be limited to just one color scheme. After you understand the method of tying this fly, experiment a bit with the head and wing color. Try olives, black, white, browns, and golden yellow. All these work extremely well on this master pattern.

Muddler Minnow—top, side, bottom, and front views

| | |
|---|---|
| Hook: | TDE 3xL Mustad 9672 sizes 3/O through 10 |
| Thread: | tan or white Nymo |
| Glue: | fly head cement and rod varnish |
| Tail: | section of brown speckled turkey-wing quill |
| Body: | flat gold tinsel |
| Underwing: | white and brown kip or calf tail |
| Wing: | matched sections of brown-speckled turkey quill |
| Collar: | natural dun-brown northern deer hair |
| Head: | same as collar |

*HOOK AND TAIL*

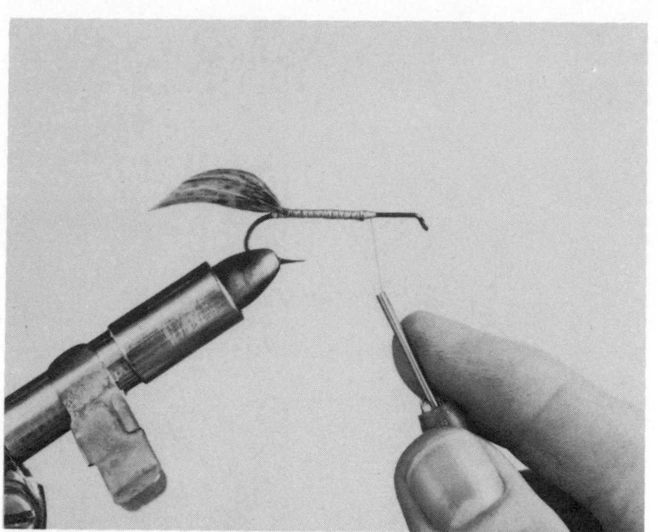

1a. Secure hook in vise, and attach tying thread and wrap hook shank from front third, covering back two-thirds of shank with thread.

1b. Cut a section from the leading edge of brown speckled turkey quill, right or left wing.

1c. Place it with leading edge pointing down parallel to wrapped hook shank.

1d. Bind down with tying thread, using same general procedure as quill wings on wet flies.

1e. Bring tying thread to front of wrap shank.

*BODY*

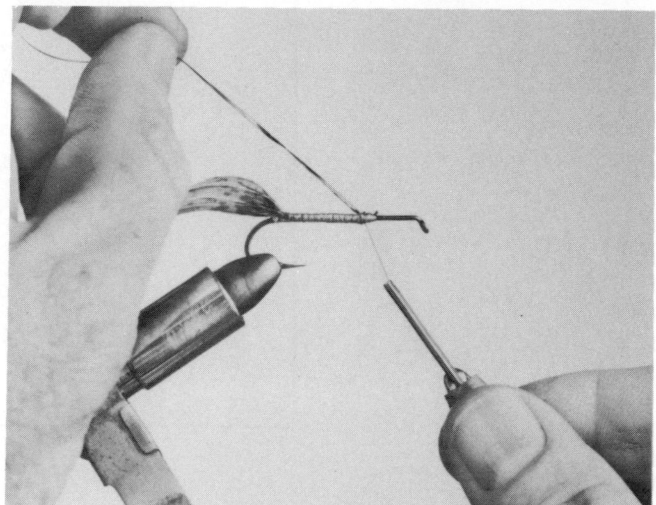

2a. Take a long piece of flat gold tinsel and tie on hook shank just behind front third of hook shank.

2b. Wrap tinsel back toward tail. Wraps should be tight and spaced very close.

2c. When tail is reached, reverse direction and overwrap tinsel back to front of body.

2d. Tie down and trim excess tinsel.

2e. With a small brush, paint tinsel body with a coat of clear head cement. Allow to dry a minute or so.

*UNDERWING*

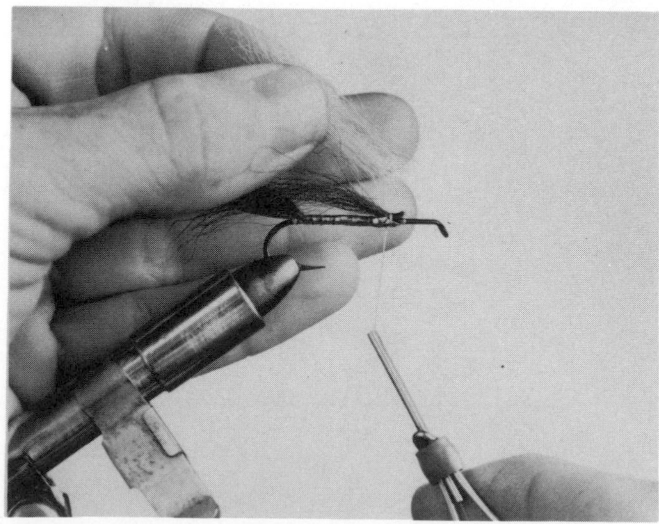

3a. Cut a small bunch of brown calf tail to length of fly body and tail.

3b. Tie to top of shank with tying thread at very front of tinsel body.

3c. Cut a small bunch of white calf tail same length and tie directly over the brown calf tail. Trim excess neatly off.

3d. Place a drop of clear head cement on butts of this hair.

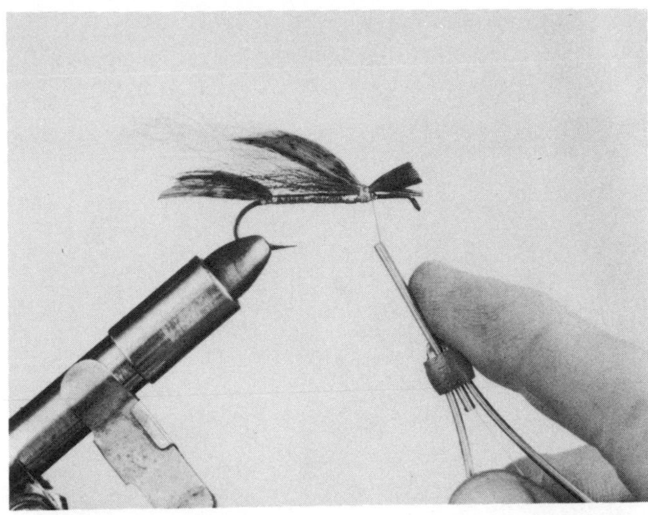

*WING*

4a. From a match of right and left brown speckled turkey quills cut two equal sections from their leading edges.

4b. Place these together with dull sides facing each other, bright sides facing out.

4c. Directly over underwing tie down this pair of wings. Make sure tips point down like tail. Use a regular procedure for quill-wing wet flies to tie wings on. Wings should be about same length as body

*COLLAR*

5a. Cut a moderate bunch of well-marked natural dun-brown northern white-tail deer hair. Remove all fuzz and short hair with a small stiff toothbrush or your fingers.

5b. Next place bunch of cleaned hair tips down in a small flat-bottomed metallic can (a 35-mm. film-roll can or empty brass rifle case will work well). Gently tap bottom a few times, which evens all hair tips quickly. Carefully remove hair.

5c. Place this bunch of deer hair along top of hook shank with tips pointing back toward tail. Tips should extend about to hook point.

5d. Take two turns of tying thread around hair and hook shank just in front of wing and body base. Slowly tighten thread but do not release hold on hair until thread begins to flare hair.

5e. Release hair and continue to tighten thread (hair will flare and roll around hook shank to form collar).

5f. Take three or four more wraps on exact plane to further secure collar, then advance thread directly in front of collar hair.

5g. With right thumb and index finger push collar back very snugly against body and wing fronts.

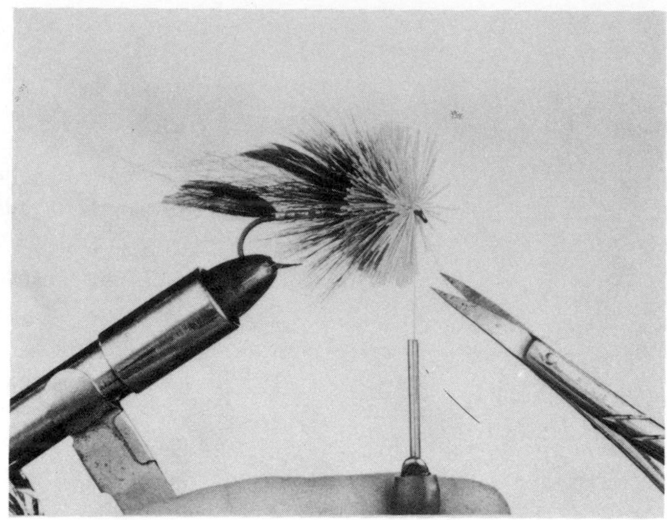

*HEAD*

6a. Cut another bunch of deer hair and repeat the steps A, C, D, E, and F in Figure 6.

6b. Pack second bunch of hair firmly against collar hair. If shank is not full, add another bunch of deer hair. A full tight head is necessary for best results.

6c. Whip-finish at hook eye with thread and cut off thread's excess.

*SHAPING HEAD*

7a. With a pair of scissors (I prefer those with curved blades), trim deer-hair head to a blunt bulletlike shape. Remember to hold scissor blades in a general parallel plane to head in order to accomplish a neat smooth job. Leave most of the collar tips intact as they are important in action and silhouette of the muddler.

7b. If fly is to be fished wet, shape head rather small. For surface use, make head considerably larger. Hollow deer hair is buoyant and much of it will float well.

*FINISHING*

8. After trimming head, apply a thin coat of rod varnish to bottom of head and at hook eye to insure a durable head. By applying mucilin or silicon to head, the muddler will float like a grasshopper and can be used, with imparted action, as an excellent popping bug for bass.

# Ernest Schwiebert

## SALMON FLIES

Drawings by the Author

It rained softly through the night.

The valley below the scrollwork Victorian hotel at Dombås was filled with clouds at breakfast. There were fresh rolls and goat cheese and brislings in dill, with coffee and fresh orange juice. After breakfast the weather was clearing, and I started north in the Volvo across the high moors on the mountain road to Trondheim.

"Good weather for tourists," the hotelkeeper had said.

"It's perfect for the tour bus to Åndalsnes," agreed another guest, "but it's too bright for salmon."

"We'll see," I laughed.

It had been a warm summer with little rain, and the rivers were low except for the melting ice fields in the Trollheimen mountains. Fishing was difficult, and few salmon had entered the thin gin-clear currents of most watersheds. The road drops steeply north toward the sea at Opdal, into the headwaters of the Driva, where I was meeting the famous Charles Ritz.

The river is moody and difficult, but its valley has an unsurpassed beauty. The mountain walls are massive above the churchyards and haymeadows and farms. Snowfields and glaciers crown the escarpments that enclose the narrow valley floor. The best fishing begins with the beats at Storfahle, the charming seventeenth-century farmstead where I was staying, and the valley is threaded with the delicate lacework of countless waterfalls.

There was a note from Charles Ritz at the farm. "Please join us at lunch on the Cappelen water," it read. "Gailliard is here with his family—and please bring some of your flies."

Ritz is an old friend, and Gailliard is another legendary French angler who holds the record salmon at Målangsfossen with a fish of fifty-seven pounds. It was an exciting prospect to meet such fishermen at the Cappelen fishing hut, and I threw my fly boxes into the Volvo.

The valley opens as it reaches the village of Sunndalsora, where the Driva meets the fjord. There is an unobtrusive gravel road that winds past a somber little cemetery. Its moss-covered walls enclose the unmarked graves of Russian prisoners who died in the valley, forced to load ships and clear the roads in the bitter subarctic winters without enough clothing and food.

The road works down through the potato fields to the Driva, where the Cappelen fishing hut stands in a beautiful grove of silver birches. "Ernest!" Ritz came running toward the car before I had cut the ignition. "Where are your flies?"

"I've brought them," I laughed.

"Fishing has been poor." Ritz was searching my flies hastily. "Perhaps your hairwings will change our luck!"

"Petri heil!" I grinned.

Gailliard came out across the sun-dappled clearing. "Charles is crazy for hairwings," he laughed. "He is decimating your fly boxes—perhaps we should introduce ourselves without him."

Ritz had several 2/0 hairwings in his mouth and could only roll his eyes and arch his eyebrows at our laughter, while he continued to rummage through the last Wheatley.

"Voila!" he waved a hairwing Orange Charm.

"It's a good pattern," I nodded.

Their fishing had failed after three days to produce a fish. The water was bright, and the huge traditional flies on 4/0 and 5/0 irons had proved worthless. Ritz liked the hairwings and simplified patterns evolved on Canadian and American waters, having first used them on the Romaine.

"They are more alive." Ritz had collared Gailliard with a tumbling flow of French. "They are more translucent, they move in the water, and the hair glitters with tiny bubbles!"

Gailliard shrugged. "Perhaps," he smiled.

"Try one!" Ritz insisted.

The boatman Kjell pushed off into the swift current and worked into the meadow pool below the fishing hut. Sunlight glittered on the waterfalls high above the river. The cool wind moved in the silver birches. The gillie settled into a steady pattern at the oars, rowing to lower each successive cast a yard downstream. Gailliard adjusted his rhythm, working the slender Ritz parabolic in the sun.

Ritz and I walked in the barley-field path above the current and watched the fishing. The wooden oarlocks creaked slightly and we watched the pleasant rhythms of the fly line working.

Suddenly the rod dipped and a spade-sized tail scattered spray on the wind. "Salmon!" Gailliard shouted.

"Perfect!" I laughed. "He's into a fish!"

"It's the American hairwing," Ritz was shouting. "It's La Mouche Americaine—the drought is ended!"

"Mais oui!" Gailliard was laughing too.

Their change of luck that noon hour on the Driva has not proved unusual these past dozen years. Such simplified patterns and American hairwings have migrated to salmon rivers on both continents as well as to Iceland, and have been readily adopted by European anglers. Although their origins are still recent, their full history has already become obscured and embellished by popular legends.

Both the hairwings and the simplified patterns have an interesting background in the folklore of salmon fishing, and there is more than a little irony in their effectiveness. The traditional salmon pattern like the Jock Scott, with its mixed palette of colors from exotic plumages of Indian crow, black ostrich, yellow toucan, speckled gallina, turkey, blue chatterer, jungle cock, blue and yellow macaw, barred wood duck, and teal, and a wing of married feathers from the peacock, golden pheasant, brown mallard, swan dyed scarlet and yellow and blue, florican, and African bustard, is a typical fly with centuries of history behind it. Such intricate constructions of exotic feathers have a direct relationship to the British naval power that followed the defeat of the Spanish Armada in 1588. Rule of the seas led to both a matchless merchant fleet and great trading companies, and ultimately to the British Empire itself. Mixed with the flow of spices and jewels and jute were bright-feathered skins of tropical birds for fashions and flies.

"The fly-dressers of the time were like a medieval guild," says Charles DeFeo, an artist who is also one of the finest salmon-fly artisans alive. "They encouraged the complicated traditional patterns because they were too difficult for an amateur."

Their exotic feathers were also expensive.

Canadian fishermen a half century ago were unable to purchase the materials specified in traditional salmon flies, and the cost would have been prohibitive. Similar constraints undoubtedly led simple Scottish flytyers on the remote rivers northeast of Edinburgh, without ready access to major seaports, to develop the more somber strip-winged Dee patterns and the dark heron-hackled flies popular on the Spey. Guides and poachers in Canada were forced to develop similar less intricate flies on their waters.

"They're still called guide patterns on some rivers," comments Colonel Henry Siegel, one of our most knowledgeable angling historians, "and the guides are proud of the fact that their flies often outfish the expensive traditionals sold to their sports."

Certainly the wealthy anglers who traveled to fish Canadian rivers from the major eastern cities of Canada and the United States continued to fish the expensive British patterns out of an exaggerated sense of tradition. Some British fishermen who have fished with me on Norwegian rivers still refuse to fish the hairwings in spite of their success. "They're simply not elegant enough for salmon," they insist, ending the conversation.

Charles DeFeo believes that the salmon hairwings have their roots in Newfoundland and patterns dressed from reddish calf tail, and his judgments are confirmed by Herbert Howard, another well-known American flytyer and fisherman. Howard tells of a Bible he examined on a backcountry Newfoundland farm that included a description of such a Hereford hairwing and its success in 1795.

However, most hairwings and reduced patterns are of more recent fly-dressing vintages. George Kelson compiled his monumental *The Salmon Fly* at the zenith of Victorian England in 1895. It codified the old gingerbread patterns into a list of three hundred flies, each a rich fruitcake of exotic feathers fully equal to the florid aesthetics of the Victorian period. Kelson actually believed that salmon liked local species of butterflies indigenous to each river, and that this diet explained both his bright collection of flies and the emphasis on locally favorite patterns. It is surprising that such nonsense could be widely believed only eighty-odd years ago, but Kelson achieved a brief renaissance of the traditionals that was further reinforced in the beautiful little *How to Dress Salmon Flies,* which T. E. Pryce-Tannatt published in 1911. Their influence undoubtedly delayed the evolution of simplified patterns and hairwings.

Colonel Lewis Thompson and Carter Harrison, the celebrated mayor of Chicago, both fished the Trude Ranch on the Snake in this same period. A. S. Trude was a well-known Chicago attorney whose friends often journeyed with him to Idaho, and it was Carter Harrison who dressed the first hairwings in that circle of friends. It was done as a joke in the summer of 1903. Harrison tied his joke on a huge muskellunge hook, using hair from a ranch dog for its wings and wool from a rug and a simulated hackle of bucktail. The joke was an immense success with an ironic turn. Trude and Thompson liked the coloring and configuration of the pattern and soon talked Harrison into dressing serious versions with dubbed bodies and squirrel-tail wings. These primitive hairwings worked perfectly on the big Idaho rainbows and cutthroats, and the diaries of Carter Harrison tell us that the party struggled to carry their catches back from the river.

Thompson carried these flies with him to the Restigouche and, during a time when the salmon were dour, he tried them in desperation and found they worked. Colonel Thompson continued to experiment with hairwings in later years, and it was with a big 5/0 Abbey on the Restigouche that he discovered his Thompson patent—a deadly method of fishing a hairwing on a wet slack-line drift like a huge nymph or dead-drift bucktail.

Since its genesis in the hands of these pioneers, the reduced pattern and its hairwing cousins have continued to evolve. Famous tyers include Roy Steenrod, Ira Gruber, Bert Miner, Herb Howard, Harry Darbee, Charles DeFeo, Everett Price, Fred Merseau, Charles Conrad, Everette Lyons, Van Storey, Harry Smith, Joseph Auclin, Wallace Doak, Roy Thompson, John Cosseboom, Carmelle Bigaouette, and the well-known Lapointe brothers who supplied flies on the classic Matapedia.

There have been many others since mid-century. Perhaps the best method of discussing present reduced patterns and hairwings is to describe the flies that I dress and carry on the river. Since my time at the fly-vise is limited these days, it might also prove valuable to cover patterns that I use and have seen producing impressive catches. These are the flies I carry, and their dressings are personal variations on older themes.

The traditional flies came first, and a sense of chivalry leads me to discuss feather-winged reduced patterns ahead of the hairwings. There are anglers in the United Kingdom, Ireland, Norway, and Iceland who rank the Blue Charm at the top of their fly books. Such men have a large number of colleagues in the United States and Canada who agree, and I am almost one of their number. It was the favorite of Arthur Wood, who developed the greased-line method of fishing salmon at Cairnton on the legendary Dee, and it became the title of a famous angling story by Paul Hyde Bonner. Its pattern follows in the order that its materials are used.

DRESSING A TYPICAL SALMON FLY

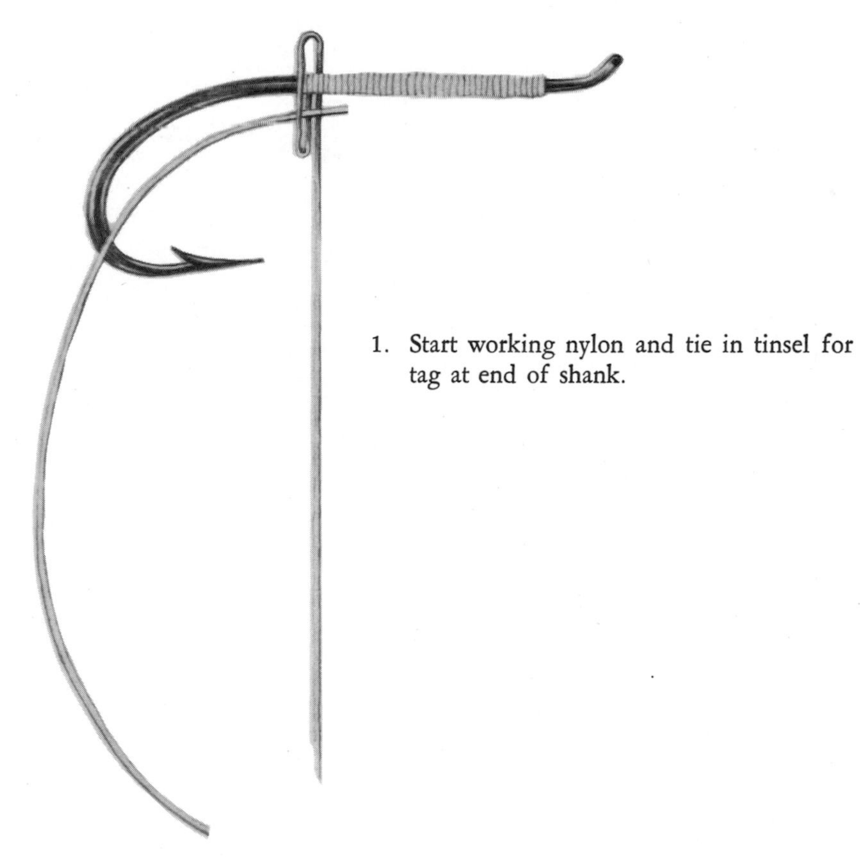

1. Start working nylon and tie in tinsel for tag at end of shank.

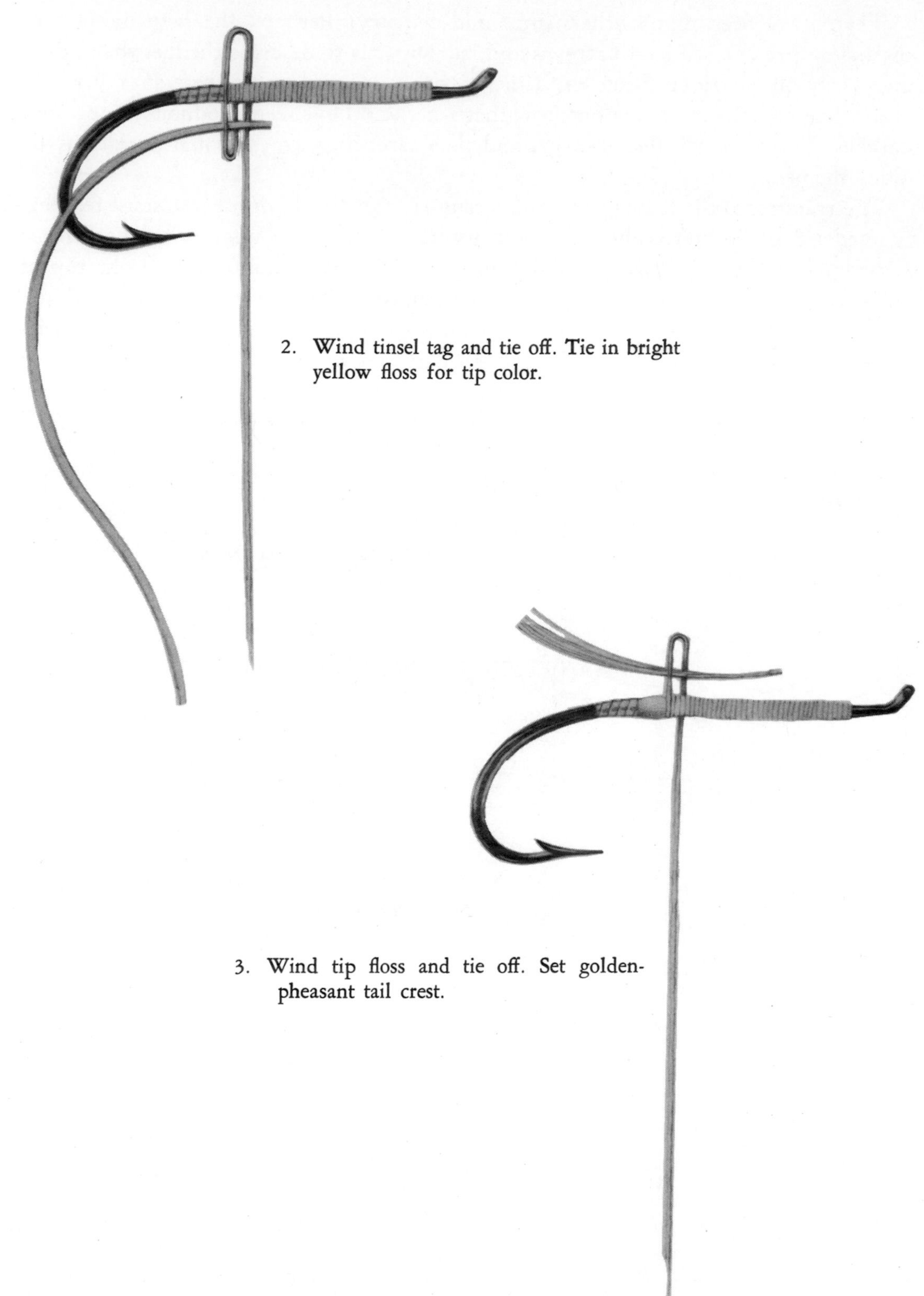

2. Wind tinsel tag and tie off. Tie in bright yellow floss for tip color.

3. Wind tip floss and tie off. Set golden-pheasant tail crest.

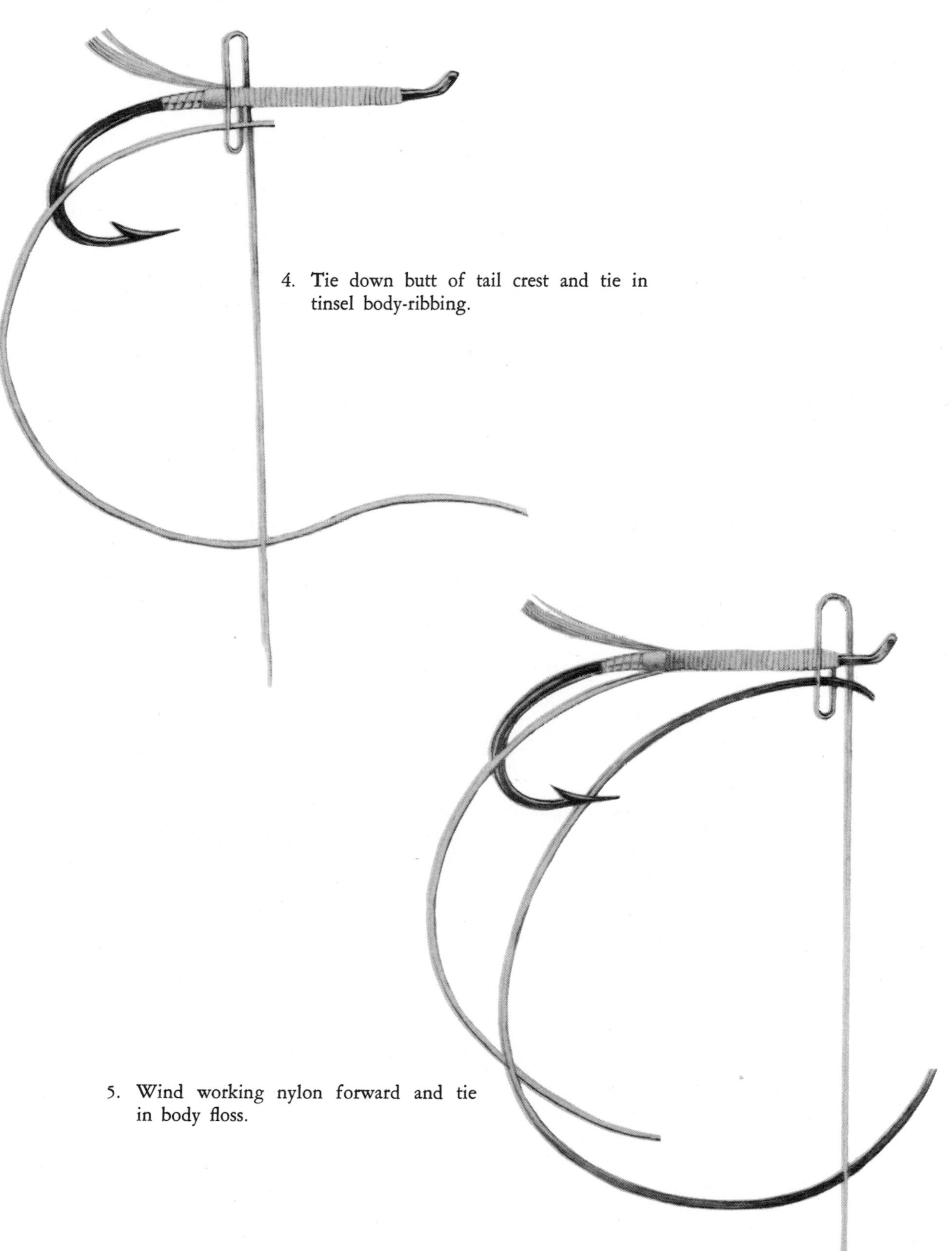

4. Tie down butt of tail crest and tie in tinsel body-ribbing.

5. Wind working nylon forward and tie in body floss.

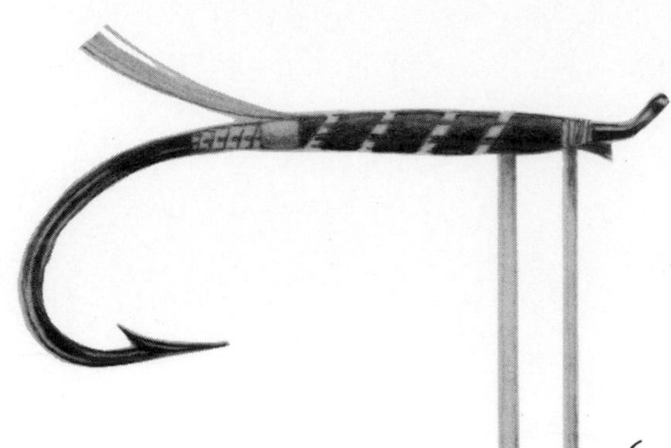

6. Wind body floss and taper neatly before winding body tinsel.

7. Cut hackle section in style of Charles DeFeo. Set under throat of hook eye.

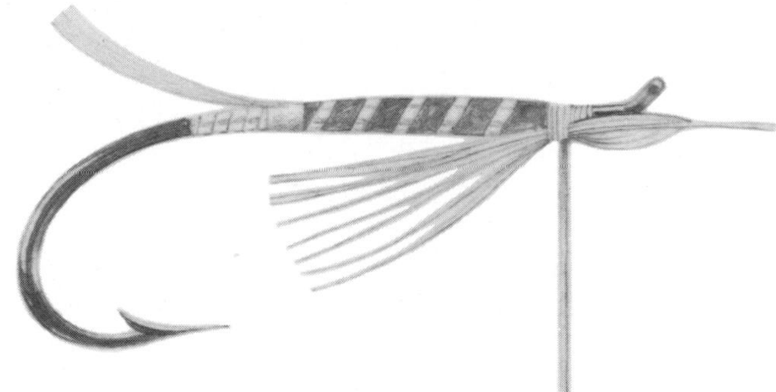

8. Pull hackle section forward, spreading hackle fibers into full throat, as drawn.

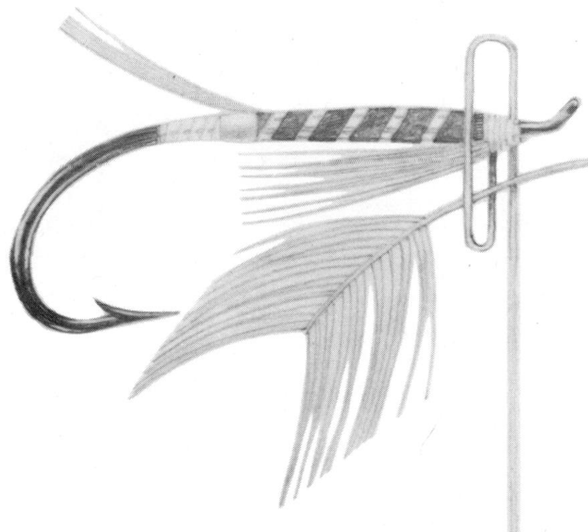

9. Set second hackle section as shown, and pull forward gently.

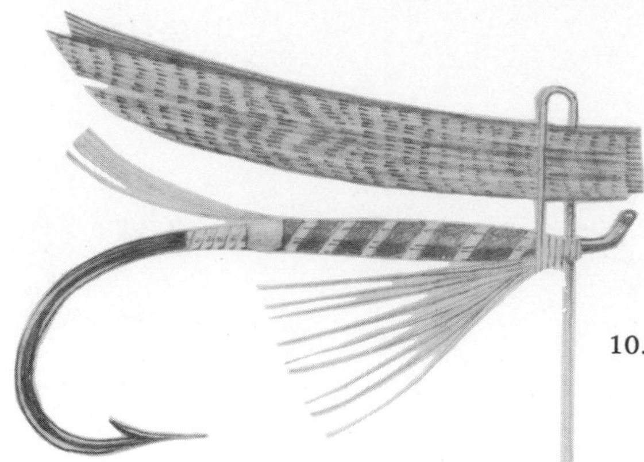

10. Fluff hackle throat into full configuration and set matched pair of brown mallard sections as downwings.

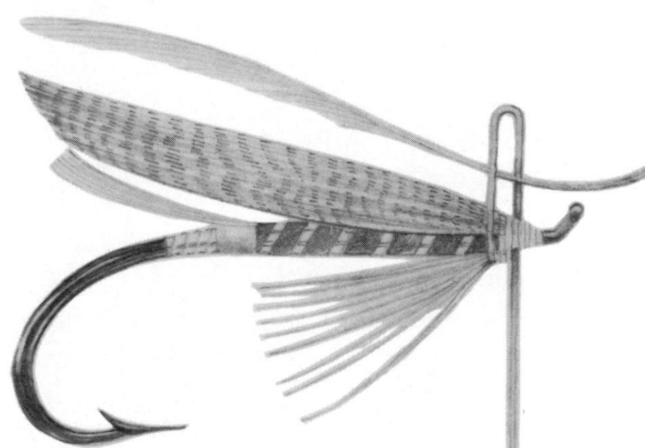

11. Complete wings with a topping of golden-pheasant crest, set as drawn.

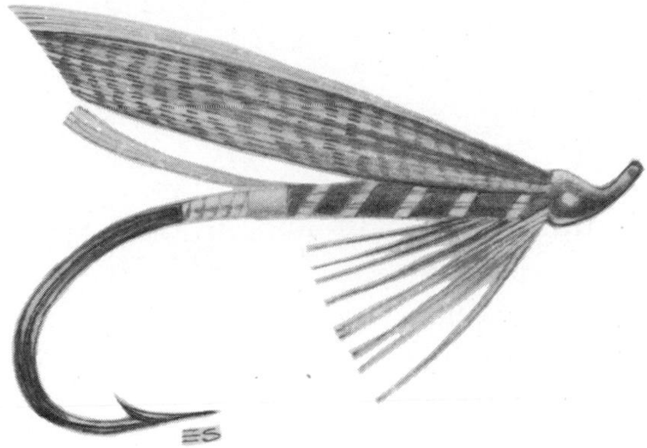

12. Whip-finish head and lacquer with black Cellire.

*Blue Charm*

| | |
|---|---|
| Tag: | flat silver tinsel |
| Tip: | yellow fluorescent floss |
| Tail: | golden-pheasant crest |
| Ribbing: | flat silver tinsel |
| Body: | black rayon floss |
| Throat: | bright-blue hackle fibers |
| Wings: | brown mallard sections |
| Topping: | golden pheasant |

This dressing abandons the mixed wing, jungle cock, black ostrich, and teal feathers found in its traditional versions. However, it retains the bright-yellow flash of the golden-pheasant crests, and adds the hot-yellow highlight of yellow floss.

The March Brown is a very old British pattern that has proved valuable on many occasions, particularly in low water when the fish are skittish. Arthur Wood once fished it solely through an entire season with only a slight decline of his average annual score.

*March Brown*

Tag: flat gold tinsel
Tail: golden-pheasant crest
Ribbing: flat gold tinsel
Body: first turns of pale-tan dubbing and remainder of body-mixed hare's-ear dubbing with guard hairs
Throat: partridge-back hackle fibers
Wings: hen-pheasant tail sections

This classic pattern is usually dressed in small sizes only, and I have seen it deadly in sizes 1 through 12. It is especially effective on sea trout when dressed with a silver tip and body of flat tinsel ribbed with fine oval silver in small sizes.

The Silver Grey is another famous old pattern. Pryce-Tannatt was an early experimenter with reduced patterns, and an example of his work is illustrated in *Salmon Fishing*, which Eric Taverner compiled in 1925. It is a pale pattern with a strong flash of silver that the fish take easily in certain moods, and my version is similar.

*Silver Grey*

Tag: flat silver tinsel
Tip: yellow fluorescent floss
Tail: golden-pheasant crest
Butt: black ostrich herl
Ribbing: fine oval silver tinsel
Body: flat silver tinsel
Throat: barred mallard flank fibers
Wings: barred mallard flank sections
Topping: golden pheasant

Experienced tyers will recognize that I have retained the ostrich herl and golden-pheasant topping. The accent of black in its pale configuration is the opposite coin of providing tinsel accents of light, and the golden pheasant is added for its gleam. My version has dropped the jungle-cock eyes, since they come from an endangered Asian bird species and should be protected in the future.

The Black Fairy is a great favorite everywhere. Its popularity holds on rivers from Lapland to the Labrador, and it is a standby in rainy weather on the Laxamyri in Iceland. Its coloring is uniformly dark except for the tiny accent of bright orangish-yellow floss, a combination that is often effective. Since it killed my first salmon, it has long been a favorite in my fly books.

---

*Black Fairy*

Tag: flat gold tinsel
Tip: yellow fluorescent floss
Tail: golden-pheasant crest
Ribbing: flat gold tinsel
Body: black fur dubbing
Throat: black hackle fibers
Wings: brown mallard sections
Topping: golden pheasant

---

The Lady Caroline is a typical dull-colored Scottish development, long valued for its low-water performance. It provides a fine counterpoint to the more brightly feathered flies to give the experienced angler a quiet change-of-pace pattern.

---

*Lady Caroline*

Tag: flat gold tinsel
Tip: small touch of yellow fluorescent floss
Tail: reddish-brown golden-pheasant crest
Ribbing: oval gold tinsel
Body: light-brown fur dubbing mixed with olive
Throat: medium blue-dun hackle fibers
Wings: brown mallard sections

---

The Crosfield is another of these sparsely dressed flies of simple materials. It provides a dour coloring that veils a bright flash of silver in its configuration. Past experience found it was a locally popular pattern that Ernest Crosfield, the master of modern British low-water tactics, had developed on the rivers of Iceland. It remains popular there today, and I had long felt it was a minor variation of the older Teal and Silver. My opinion was changed abruptly when my friend Bill Kent outfished our entire party during a difficult week on the Laxá in Pingeyjarsysla, when he was given a Crosfield by riverkeeper Heimir Sigurdsson.

---

*Crosfield*

Tag: flat silver tinsel
Tail: golden-pheasant crest
Ribbing: fine silver oval tinsel
Body: flat silver tinsel
Throat: medium blue-dun hackle fibers
Wings: barred mallard flank

---

The Brown Fairy provides a black-bodied pattern veiled in rich chocolate feathers, another mix of color essential in the spectrum of a well-stocked box of flies. Like its cousin the Black Fairy, it is an ancient pattern of modern importance.

*Brown Fairy*

Tag: flat gold tinsel
Tip: yellow fluorescent floss
Tail: golden-pheasant crest
Ribbing: fine gold oval tinsel
Body: black fur dubbing
Throat: fiery-brown hackle fibers
Wings: brown mallard sections

The Teal and Silver is another old pattern that still holds an important place on any salmon river in low water. It provides a glittering body sheathed in barred teal and bright blue, a combination that has long proved its mettle around the world.

*Teal and Silver*

Tag: flat silver tinsel
Tail: golden-pheasant crest
Ribbing: fine oval silver tinsel
Body: flat silver tinsel
Throat: bright-blue hackle fibers
Wings: barred teal sections

The Oriole is a Canadian original. It was first dressed by Ira Gruber, and is a great favorite on his beloved Miramichi. It is a simple pattern in spite of its mixed wing colors. Many knowledgeable anglers consider it the best of his many flies. Gruber was a retired American manufacturer who learned his fly-tying from Everett Price, a professional who lived on the river, but Gruber became the master of the many fly-dressers and guides in its watershed. His flies and methods solved the enigmas of summer fishing on the Miramichi, and are especially effective in small sizes. Knowledgeable fishermen will recognize my addition of a bright tinsel tag and a scarlet silk core in the dubbing.

---

*Oriole*

Tag: flat silver tinsel
Tail: reddish golden pheasant
Ribbing: fine oval silver tinsel
Body: black fur dubbing mixed on bright red silk
Throat: medium-brown hackle fibers
Wings: underwing of reddish-violet hackle fibers and overwing of barred mallard dyed pale olive

---

The Orange Charm is a great one. It changes its cousin the Blue Charm into the coloring of the older Thunder and Lightning, with its mixture of orange and black. It apparently evolved in the Labrador among early floatplane pioneers who accompanied Lee Wulff, and it was first given to me by Ted Rogowski, an attorney who doubled as Wulff's cameraman on several films. Since it was responsible for most of the salmon in a fifty-six-fish week in the Labrador, and once took sixteen in a single afternoon, it is permanently in my collection of flies.

---

*Orange Charm*

Tag: flat silver tinsel
Tip: yellow fluorescent floss
Tail: golden-pheasant crest
Ribbing: flat silver tinsel
Body: black rayon floss
Throat: bright-orange hackle fibers
Wings: brown mallard sections
Topping: golden pheasant

---

The Dusty Miller is an old and justly famous pattern that combines orange and silver with a darker wing. It is a favorite of many famous anglers on many famous salmon rivers. It is perhaps the most consistent pattern on the storied Alta in arctic Norway, and it killed the world fly-record of sixty-eight pounds for Nicholas Denisoff on his legendary Årøy steeplechase. It was also a small Dusty Miller that took my best salmon, a bright fifty-one pound cockfish on the Vossa in Hordaland. It is obviously a favorite.

*Dusty Miller*

| | |
|---|---|
| Tag: | flat silver tinsel |
| Tip: | yellow fluorescent floss |
| Tail: | golden-pheasant crest |
| Butt: | black ostrich herl |
| Ribbing: | fine oval silver tinsel |
| Body: | half flat silver tinsel and half orangish-yellow floss |
| Throat: | orange hackle fibers |
| Wings: | barred lemon wood duck flank |
| Topping: | golden pheasant |

This dozen patterns of the reduced type are old favorites in my fly books, but sometimes the simpler hairwings fish even better. Since the hairwing pattern was developed on Canadian and American rivers, its evolution has spread to the United Kingdom and Iceland.

Such tyers include James Younger, Geoffrey Bucknall, Colin and Alex Simpson, Harry Willcox, Esmond Drury, John Wright, John Reidpath, Douglas Pilkington, John Mackensie, Peter Dean, Gerry Curtis, and the incomparable Megan Boyd. James Younger is a descendant of John Younger, whose *River Angling for Salmon and Trout* has been a classic for more than a century. Megan Boyd is a lady fly-dresser at Kintradwell near the Brora in northern Scotland, and only the United Kingdom could justly bestow a British Empire Medal on someone of her obscure profession.

"For her singular contribution," read the honors list presented by Queen Elizabeth, "to foreign exchange through the creation of exquisite salmon flies for anglers across the world."

Megan Boyd is famous for both traditionals and hairwings, and I have witnessed the effectiveness of her flies in the hands of British friends in Iceland. Her own pattern, christened the Arndilly Fancy, was the best single pattern in the record week of 157 salmon that I experienced with Bill Kent and Lawrence Banks on the Langá in 1970. Our record in the fishing log at the Langarfoss farm produced a desperate telephone call from Iceland.

"What in hell is an Arndilly Fancy?" yelled an American friend whose party was fishing Langá a week later.

Although my fly-vise time is scarce these days, and my supply of reduced feather-winged patterns sometimes runs thin, my boxes are never without hairwings like the Arndilly. Such flies seem more effective on most rivers, and I tend to agree with Charles Ritz that their success can be explained: the hair comes alive in the current, working and breathing with a pumping fly-swing. It entrains bright clusters of bubbles, and its silhouette is more translucent than the traditional dressings.

Among the hairwings I use, the Blue Charm is again the number-one performer. Last season I accompanied a party of six beginners to the Langá in Iceland during one of its best weeks. Their score for the week was seventy-six fish weighing between four and thirteen pounds. Forty-three of those salmon were killed on small Hairwing Blue Charms I dressed in the farmhouse. Performance like that assures them a permanent place in my tackle vest.

---

*Hairwing Blue Charm*

Tag: flat silver tinsel
Tip: yellow fluorescent floss
Tail: golden-pheasant crest
Ribbing: flat silver tinsel
Body: black rayon floss
Throat: bright-blue hackle fibers
Wing: barred red squirrel tail

---

This pattern is virtually the same as the Scottish Hairy Mary, popularized in the United Kingdom about ten years ago through the efforts of John Reidpath, a fly-dresser in Inverness. Similar flies had been used on Canadian rivers more than a decade earlier.

The Black Fitchtail is simply my version of the coloring found in the traditional Black Fairy or Black Dose. It is similar to the Orange Butt popular on the Miramichi, although I have never liked the look of the coarse bear hair used in such patterns, and prefer the softer fitchtail specified below. The pattern has often teased a fish into taking under difficult conditions. During a camera session on the Stryn in Norway, fishing with the American salmon fisherman Edmund Monell, the *Life* photographer George Silk expressed concern over the beautiful weather and scarcity of salmon.

"What do you think?" he whispered.

"Black Fitchtail," I said.

Monell agreed to change of fly, and I selected a big 3/0 from my fly book. The big two-handed Payne that Colonel Ambrose Monell had once used on the Upsalquitch with Hewitt and LaBranche worked a long cast out across the run, and a big salmon took it hard. It weighed thirty-six pounds, and the Fitchtail continues as a great favorite.

---

*Black Fitchtail*

Tag: flat silver tinsel
Tip: bright orangish-yellow fluorescent floss
Tail: golden-pheasant crest
Ribbing: flat silver tinsel
Body: black rayon floss
Throat: black hackle fibers
Wing: black fitchtail

---

The Orange Blossom is a popular hairwing based on the color-mix of the traditional Dusty Miller. It originated on the Restigouche and Matapedia rivers in Quebec, where it was used primarily as a spring pattern for the big cockfish that enter the rivers in June. However, it has also produced many good fish for me in Europe, including ten salmon averaging twenty-six pounds in a single night on the Alta.

*Orange Blossom*

Tag: flat silver tinsel
Tip: bright orangish-yellow fluorescent floss
Tail: golden-pheasant crest
Ribbing: fine oval silver tinsel
Body: flat silver tinsel and half bright yellow floss, palmered with yellow hackle
Throat: orange hackle fibers
Wing: brown fitchtail mixed with a few blue, yellow, and red-dyed hairs

Green patterns are strangely successful at times, and their productivity seems to occur in streaks. Cornelius Ryan once had an impressive run of fish on the Jöraholmen beat at Alta that soon had the river full of Green Highlanders. Ralph Strauss and John Hilson put a pair of four-fish nights together on the Laxamyri in Iceland with traditional Highlanders. Their exceptional luck soon had me at the fly-vise long after curfew.

*Hairwing Highlander*

Tag: flat silver tinsel
Tip: bright yellow fluorescent floss
Tail: golden-pheasant crest
Butt: black ostrich herl
Ribbing: flat silver tinsel
Body: half yellow floss and bright-green fur dubbing
Throat: bright green and yellow hackle mixed
Wing: brown fitchtail mixed with a few bright-blue, yellow, and green-dyed hairs

Megan Boyd created the Arndilly Fancy, a delicate example of modern Scottish hairwings. It was introduced to me by two British friends, Lawrence Banks and Billy Ropner, who were convinced of its killing qualities. Banks is a young banker in New York who had caught something less than ten salmon in his entire life on British rivers. His first day on the Langá in Iceland equaled that lifetime score, and the Arndilly was the catalyst.

*Arndilly Fancy*

Tag: flat silver tinsel
Tail: golden-pheasant crest
Ribbing: fine oval silver tinsel
Body: yellow silk floss
Throat: bright-blue hackle fibers
Wing: dark-brown fitchtail

The classic Miramichi is the source of the Green Butt pattern, with its bright spot of fluorescent color. It is another fly that has its innings, and I have often used it successfully with a riffling-hitch retrieve in both Iceland and the Labrador.

*Green Butt*

Tag: flat silver tinsel
Tip: bright-green fluorescent floss
Tail: golden-pheasant crest
Ribbing: flat silver tinsel
Body: black rayon floss
Throat: black hackle fibers
Wing: black fitchtail

The elegant little Minktail is a pattern of obscure origin that owes its popularity to *The Fly and the Fish,* the poetic book written by the late John Atherton. It has taken many salmon for me on widespread rivers in Europe and Canada, and is most effective in small sizes in Iceland.

*Minktail*

Tag: flat silver tinsel
Tip: yellow fluorescent floss
Tail: golden-pheasant crest
Ribbing: flat silver tinsel
Body: black rayon floss
Throat: iron blue-dun hackle fibers
Wing: light-brown mink or fitchtail

The Orange Charm is a particular favorite of mine, with a color spectrum echoing the timeless Thunder and Lightning. It has killed salmon from Labrador to Lapland, and it once teased eight fish in a single morning from the Tonjüm pool at Laerdal.

*Hairwing Orange Charm*

Tag: flat silver tinsel
Tip: yellowish-orange fluorescent floss
Tail: golden-pheasant crest
Ribbing: flat silver tinsel
Body: black rayon floss
Throat: bright-orange hackle fibers
Wing: barred red squirrel tail

The Ackroyd is a hairwing adaptation of a fine old pattern from the Spey in Scotland. It provides a simplified configuration and color-mix that echoes such flies as the Jock Scott, and it has proved its worth on many rivers over the years.

*Ackroyd*

Tag: flat silver tinsel
Tip: bright-orange fluorescent floss
Tail: golden-pheasant crest
Ribbing: flat silver tinsel
Body: half yellow and half black rayon floss
Throat: dark blue-dun hackle fibers
Wing: medium-brown fitchtail

The Pale Torrish is a hairwing version of the Scalscraggie pattern long traditional on the Scottish Helmsdale, in the Strath of Kildonan. It is particularly effective in such dark tea-colored rivers. It was not a pattern I carried until Clare de Burghe gave me one at lunch in Oslo after a particularly exciting week on the Alta in arctic Norway.

"It was our best pattern," she said.

"Clare had thirty-seven fish!" added Charles Woodman. "The best went fifty-seven pounds!"

Its magic still worked the following week, and on a less exalted beat it killed a brace of immense salmon for me in a single night. The fish were both taken in the Velliniva at Alta, and scaled forty-one and slightly better than forty-five pounds. It is in my fly books now.

*Pale Torrish*

Tag: flat silver tinsel
Tip: bright yellowish-orange fluorescent floss
Tail: golden-pheasant crest
Butt: black ostrich herl
Ribbing: fine oval silver tinsel
Body: flat silver tinsel
Throat: bright-yellow hackle fibers
Wing: light-brown fitchtail mixed with a few bright scarlet, blue, and yellow-dyed hairs

The Squirreltail is a basic Canadian hairwing. The pattern I dress and fish is similar to the type described in *The Fly and The Fish.* Jack Atherton was particularly fond of this pattern, and this type of dressing has long been a standby on most Canadian salmon rivers. It has produced many fish for me in several countries, including a brace of thirty-pound cockfish on the moody Vossa in 1961. I call it the Atherton Squirreltail in this variation of its dressing.

*Atherton Squirreltail*

Tag: flat silver tinsel
Tip: bright-yellow fluorescent floss
Tail: golden-pheasant crest
Ribbing: fine oval silver tinsel
Body: black fur dubbing
Throat: fiery-brown hackle fibers
Wing: brown fitchtail

The Hairwing Onset is another old pattern that has proved remarkably successful on several rivers. Its white-tipped turkey wing is a perfect color-mix for grey squirrel tail, and its hot orange and yellow body seems to glow inside its darker hair and hackles. Like the other pale-bodied flies, it works best over a hook shank lacquered white and with white working-nylon. The bodies take on a rich translucence without the dark silhouette of the steel shank inside. The pattern once took three big salmon from the Upper Bridge Pool at Bolstadøyri on the Vossa in less than two hours. It was a bright morning in relatively low water, and the fish took the working fly as it passed the dark abutment shadows of the bridge, teasing and swimming in the sun. The fish averaged twenty-four pounds, and two were over thirty. Perhaps it was the orange rayon glowing in the bright water.

*Hairwing Onset*

Tag: flat silver tinsel
Tail: golden-pheasant crest
Ribbing: flat silver tinsel
Body: one-third bright-yellow fluorescent floss, and two-thirds bright-orange rayon floss
Throat: medium blue-dun hackle fibers
Wing: white-tipped grey squirrel tail

These two dozen patterns are the nucleus of my arsenal of salmon flies. Strangely enough, the popular Rat patterns devised by the late Roy Angus Thomson (their name came from his full initials) have never been particularly kind to me, and I seldom use them. There are times, when the fish are uncooperative and dour, that a bright-orange Chilimps or prawn fly like the General Practitioner will excite a disinterested salmon into a savage strike. Big mylar marabous are another offering that will sometimes trigger an abrupt change of mood, and once on the Langá I had an entire pool of fish churning and spiraling under a retrieve. There are also times when unresponsive salmon can be taken on tube-fly variations of these patterns. However, these are tactics and fly-dressings that seem a little unworthy of the salmon, and I seldom use them. They can also put fish down if they are used too much.

Experienced fly-dressers will recognize that my patterns are tied slightly low-water in style. The tags and tips are started above the hook points, and the butts always occur well into the straight section of the shank. The wings and tails are stopped short of the bend, although the size of the fly is not as exaggeratedly small as a classic low-water dressing. However, such proportions discourage short pulls and takes that occur when the fly extends beyond the hook, and a relatively small pattern has the weight and holding qualities of a bigger fly. This style of dressing has worked well for me on many rivers. My flies are usually dressed on English hooks, and although I prefer singles for aesthetic reasons—they layer beautifully in a Wheatley box—there are more and more small doubles in my collection these days, particularly in smaller sizes.

Sizes can vary widely. Rivers in the United Kingdom that fish from late winter runs in February to low water in the end of summer will find 5/0 irons useful in high spring flowages, and delicate size-ten dressings at the opposite end of the spectrum. Norwegian fishing during my seven summers of experience has ranged from 5/0 doubles at midsummer even in Finnmark to size-ten low-water patterns on the Laerdal in August. Canadian and American fishing has ranged between 1/0 patterns and tiny size-twelve doubles in September on the Miramichi, and several summers in Iceland have found the salmon partial to sparse dressings on sizes 1/0 to size-ten doubles. Fishing in Iceland more nearly resembles the small-fly techniques most American and Canadian fishermen have mastered, except for the handicap of frequent high winds.

Two or three minor items are worth mention. While dressing a fly I usually pause once the ribbing is wound in place, and lacquer the dorsal surface of the body to secure the position of the tinsel on either floss or tinsel bases. Before seating the wings I place a healthy drop of clear head lacquer where they will be wrapped. This step is particularly needed to seat a hairwing well. My heads are usually coated with the superb black Cellire sold through Veniard in England.

The effectiveness of these reduced patterns and hairwings has been acknowledged in virtually the last bastions of tradition. The Alta is a perfect example. Twelve years ago the Duke of Roxburghe, whose family has fished the river every summer since 1863 with the exception of the Occupation years, refused to fish the big hairwings his American friends used so effectively. The big hairwing doubles continued to outfish the bright-feathered confections of exotic feathers that are traditional in salmon-fishing. Two summers ago I fished the Sandia beats at Alta again, and when the subject of fly-choice came up that evening it was different.

"We use only hair-flies," said the gillies.

Andreas Olsen, who once dressed flies for Prince Axel of Denmark, is the father of Olav Olsen, the famous flytyer on the Laerdal in Norway. Olav Olsen ties salmon flies for the young Crown Prince Harald of Norway, a skilled fly-fisherman who often fishes with the Astrup family from the charming Ljøsne farmstead above Laerdalsøyri.

Andreas was riverkeeper for Thomas Falck, whose classic Rikheim water included the legendary Tonjüm Pool. The first summer I fished Tonjüm the river was low and clear after two weeks of bright weather. The regulars had stopped fishing their big two-handed rods and flies in the usually productive midday hours.

"Too bright!" explained Falck. "We fish the evenings."

"I'd like to try an experiment," I said. "Could we fish a smooth-flowing pool with light tackle and a hairwing?"

"Tonjüm is perfect," he said.

No fish had been taken for several days, but a delicate little Hairwing Orange Charm rose three salmon and killed two in about two hours under the cloudless skies. Andreas expressed great interest in the hairwings, and insisted that I sit down with his son Olav to show him the dressings for the strange new flies I carried.

Crown Prince Harald was equally intrigued with the Canadian and American techniques, and quickly tried the hairwings on a Winston that he usually used for sea trout. The delicate almost-somber little patterns worked, and three weeks after my return to New York there was a brief note telling me that the Crown Prince had killed three salmon on the legendary Bjorküm Pool at midday, using one of my little Orange Charms.

# Lefty Kreh

## SALTWATER FLIES

Photographs by the Author

The freshwater fly-fisherman must alter somewhat his approach to the subject when he begins to work with saltwater flies, for they are different in many ways. For generations, fly-rod anglers have spent a great deal of time studying insect and aquatic life in streams and lakes. Then exhaustive searches have been made to find materials that enable the tyer to construct flies that he feels faithfully reproduce the food the fish are feeding upon. Nearly every trout fisherman has among his materials inventory a long list of such exotic materials as furs from Africa, feathers from the Orient, synthetics, and all sorts of trappings that are used to build the flies he feels necessary for his sport.

Heavy emphasis has been laid in freshwater fishing on tying delicate flies that match the food fish eat. What has arisen are guidelines for all tying—even names for the various portions of the fly. Much of this is unimportant in tying saltwater flies, although basic techniques are the same. Indeed, an accomplished fisherman can make the switch to saltwater tying more quickly than the man from the salt can make the transition.

Many of the components of freshwater flies are not used in tying saltwater flies. A tag or tail is rarely used. Hackle, as wound for tying a dry fly, is almost never employed. Shoulder, butt, and cheek are not used at all. Ribbing and tinsel bodies are infrequently used. In fact, most saltwater fly-fishermen build on their hooks a wing, a body, and occasionally a beard or topping—that's it!

Even the hooks are different. There are no turned-down or turned-up eyes, and the trend today is to build the flies on hooks not from the best forged steel, as in fresh water, but from stainless steel, to resist corrosion.

So, the man who comes to saltwater fly-tying must think a bit differently. It might be best to call the various types of flies "styles" instead of patterns, so that the angler clearly understands that a distinct difference does exist between the two worlds.

The sea is a vast body of water and the types of fishes are so numerous that many have not yet even been discovered or cataloged. In any given area there might be many kinds of baitfish that predatory fish feed upon. The baitfish may range in color from yellow to blue and silver, to all green, even bright red. The baitfish may also vary in size.

To compound the fly-fisherman's problem, the sea produces no hatches. Experienced trout anglers can sometimes predict to the day and maybe the hour when certain insects will appear on the water for the fish to feast on. The angler may even be aware that, during the hatch, subtle color changes will occur in the insects. In such cases he will build imitations to suit conditions. A trout, in the relatively captive environment of its own pool, will unhurriedly examine the drifting insects and select only those that a cautious inspection deems correct. If the fly it is looking at does not pass muster, the fish simply allows it to drift by. It knows that during the hatch more flies will pass through the pool. In short, the trout has no need to rush and can take its time. Under such fishing conditions a good imitation can spell the difference between success and failure.

Saltwater fishes do not share the luxury of having a slow-moving, reliable bait supply. They must rush about and grab what they can eat when it is available. Since there are few hiding places where the prey may escape from the predators, the smaller fish can only escape by going away quickly. A rapid retrieve by the angler, and no real need to tie exact imitations, usually succeeds in the salt.

Naturally, if there is, in an area, an abundance of three-to-four-inch baitfish that are silvery on the lower part of the body, with a dark green back, then an imitation of that baitfish will surely help. Yet those same baitfish may be gone tomorrow, moving to another part of the mysterious sea.

I do not completely discount exact imitation, since there are places where it can be important, but certainly it never shares the same status it has acquired in fresh water.

Probably the most important factor in building successful saltwater flies is attention to overall size of the fly. It is vital to know what size fly the fish you seek will strike. Amberjack, king mackerel, cobia, big roosterfish, sailfish, and other ocean roamers are not going to get excited when they see a two-inch fly swimming in front of them. Such fish need a mouthful—and that could mean a fly with a 5/0 to 7/0 hook on which twelve to twenty full-length saddle hackles have been tied. These fish will inhale a three-pound fish if they can get it, and they'll pay little attention to an exact imitation of a four-inch baitfish.

A rough guide to the size of the fly you want to tie for specific fish can be obtained by observing the size of the fish the quarry feeds upon. Bonefish have a tiny mouth and obtain small crabs, little minnows, shrimp, and worms from the bottom of shallow warmwater flats. These fish would have difficulty trying to eat a six-inch fish. Therefore, flies of one to one-and-one-half inches in length are recommended. Snappers and other fish that feed on little baitfish rarely take a fly longer than four inches. Bluefish are particularly fond of three- to four-inch flies.

Cobia, with a mouth like a water bucket, and others such as grouper, amberjack, and big striped bass will swallow flies larger than we can reasonably cast. A favorite lure for amberjack and cobia, for example, is a popping bug fully one-and-one-quarter inches across the face. Such a lure gulps gallons of water on the retrieve, creating a foaming disturbance that convinces the cobia and amberjack that struggling on the surface is a fair-sized meal.

King mackerel that grow to more than sixty pounds (fish exceeding forty pounds have already been taken on the fly rod) often feed on baitfish in the six- to eight-inch size. Since this is their favorite food size, the angler seeking kings should build flies this long.

Perhaps the second most important factor in constructing saltwater flies is the lack of air resistance built into the fly. There is almost always some breeze on the oceans and bays, and the fish usually seem to approach from an upwind direction. Also, the fly must often be delivered over a great distance. Contrary to what many outdoor writers have written, the top saltwater fly-fishermen make many full-line casts. They believe the more area you can search, and the longer the fly is in the water, the more effectively you can fish. Hooks used in salt water are much larger and heavier than those used in fresh water, which further complicates the casting problems. Add all these casting liabilities together and you can see that the fly itself must have a minimum of air resistance. Regardless of how effective the fly, if you can't cast it, it won't catch fish. Saltwater flies should arise from the water on the backcast as sleek missiles, the wings clinging to the body like a pointed projectile.

If air resistance is important, and it is, then heavily palmered flies are generally disregarded, except in very special situations. Feathers tied to the hook so the fly swims on the retrieve with a frog-kicking motion were standard patterns in the early days of saltwater fly-fishing. Because such patterns are so wind-resistant they have fallen into disuse. Most flies used by modern anglers move through the water in an undulating, swimming motion, rather than the older pulsating, frog-kicking motion.

The third most important consideration when building saltwater flies is to construct them so that the wings and other materials do not foul on the hook during the cast. Long, limp wings and other such materials often underwrap the hook shank or fly body and spin violently, twisting the leader and ruining the retrieve. As stated before, saltwater fly-rodders make frequent and long casts. Change of direction casts are constantly called for. These two factors cause serious fouling of the fly unless the pattern is properly designed. Thus, wings on most saltwater patterns are attached at the rear of the hook shank, so that they won't curl under. If a wing is to be tied forward near the hook eye, it is possible to add another wing near the back of the hook to offer support to the forward wing. This deters fouling. Joe Brooks's blond series of patterns are a perfect example of fish-taking flies that rarely foul when properly tied.

Naturally, very limp materials are avoided when tying in the wings, since this simply compounds the problems. Capra hair, for example, is simply too soft and pliant; marabou, a superb wing material, is so supple and fluffy that it is generally used as a forward wing, trimmed so its total length is no longer than the hook shank.

Fourth in importance in tying saltwater flies is what experienced fly-fishermen call "sink rate." Of little importance in freshwater fishing, sink rate is vital to saltwater angling.

Occasionally a fish will rise to accept a saltwater fly, but I have never known of a fish that will descend to snap at one. Ideally, the fly and the fish should arrive at the same junction at the same time. Therefore, an angler needs to control how fast or how slow his fly will sink. A tarpon fisherman anchored in eight feet of water sees a 100-pound, six-foot fish approach, four feet under the surface. The angler's problem is to toss the fly far enough in front of the fish so as not to frighten it; and the fly must sink at a rate so that it arrives right in front of the tarpon. Obviously the fly's sink rate has to be understood.

Another example of a totally different application of sink rate is when you are fishing a shallow-water flat where the bottom is covered with grass. You need a fly for such fishing that will attract the fish's attention, and it must remain almost suspended in the water, sinking extremely slowly or it will be buried in the grass. This is one of the few cases where a heavily palmered fly is necessary. (Heavily palmered means that the feathers have been wrapped many, many times around the hook shank in a circular fashion. The fly resembles a huge caterpillar with several hackles protruding out the rear of the fly as a tail. This creates a fly that will sink very slowly.)

When fishing for striped bass or bluefish that are feeding on the surface, it would be foolish to use a fast-sinking fly. Bucktail, which floats, as most flytyers know, is a good material with which to build wings for fishing near the top.

Visibility is important, too. Bivisible flies are used infrequently in freshwater trout angling, but there are times in saltwater fishing when visibility is more vital. Sharks, which can barely see, are among the most difficult fish to take on a fly. Manipulation of the fly is critical on the retrieve, so that the fly is kept not in front of the fish but exactly beside the shark's eye. A bright fly, dressed with flashy mylar, allows the shark to locate the fly. But you need more than that; most experienced shark anglers will tie into the fly some orange or red, enabling the angler to better diagnose his retrieve.

The color of the fly is sometimes important, but not nearly as much so as it is in freshwater angling. The saltwater flytyer will soon discern that most flies used in the salt are either white, yellow, or a combination of red and white or red and yellow. Grizzly and occasionally brown are used less frequently. For probably 80 percent of your saltwater fly-fishing you could use an all-white fly, shifting to a yellow one as a substitute when things are not going right. Brightly colored flies will usually produce poorly when saltwater fishes are swimming over bright sand; at such times the fish seem to be badly frightened by bright flies, and grizzly and subdued brown seem more effective.

## MATERIALS USED IN SALTWATER FLIES

You'll need a strong vise for serious fly-tying, and fortunately one of the very best is one of the least expensive. It is a vise of stout proportions that is closed firmly with a cam-type lever. Such a vise can handle the normal range of hooks demanded for the chore. The very best vise for saltwater fly-tying is a pair of Vise-Grip pliers welded to a shaft that can be inserted into the standard vise clamp. Use the smallest size (approximately 5¼ inches) Vise-Grip, which should be welded to sit at right angles to the shaft. Vise-Grips will handle any hook from size 12 to 9/0. And they hold them so firmly that even giant hooks never move. This same vise is a dandy for streamer fly-tying in freshwater work.

Other tools required for saltwater fly-tying are few: dubbing needle, hackle pliers, whip finisher, medium-size scissors, bobbin, and thread.

The basic mistake made by many saltwater flytyers is that they use thread far too large in diameter. Size A thread is about the largest that should be employed, and a size smaller will produce flies that are better tied, stronger, and much more pleasing in appearance. I like Nymo or mono-thread rather than silk or plain nylon, in black, red, and white. Then, when I tie a fly that has a red head, I use red thread. When painting heads I use the common model paints that come in tiny jars. Tyers who have plenty of time will get a stronger head with an epoxy paint.

With the exception of popping bugs, most saltwater flies resemble some form of streamer pattern; no nymph, dry, or wet patterns are tied. Some anglers will try imitating some of the small shrimps, but that's as close as they come to imitating actual bottom life.

The bodies of saltwater flies are formed mainly from chenille, wool, or silver tinsel. Of late, mylar has been substituted for all tinsel, to resist corrosion. There are many fly patterns that simply leave the hook shank bare.

Mylar has revolutionized much of saltwater fly-tying. This plastic material, which can be had in ribbons as thin as 1/64 inch in width to wide sheets, is the salvation of the flytyer. The uses mylar are put to in saltwater fly-tying are just as effective for freshwater applications.

Mylar resembles tinsel, and comes in smooth gold or silver. It will never tarnish and is incredibly thin and strong; it has banished regular fly-tying tinsel from my bench. You need only two sizes of mylar for all your tying needs in salt water, and for most freshwater requirements. I use the 1/64 inch to be added to wings and for thin ribbing on smaller flies. The ⅛ inch works well on very large flies and for body construction. Anything wider than ⅛ inch should never be used as a wing material, since it flutters badly, setting up too much air resistance and being so wide it doesn't flex easily on the retrieve. I've seen mylar wings ¼ inch in width, but this definitely inhibits the fish appeal of the fly; in most cases the 1/64-inch width is best for wings. Seldom, too, should more than five or six strands be added to either side of the wing. In many cases the mylar is best placed deep inside the wing, so only the ends really flash. Bluefish, kings, and mackerel love very flashy lures, hence so many are taken on small silver spoons trolled with regular gear; mylar tied in multiple strands on a hook (with no other material used except the thread) can be very effective for such fish.

I cannot stress too strongly how much more effective a fly becomes if it has mylar attached. Any fly that is supposed to resemble a baitfish is much better if the mylar is added to the fly to give off those seductive flashes.

Nearly every needlepoint store or sewing-needs outlet sells mylar piping, a rope-like tube of braided mylar with a string core. It is very inexpensive, and you can purchase a yard for a few nickels. Cut a short section, about three inches long for the average fly, from the piping, and remove the strings from the center. Take a needle and tease apart the braids and you have many strands of mylar to use for ribbing, body, and wings.

There are three basic types of popping bugs used in salt water. Sliders (which have a pointed nose) are worked silently across the water; they are supposed to imitate a struggling, helpless minnow. Sliders are simple to make. A bullet-shaped cork is cemented to the hook, with the small end next to the hook eye. Then either saddle hackles or bucktail is tied just back of the bug body; often mylar is added to the tail. Such popping bugs are excellent in shallow water where fish are often frightened by a loud, blurping popper.

The second type of bug is similar to a bass popper, with or without the scooped face. These range in size from very small, half the size of a peanut shell, to those with a face on the front as large as a nickel. The bugs are made from balsa or cork. Saltwater popping bugs have to stand more abuse than freshwater varieties, so they must be strong. The general procedure is to wrap bucktail or feathers firmly on top of the back of the hook shank, then wrap the rest of the hook shank with thread. A hole slightly smaller than the hook eye is drilled through the center of the cork. Then epoxy glue is smeared over the hook shank. The eye is inserted through the rear of the bug body and shoved forward until it protrudes out of the front end of the cork. Extra glue is wiped from the bug body and the glue allowed to dry before painting with epoxy paint. (When purchasing epoxy paint or glue, buy the two-part kind, where the amount needed is mixed separately each time. Two-part epoxies give much greater strength.)

The third popping bug made for saltwater fly-fishing is a specialty bug, used primarily for sailfish, amberjack, cobia, and any other large fish that can be deceived into believing that the bug is actually much larger than it is. These loud noisemakers, measuring a full 1¼ inches across the face, are made from styrofoam and are dressed on 5/0 to 7/0 stainless steel hooks. Naturally they are glued with epoxy cement, since they are subjected to severe punishment. The bugs, rarely painted, have about 15 to 20 saddle hackles (butts and all to obtain maximum length) and are attached to the rear of the bug body.

Among the most favored materials used by flytyers of saltwater patterns is bucktail. This is a general-purpose wing material for smallish flies. Polar bear, difficult to obtain, is considered the finest wing material available for many patterns.

Feathers are perhaps the single most used material. Neck feathers are rarely used by highly experienced fly-fishermen; the stiff hackles are simply too hard to cast, and stiff and unyielding on the retrieve.

For larger flies, hackles that range from six to eight inches are ideal; shorter hackles will work fine on smaller flies. Strung saddles are the easiest method of handling the feathers. Rather than buy many colors of feathers, some tyers will purchase a half pound or a pound of white strung saddles, since this is the cheapest way. If red, yellow, or other colors are needed, they use Rit dye, following the instructions on the package. Add a half cup of white vinegar to the dye to prevent the colors from running when the fly is later used. Bucktails that have been washed with a detergent before dyeing can be handled in the same manner.

Some nylon materials make fine wings. They can be used solely as a wing, or added as topping. Rolling strands of mylar inside the nylon is often a very effective treatment. Nylon that has been saturated with a fluorescent dye gives off bluish flashes of light that closely imitate the silvery reflection of swimming baitfish.

Two stainless-steel hooks have found great favor among anglers who tie saltwater flies. The most popular general-purpose hook is the Wright and McGill 254 SS. This hook resists rust, has a round bend and round eye, and is the standard among tyers; it has a regular-length shank. When anglers tie a fly on a little longer shank hook, they generally use the Shakespeare L126C model, a hook with a superfine steel, a fairly sharp point, and a round bend and eye.

The mechanics of tying a saltwater fly are the same as for freshwater patterns, except that epoxy glue and paint are often used to obtain greater strength. The extreme care that is generally taken in dressing freshwater flies is often disregarded, for saltwater flies usually have a short life: the teeth and raspy mouths of the fish soon tear the fly to pieces. I have frequently seen a fish destroy a popping bug on the strike, and a barracuda, bluefish, mackerel, or kingfish usually leaves nothing on the hook shank but a few traces of thread.

Fortunately, the saltwater flytyer need not be as neat or as adept as the freshwater man. He need only make a fly that has the correct size, proper sink rate, and acceptable color: it should not foul in flight, and it should have little air resistance.

*Lefty's Deceiver*

This fly, which swims with a fishlike motion, is of the general shape of a baitfish, and is nonfouling and offers little air resistance. It is a general-purpose fly for either coast and almost any saltwater fishing situation; only the size or color need be altered. It is generally tied in all white, or with white hackles and red collar, or yellow hackles and red collar.

1. Tie in six to eight hackles at the rear and then tie on each side several strands of mylar, preferably smaller than ⅛ inch in width.

2. Wrap thread forward to within 3/16 inch of the eye, then tie in a piece of tinsel (or, better, mylar); then wrap this material down to the end of the hook shank and back to the front again.

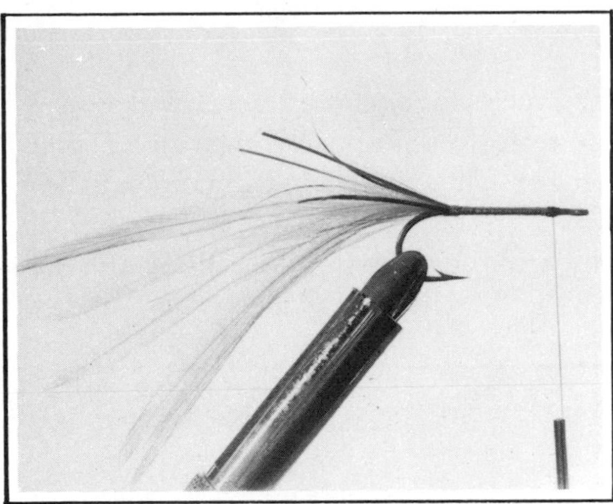

3. After tying off it will look like this.

4. Build a collar around the front of the hook as shown, taking care to get the material evenly distributed around the hook shank. The collar is generally made from polar bear or calf tail, but marabou or bucktail is also often used.

*Monofilament Fly*

This fly, due to the mylar or tinsel used in combination with the monofilament, gives one of the most realistic imitations of a small minnow of any fly I know. It is useful in both fresh and salt water. The wings are usually made to resemble local baitfish; if the bait has a greenish back, then topping of the appropriate color is placed above a usually white underwing. The fly is also sometimes called a Glass Minnow.

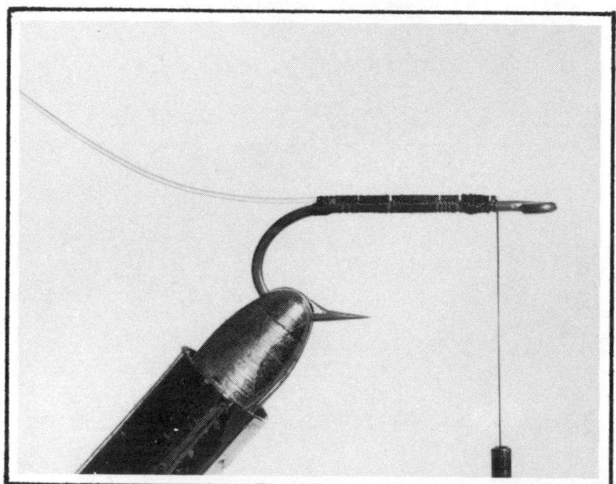

1. For hooks from size 1 through 5/0 use 30 pound monofilament: for smaller hooks, use 20 pound monofilament. Wrap the mono securely on the top of the hook shank as shown, leaving about $\frac{3}{16}$ inch of space at the front near the eye, to tie in the wing.

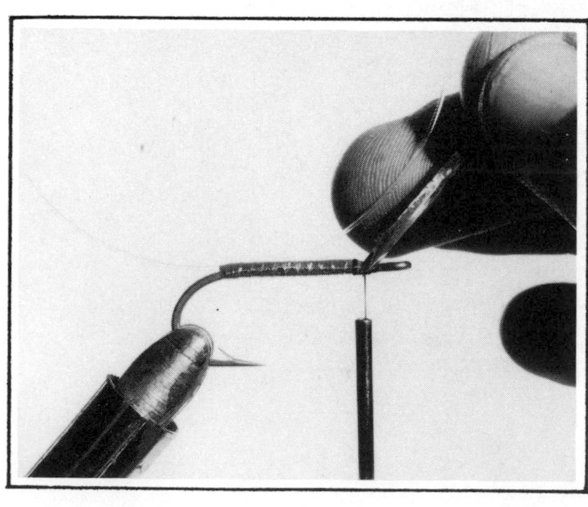

2. Wrap a tinsel (or, better, mylar) body over the length of the hook. Note that about six inches of monofilament protrudes from the rear at the top of the hook shank. Mylar or tinsel is tied in at the head and wound down the length of the shank over the mono and back again, as shown.

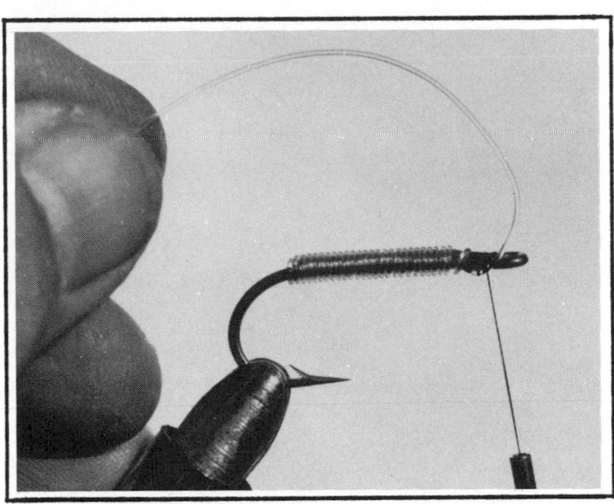

3. Wrap the monofilament in tight spirals the length of the shank and tie off as shown.

4. Attach a wing, usually of calf tail or polar bear; generally the upper portion of the wing is either brown, blue, or green. Several strands of mylar, $\frac{1}{64}$ inch in width, are tied in on either side of the wing to complete the fly as shown.

### *Joe Brooks's Blond Fly*

This fly is nonfouling, and the rear wing tends to support the front wing. It is a simple fly to tie and most effective.

1. Tie in some bucktail with the stub ends of the bucktail extending clear to the front of the hook shank as shown. Add some strands of mylar to the rear wing. Then wrap a tinsel body as was done for the Lefty's Deceiver pattern.

2. Tie in another wing on top. Do not add mylar to this wing. Then finish off the fly.

### *Keel Hook Fly*

Keel hooks allow the saltwater angler to fish in some of the most productive angling spots. Heavy grass on the bottom, coral rock, and floating vegetation plague the saltwater fly-fisherman. The keel hook is not quite so effective in hooking a fish as a standard pattern, but it certainly allows the angler to fish areas effectively that he could not fish with conventional hooks. One word of caution: to increase your chances of hooking the fish on the strike, bend the point open about ⅛ inch on a keel hook before you begin tying.

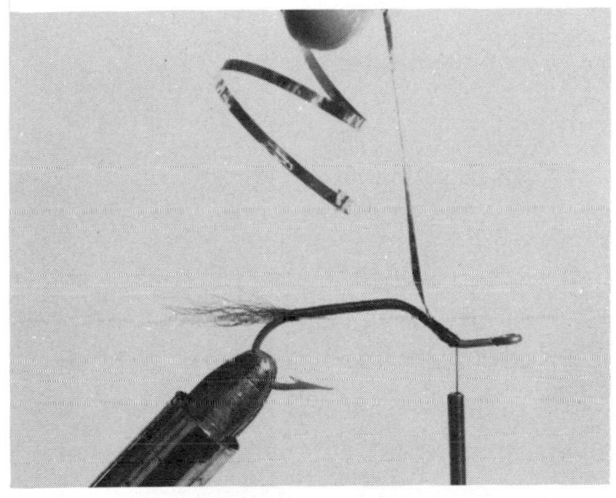

1. After opening hook slightly, attach a tail, wrap thread forward, and tie in mylar or tinsel as shown.

2. Wrap shank back and forward with mylar, tie off, and add a wing of bucktail or calf tail, with several strands of mylar.

3. Add whatever additional wing material you want to the top and finish off the fly.

*Basic Tarpon Fly*

For giant tarpon, 80 pounds or more, use a 4/0 or 5/0 hook. For smaller fish, scale hook size. Overall size of the fly should not exceed four inches.

1. Attach six saddle hackles, three to a side.

2. This is a top view showing how the saddle hackles should be spread.

3. Thread is wound forward and brown bucktail from topside of the deer tail is evenly tied around the hook shank. Fly head is generally painted either brown or red.

4. A variation of the standard fly pattern. The bare hook in no way affects the fish. In this case, grizzly hackles are used with red collar.

# Dave Whitlock

## NEW TOOLS and MATERIALS

Recently I was fortunate enough to make an extended tour of the United States to obtain firsthand information about fly-fishing and fly-tying. I interviewed, visited, and fished with many of our great tyers; whenever possible, I watched them at their vises. I had grown up in Oklahoma, an area practically sterile in the knowledge of fly-fishing and fly-tying; thus, what a revelation it was for me to learn or confirm so many of their ideas and methods!

The wealth of information derived from visits and similar contacts at the Federation of Fly Fishermen conclaves, plus hundreds of letters and phone calls, have allowed me to obtain an extremely broad insight into modern American fly-tying—both professional and amateur. Art's book seems the perfect place to relate this knowledge, as his book represents an extremely useful and broad look at contemporary fly-tying.

Here, then, are many of the "now" and "coming" attractions that we will all be needing to know or learn if our flies are to continue to be consistent producers for a growing population of selective game fish.

### TOOLS

The single most important tool, our vise, hasn't changed much in the last twenty years. Just recently there have been a number of new designs showing up at the conclaves and in the catalogs. Sooner or later many professional tyers have a custom tool made that accommodates their individual needs better than standard vises. The new vises are usually copies of these prototypes, or incorporate some part of their design. A handful of pros manufacture and sell their own vise prototypes.

It is a recognized fact that the Thompson A model is the most popular quality tool on the market. It is a standard of design and reliability, and I use one myself for 80 percent of my tying. It will hold a wide range of hooks and has several basic mechanical adjustments to accommodate most of our needs.

Considering the Thompson as our basic model vise, let me relate the changes evident in other new models. Jaws that are longer and finer, to hold smaller hooks and provide more room around the hook for working, are definitely an advantage for the new generation of miniatures, both aquatic and terrestrial. The new Swisher-Richards vise is an example of this—and they are now making an improved version of their basic design to further this principal.

A lot of tyers have had skilled machinists make these "finer" jaws to fit their Thompsons. That route can be very expensive and/or disappointing unless you know your machinist or metallurgy and design pretty well yourself. Perhaps Thompson itself can soon be persuaded to build a "fine" set of jaws for the Model A and ultra vises for the smaller hooks, sizes 12 to 28. People have approached them about the possibility, but I am not sure it will come to pass in the near future.

The Universal Rotating vise is not entirely new, but it is certainly a departure from stationary jawed vises. It is particularly useful if the tyer does much work with chenilles or other yarnlike materials. The rotating jaw assembly enables you to quickly and neatly wind bodies such as those used on the popular woolyworm or crappie jigs. Walt Burr, an outstanding tyer, uses a custom rotary vise with magic quickness—and his flies are beautiful to behold. The Universal vise is available in most material catalogs. It is quite compact for so much machinery, and has a more than reasonable price tag.

In the opposite direction, the increase in saltwater fly-fishing has vises strangling to hold the big "O" size hooks. Tying jigs for freshwater and saltwater spinning has also choked some good vises to death. Veniard's Salmo vise is an excellent quality vise and will handle these beastly hooks better than any other I know. If it can't accommodate a large enough piece of bent barbed iron, I'd suggest you try a pair of vise grip pliers to hold your large hooks!

We all travel and tie more on the move, at motels or camps. We even struggle to wind a fly at streamside, if we have lost our minds or our last size 24 Blue-winged Olive No-Hackle. Did you know there is a secret conspiracy, ladies and gentlemen, among all motel owners never to provide a tabletop that you can clamp your vise on? Nothing can be done to foil this conspiracy except for you to buy a pedestal type vise that will hold itself. Several companies have such models. I have a Swisher-Richards and a Herter's, which sit erect by use of a heavy pedestal on a flat surface.

Someday a company will marry the suction pedestal to a tying vise and we won't have to carry ten pounds of extra pedestal weight with our kits. If you don't want to wait, I'd suggest you get a suction pedestal vise and alter its jaws to hold your Thompson A's stem and jaws. The price and work for the job are cheap, considering the satisfaction obtained from outsmarting all those motel managers.

Streamside kits can save the day if you are caught short of the right pattern. Of the several vises that can be used fairly well on the bank, the most popular is the Croydon Onehand vise, which will bite a size 6 or smaller hook well enough to bind materials to it—provided you have spent some time at home learning how to use it. The finger stall limits the use of one hand considerably, so I'd suggest a few trial runs while sitting on the den floor before you count on it when the pressure is on. Better still, you might practice in your backyard.

The Streamside Porta-Vise is somewhat better to use, for you can strap it to your leg or any other leg that might be available at streamside. It uses the same jaw design as the Croydon; though it has a little more bulk and a higher price, it has to be a more efficient tool at streamside. Shouldn't be a bad motel or camper vise, either. You can find it listed in the Flyfisherman's Shoppe, Inc. catalog.

## BOBBINS

Since I learned to tie flies without a bobbin, perhaps that is the reason it took me twenty years to learn what others learn in two years. Many pros still shun a bobbin. Polly Rosborough is such a person, and his work is perfection without a bobbin—though his flies have the faint aroma of Corn Husker's Lotion. That's right, he uses this hand lotion to keep his skin soft so that the thread will not fray as it rubs over his tying fingers. Maybe the lotion is the reason that fish find his flies so very attractive.

However, bobbins do make tying much easier, and I'm convinced I produce a better fly with than without one. A bobbin should be simple in design and use. It should have a thread barrel of high-quality steel that does not groove under the friction of nylon thread use. It must not tangle every time you make a move with it, and if it should foul, it should not require a mechanic to disassemble and free the thread. Screws, springs, levers, and sharp edges are out; such bobbins will drive you back to the bare-handed methods.

The drag should be easily adjustable so that even 8/0 silk will not pop its stitches under use. A coarse drag will also cause you to bend the small hook sizes if you are heavy handed.

There are several wonderful little bobbins on the market that meet every one of the above requirements and then some. They are basically a thread barrel connected by a loop of spring steel. Each end of the loop has a ball-like knob that fits into the spool hole. Though various catalogs list them differently, their common names are: Custom Clip bobbin, F & M Stainless Steel bobbin, and Orvis bobbin.

Since I began using these bobbins, many of my tying faults were corrected and my work improved consistently. Also, as a pro tyer I had to fill orders despite rough, cut, or chapped hands. With a good bobbin I lose no time even if my hands are out of shape, and I can handle many types and sizes of threads without much delay.

## LITTER CONTROL

No flytyer is neat. When at the vise the fur and feathers fly in all directions unless they are tied to the hook. We all spill paint and cement and manage to drop hooks and tools and materials on us or on the floor. This live and growing trash dump surely creates an eyesore in and around the tying area. Since we usually set up shop in the family room, den, or bedroom, it causes some hard feelings unless your wife is a tyer too—or away at her mother's.

Recently, while in Visalia, California, Darwin Atkins, a talented professional tyer from Fresno, showed me what must be the greatest tying aid since the vise was invented. Darwin calls it "Waste-Trol." It is a frame and plastic bag uniquely designed to fit around any vise and catch 99 percent of all excess or dropped material. Whatever materials miss the perimeter of the bag are attracted by the static charge on the plastic bag, creating a magnetic vacuum to snap up flying fuzz and frazzles. I've been using one now for a year and couldn't do without it. I'm rather unorganized and clumsy, and the Waste-Trol catches my droppings without fail. By the end of a tying session it has saved me a lot of time and nerves. Often the floor around my desk is as clean as when I began hours before.

The Waste-Trol is a no-nonsense tool, a terrific accessory that is easy to use and makes tying a neat hobby. They are now available in several catalogs and the price is less than a Grade B cock neck. Use one for a while, and I can almost guarantee it will improve your tying, improve relations with the woman in your life, and prevent gray hair. Can you think of anything else that will do all that for less than five bucks?

## HOOKS

In spite of the great increase of hook sales, fewer hook manufacturers exist now than was the case some years back. Becoming President is easier than succeeding in having a new hook style made—and it almost costs less money, too!

There are several pro tyers and materials firms that have had new hooks specially made, but there is still need for more new designs. If hooks and flies didn't suffer from underpricing their worth, we would see a lot more quality in both. When we are willing to pay a nickel for a super hook, then one will be made; but as long as we nearly faint at the two-cent limit we won't see much change in design or quality. There is a need for a new hook for the new No-Hackle flies; available models do not suit this unique fly design properly. I predict the manufacturers of these new patterns will soon make available such a hook to tyers.

Otherwise the Keel hook, Orvis Special and Premium Dry Fly hooks, Plated Steelhead and Shad models by Buszeck's, and the new Saltwater Stainless models are about all that is new in tying hooks.

With a swing of popularity to fly tackle that is designed to fish fine and far, nymphs are enjoying a big play. A standard heavy wire hook is too coarse for superlight tippets, so a problem has developed about how to sink the fly and still have good soft hooking. Some of us are going to dry-fly wires and wrapping the shank with a few turns of lead. This enables the fisherman to use even large nymphs with very light 5X to 7X tippets, with good hooking results from the thin wire, supersharp points while bouncing the bottom. The single objection raised is: The weight causes the nymph to keel up the point and look distasteful to the trout. I've had terrific results with nymphs so weighted, and don't feel this is a serious fault in most cases. Also, if the nymph is properly balanced with materials, it will swim or drift upright unless a pound of lead is used. The turle knot also helps ride a turn-down-eye hook straight.

While I'm on body weighting let me pass along another hint. For some reason I've never been able to discover why lead wire is so unbelievably expensive. At times it is also very hard to find. So I use small-diameter solder that I buy in quarter-pound or pound spools. It works as well and costs only about one-third what lead wire costs. It is available in small diameters (.012″ to .032″) at electrical or electronic shops or through various electronic equipment catalogs.

## CEMENTS

In the last few years a vast number of new cements and glues have come on the market; many are extremely useful to the flytyer.

Vinyl cement in liquid form has terrific uses for reinforcing various quill-wing materials. A thin coat of it on one side of each wing of a duck quill No-Hackle or standard dry fly increases the durability tenfold. Yet it does not discolor nor distort the wing. It is great for quill bodies and as an undercement on dubbed bodies.

Epoxy glues have many applications when making plastic, wood, or cork bass bugs. They will hold a body to the hook indefinitely and eliminate twisting of the shank inside the body. Epoxy also can be used on deer-hair bugs to increase durability and prevent the hair from spinning around the shank or becoming loose after a little use. Simply put a small amount at the base of hook and hair after flaring each bunch. The next bunch of hair will squeeze the epoxy into the hair behind it. Lay the bug aside for about twelve hours before you trim it to shape. Muddler heads can also be made extremely durable by using this method.

Varnish is not new, but it has to be considered a much neglected finish that has a lot of superior qualities. A good rod, spar, or head varnish that dries fast is an extremely good coating for fly heads, cement for deer-hair bodies, hackle reinforcer, and coating over hooks and tinsels to prevent corrosion or tarnishing. Its ability to penetrate materials before it dries assures a very deep, durable, and flexible coating. A thin drop at the base of the hackle on a dry fly will make the hackle fibers many times more durable and less likely to bend back while in use, and will not mat them like regular head cement. It will discolor some materials—usually making them darker and transparent. I like the translucence that varnish gives colored threads for a flyhead; it also lends a transparency to feather fibers, creating a very natural sheen similar to real insect wings.

## SPRAY-CAN PAINTS, LACQUERS, AND VARNISHES

This new generation of coating applicators has infinite uses for the flytyer. They can be applied quickly, smoothly, and easily to materials; most of them dry in seconds. The acrylic-base spray paints are perfect for coating wing quills to make them split less while tying and wear well while fishing, yet they add little weight to the feather.

Spray lacquers provide the bug or jig maker with slick paint jobs that dry in seconds. Other colors or designs can be applied without long waits between drying periods. The color range is almost infinite, from opaques to transparent to metallic to pearls.

The waterproofing product "Scotchgard" is now available in spray can. It is applied to a dry fly or hairbug to make it waterproof and durable. Spray your flies a day or so before you use them; the best procedure is to give them two light coats as soon as you tie them.

## FELT POINT PENS

Felt-point inking or marking pens that have a waterproof transparent dye have some interesting uses for the flytyer. They come in all the popular colors and various wood-stain tints. The rapid-drying pen ink does not mat or build up on surfaces the way most paint will.

My first introduction to them came from a reprint of an article by John Veniard sent to me from England. It described a method of marking hackle with the pen to simulate grizzly or badger hackle. Even though this technique seemed to mark feathers fairly well, it fell short of a decent substitute for the naturals. However, for marking various quills and hair it works quite well.

The most practical application I've discovered thus far is the marking of hair-bugs with stripes or bars; this eliminates the tough tying job of making these color variations by blending different colors or hair.

These pens also mark mylar or chenille bodies beautifully. Vertical bars can be made on marabou or hair streamer wings; fur nymphs can be darkened on top with these pens with perfect effects. You can color a few yards of thread in seconds. Plastic and foam-plastic bug bodies are easily colored or marked with these pens without damage to solvents. You will surely find many other applications for these quick-drying inking stains; they are quite reasonable and are sold in most drug or stationery stores. Be sure, though, to check the label for the waterproof type.

## DYES

Being able to dye materials is extremely important to any serious flytyer. Without this ability a tyer is really handicapped. Throughout my travels I saw that all the good tyers had learned the art of tinting and dyeing their materials. Today there is no reason not to know how to use dyes. It is impossible to find all the colors and shades in catalogs; suppliers can't begin to keep such inventories, and usually have just natural and a range of standard colors. But few pure colors are found on naturals; we must be able to dye to match or forever be frustrated looking for and ordering the right shades or duns of colors.

There are at least three reliable and reasonable fabric dyes on the market to use which you do not require a master's degree in chemistry. These dyes have various salt and acid crystals mixed in the ready-to-use packs; these are the setting and fixing agents. The dyes come in a very wide range of pure colors and mixed shades. With additional mixing of two dye colors or two-step dyeing, an infinite number of colors can be obtained.

Before dyeing any feather, fur, or synthetic material, it must be wetted for a good quick dye penetration. I use dishwasher detergent or liquid washing detergent in hot water to wet and remove all oils and fats. The longer these materials are soaked the better they accept the dye pigments. Remember to rinse well.

The dye is added to a container of water and heated to 180° F; then the soaked and rinsed materials are added. I use a coffee can. Stir frequently and *do not over-*

*heat to boiling*, as many protein-based hairs and feathers will be badly damaged by the heat, which cooks the protein and breaks it down. The texture is easily destroyed and often the hair or feather is badly distorted. Rinse materials and allow to dry in a well-aerated area. If you dare, use your wife's hair dryer or clothes dryer to dry and restore materials to shape. Put materials in a woman's nylon stocking, a cloth bag, or a box so that they don't scatter all over the house while drying.

You can purchase these dyes, which come in convenient packs, in any drug or food store. I prefer Putman, but Rit and Tintex both work well too. A little experimenting with sample materials will be easy, and in no time good results are possible. The use of home dyes will expand your ability to build great imitations, I assure you.

## TYING THREADS

Silk held the limelight as the best material for fly-tying thread for many, many years—even after nylon became available; but recently it lost its popularity to the new improvements in nylon tying threads, and I found only a small group of tyers still using silk for the majority of their work.

The reasons for this shift are that the new nylon threads are reasonable in price, more resistant to fraying, and much stronger than silk, and have superior tying properties. The last reason is due to the fact that nylon has been made softer or more flexible than earlier stock and the filaments are not braided, as earlier nylon was. Now the thread lies flat on materials, giving less bulk per wrap and holding the material down better per wrap. Excessive stretch has also been processed out. Nylon has a slower tendency to age or rot and does not adsorb water readily.

The leaders of this new generation of threads are Nymo, Monocord, Buz's Super Mono, and Herb Howard or Danville's. Though all have outstanding properties, one big advantage is the prewaxing of Herb Howard's and Monocord. Uniform waxing makes them perform wonderfully for most jobs.

Perhaps the biggest boon to those who tie small flies are the strength and size of Herb Howard's thread. It is a thread unbelievably small in diameter with even more unbelievable strength. It ties like quality waxed silk 8/0, but has three times the strength with almost no stretch! It is rated between 6/0 and 8/0 in diameter, but can even be used to tie deer hairbugs or dub big nymphs. It holds materials fast with just a few wraps. These new nylon threads are available in an excellent range of colors.

### MYLAR, PLASTICS, AND TINSELS

Space Age plastics are being welcomed with wide-open arms by most innovative tyers. The uses for these materials are almost infinite—from tiny trout flies to big shark streamers.

Mylar is perhaps the most popular film plastic for it is extremely light, flexible, and strong. It can be colored or have metallic films on it; the metallics are especially popular for streamer bodies. Wrapped as tinsel or braided in tubing, mylar makes beautiful and durable bodies. In thin strips, it is blended with wing materials for a superflash effect. It is just a matter of time before it replaces metallic tinsels, and that will be a blessing to any flytyer. It will eliminate all the problems that brittle, wiry, discolored metallic tinsels give us.

Fire tinsel is one of the first attempts to make a plastic tinsel, and I love it. It offers a great range of colors and finishes and can be used as a body material or with its superflexible hairlike material, for all sorts of streamer wings. Its action when blended with marabou or hair is something to behold! It is presently available from Fireside Angler, Inc.

Polyethylene, Saran wrap, and several other plastic films that we use every day for bags or covers have many applications. They can be wrapped as bodies, giving a natural sheen to the colors they are wrapped over; and they make great insect wings or nymph coverlets. Wherever you look you can find all sorts of plastic films. Experiment with them and you will obtain some "striking" results.

The only thing I've found new about tinsels in my investigations is that most dealers are having increasing problems obtaining good tinsel and holding their costs down. Both are headed in opposite directions.

A lot of tyers are using the acrylic clear sprays to coat tinsel and give added strength, prevent discoloration, and keep them from fouling up the spool. The oval style with a thread core holds up extremely well if sprayed with this clear enamel and will not unravel when cut. I have always found oval tinsel far superior to the flat types for most jobs. It will not kink and break about the time you are ready to rib a body with it, as the flat type will. In addition, oval is far less likely to be cut by a fish bite and to unravel from the body.

Most catalogs carry various mylar or mylarlike materials and describe their uses. Usually these are in tubing or sheets, or spooled. However, if there is a hobby or sewing store near, investigate what they might also have that you can use for tying. Some of the various materials made for sewing hobbies are perfect for our tying needs. I explore every shop I find, and have really discovered some great stuff. Never hesitate to explore these areas for new ideas.

## YARNS

Natural lamb's-wool yarn has been a staple of fly-tying since fly-tying began, and it is still a very practical and useful material. The last ten years of synthetic fibers have been approaching the wool as popular yarn for sewing and knitting. For fly-tying these same synthetic yarns are superior in many cases. They have textures, sparkle, and adsorbent resistance that go into making some beautiful fly bodies.

The most popular with flytyers these days is acrylic fiber orlon. It comes in several textures and blends and is very reasonable. The colors and shades rival all nature, and it is easy to pick exactly what you need from the infinite variety available. Orlon yarn also can be teased apart to make a fine dubbing, or blended with natural furs for a truly wonderful effect. Mohlon—an orlon yarn—is especially useful for dubbing in this manner. Cut yarn into half-inch pieces and drop them into a food blender. On high speed the blender will convert the yarn into furlike felt for dubbing.

Another new polypropylene fiber yarn is called Poly-Pro yarn. This recent development in yarns has dry-fly tyers excited. It has a specific gravity of less than 1, which means it floats on water and will not adsorb water or sink! It can be used to wrap dry-fly bodies and, cut into dubbing, it can be spun on thread to provide a shaggy furlike body for floating nymphs. It is extremely translucent and makes very insecty bodies. It is a perfect material for the new No-Hackle fly bodies. It comes in a good range of colors, and most materials catalogs will be stocking it by press date.

Visit your local sewing or fabric shop; you can find all sorts of useful yarns, threads, mylars, floss, and interesting tool items that can supplement your regular tying materials. It's fun to explore for new ideas.

## HACKLE

No other subject except, maybe, women causes more conversation among fly-tyers than hackle. It is the most versatile and useful feather material we have. Tyers all over the country constantly complain about shortages of good necks and, if they *are* available, their high prices. With the increase in fly-tying and the decrease in the cock chickens, the demand will never be satisfied.

On the bright side, a few American poultry raisers are trying to develop a good strain for fly-tying feathers. Dun, badger, ginger, and grizzly hackle are the most sought after. I saw several private flocks of high quality birds and necks from several other American raisers that hold a domestic-source promise in the next ten to twelve years. At least these are steps in the right direction. These special strains are not cheap, for perfect necks breeders are asking some frightening prices and having little trouble finding buyers. Outside sources seem to be improving, and our improved relations with China may enable more superior Oriental necks to be imported. Until recently, most neck importing was done by a very few dealers. But I have seen evidence that may indicate a breakdown in this monopoly; if so, more necks will undoubtedly be imported and prices will change accordingly.

The new No-Hackle dry flies should indirectly relieve the hackle shortage by giving tyers an alternative method of floating their imitations. I was not able to see this effect in my research, but in time it should be noticeable. Many of my personal dry flies are hackleless now, and I consider them superior to hackle patterns most of the time when fishing the dun and spinner stages of mayflies.

Hen hackle has always been the superior hackle for wet flies but was never very popular with tyers. The recent publicity that hen hackle received from *Selective Trout* has drastically increased the demand for it; Doug Swisher and Carl Richards reveal that it has superior qualities as a wing material for dry flies. I agree; it is a very unique feather for this purpose.

Since hen chickens are usually more plentiful than cocks, and since neck age is unimportant, a good supply of hen hackle should always be available. That fact also allows a hen neck to sell for much less. Demands for them now, however, have raised the price somewhat. Most catalogs provide us with a useful range of natural and dyed hen necks.

A new system of grading hackle and saddles should be put into effect. One is needed that classes necks simply by dry-fly, wet or nymph quality, and streamer quality. Necks that hold many small hackle should be classed in the dry and wet category; those with lots of large hackle should be classed as streamer or bug hackle. With such a system you would be able to purchase hackle to fit needs more closely and enable merchants to grade and sell more accurately. Saddle hackle would be classed as dry-fly quality, wet or woolyworm quality, and streamer quality. Recently, feather merchants have finally been obtaining saddle capes that make matching or selecting hackle by size and color ten times more convenient for the tyer, just as a neck does for the tyer.

Besides purchasing hackle from suppliers, look around your home area. Some fine feathers can be obtained at local poultry shops, farm flocks, local poultry fair shows, and gamecock fights. Some of the most beautiful hackle I've obtained was from local sources.

## DEER, ELK, AND ANTELOPE HAIR

Deer hair now competes with hackle as the most popular tying material. A whole new generation of flies have evolved that incorporate deer hair as the main material. With the introduction of terrestrial imitations, the muddler series, western and Wulff floaters, hairbugs and saltwater patterns, deer hair has come into its own as a unique tying material. Its texture and physical makeup render it extremely versatile for fly-tying.

Deer hair is easy to obtain and quite reasonable. However, the best skins come from our northern states and Canada, where the colder climates have produced the most ideal textures for fly-tying. Southern deer have short wiry hair, which has poor floating quality and is reluctant to flare. Whitetail and mule deer are the most popular and certainly the most plentiful. Most material shops sell both white and natural dun brown; either is usually easily dyed with fabric dyes to the shades you wish if they are not stocked by these shops.

Elk hair is very much like deer hair in property but has the additional advantages of being longer and tougher. However, it is generally harder to obtain and does not have the barring marks that deer has. Since it is recognized by many experienced tyers as superior, it is well that you include some along with your deer-hair stock.

Antelope and caribou are two additional hairs that have the characteristic physical texture of deer hair and are useful to us. Both make superior bodies for the Irresistible-type dry flies because their texture and weight are lighter. On larger flies, however, this hair is a bit tender for good wear. Caribou has the most superior floating qualities of all four.

Most beginning tyers will be well advised to obtain these hairs and learn their countless uses. The time spent developing a skill with them will greatly enhance your ability to create many imitations.

## FAKE FURS

There has recently been a lot of interest in synthetic furs. From a short distance it is almost impossible to tell them from the real thing. They deceive even the sense of touch. The only one, however, that seems to impress any number of tyers is the fake bear-hair type commonly used for bathroom rugs. This filament hair resembles polar-bear hair and is an excellent substitute for it on streamers and jigs. The shorter underfur, which comes close to seal in its texture and sparkle, can be used for dubbing fur.

The fake fur has a transparency much like polar-bear hair and comes in many fluorescent and regular colors. It has action superior to most bear hair since it is much softer; and it adds greatly to the appeal of natural bucktail when blended for streamer wings. Best of all, it is very reasonable compared to the price of gold and natural polar-bear hair. It is available at rug stores, craft shops, or fabric shops.

The time is fast arriving when some of our favorite furs will go the same route that jungle cock went. Wallaby or Australian opossum has already been restricted; seal and polar bear will soon join the embargoes. So flytyers will have to put some of their aesthetic values aside and begin to use fake furs or fake feathers. I don't really think most fish care which kind they strike.

## FUR BLENDS FOR DUBBING

Dubbed bodies are becoming popular with fly-fishermen as we learn how effective they are on all types of flies from nymphs to No-Hackle flies. Dubbed bodies almost always prove to have more fish appeal than the less lifelike quill or hard plastic bodies. Most flytyers around the country agree with this. Also, the trend to tie flies that are more suggestive than imitative requires use of these rough fur bodies to create the right illusion with water and light.

Making dubbing was something like making a witch's brew to most of us, and only the master pros had the magic recipes to create such blends. That is no longer the case. Blending a dubbing from fur and wool is extremely easy. By using either the water-and-detergent or the food-blender method it is possible to fashion your own blends easily. I prefer the dry-food-blender method because it mixes different materials fast and evenly into a felted dubbing that does not require drying and is perfect to spin on your dubbing thread.

By using all sorts of fur cut from the hides of rabbit, seal, otter, beaver, polar bear, mink and the like, and various yarns teased into a wool, you can blend a limitless variety of dubbing. It is usually superior to any chenille, yarn, or floss body.

I predict that most materials dealers will soon make available ready-made dubbing for many popular patterns that call for fur bodies. If so, we will not have to fool with a lot of smelly and expensive furs on skins that must be on hand to make such blends. Also, with some fur becoming increasingly difficult to obtain, ready-made dubbing will save everyone the trouble of hunting around for these rare and expensive furs.

Nothing really new in fly-tying? Can't agree with that remark these days. The foregoing will give you some idea of how much *is* new and what we can expect during the next ten years or so in American fly-tying techniques, tools, and materials.

Let's never give up the traditional wealth our sport and hobby are graced with, and always prefer wood duck to dyed mallard, jungle cock to printed plastic fakes, natural-dun cock hackle to dyed dun. But let us also admit, gracefully, that we are living in a new time, and let us make good use of what it has to offer. Compromise with an open mind and it will serve to improve our unique sport hobby.

# Reliable Sources for Fly-tying Materials

No attempt has been made to make this list comprehensive, only to offer some proven personal preferences collated from names submitted by each of the contributors to this guide. All these dealers provide catalogs, most of which are free; and most catalogs contain a wealth of valuable information for the amateur or professional tyer, as well as a thorough guide to the latest tools and materials available.

Dan Bailey's Fly Shop
209 West Park Street
Livingston, Montana 59047

George M. Bodmer
Bodmer's Fly Shop
2404 East Boulder
Colorado Springs, Colorado 80909

Mrs. Virginia Buszeck
Buz's Fly and Tackle Shop
805 West Tulare Avenue
Visalia, California 93277

Harry A. Darbee
Livingston Manor, New York

Eric Leiser
Fireside Angler, Inc.
P.O. Box 823
Melville, New York 11756

Herter's, Inc.
Rural Route 1
Waseca, Minnesota 56093

E. Hille, Inc.
Williamsport, Pennsylvania 17701

Bud Lilly's Trout Shop
Box 387
West Yellowstone, Montana 59758

The Orvis Company
Manchester, Vermont 05254

Reed Tackle Co.
Box 390
Caldwell, New Jersey 07006

Tom C. Saville, Ltd.
9 Station Road
Beeston, Nottingham
England

E. Veniard, Ltd.
138 Northwood Road
Thornton Heath, Surrey
England

# Notes on the Contributors

ART FLICK is a past president of both the Catskill Mountains Fish and Game Club and the Federated Sportsmen's Clubs of Greene County; he is a past vice-president of the New York State Conservation Council and has served on the Advisory Committees of four Conservation Commissioners in New York State. He is the author of *Art Flick's New Streamside Guide to Naturals and Their Imitations.*

ED KOCH, who lives in the limestone-creek section of Pennsylvania, is a specialist in minutiae and terrestrials, and is the author of the forthcoming book *Fishing the Midge* (Freshet Press). His articles have appeared in such magazines as *Trout, Outdoor Life,* and *The Pennsylvania Angler.*

BERNARD "LEFTY" KREH, a member of the Fishing Hall of Fame, manages the world's largest fishing tournament, The Metropolitan Miami Fishing Tournament. He is on the Advisory Board of the Federation of Fly Fishermen, and is a member of the Advisory Board of the Salt Water Fly Rodders of America. Lefty, who has written for every major fishing magazine, is the holder of six world's records for fish taken on a fly.

TED NIEMEYER was born in Seattle, Washington, and has fished for trout, salmon, and steelhead since early childhood. Thirty-five years of astute observation and dedicated practice with the fly rod and vise have given him unusual insight into fishing and fly-tying. Ted, who is six feet four, ties exceptionally delicate and meticulous flies. He lives with his wife, Phyllis, and their two children in New Canaan, Connecticut.

ERNEST SCHWIEBERT is the well-known author of *Matching the Hatch, Salmon of the World,* and the recent—and widely acclaimed—*Remembrances of Rivers Past.* He is a superb fly-fisherman, known the world over, and is one of the very few people in the world who can boast of having reduced to possession, on a fly, an Atlantic salmon weighing over fifty pounds. He is currently a Contributing Editor of *Sports Afield,* and has published articles in such magazines as *Sports Illustrated, Life, Esquire, True,* and many others.

HELEN SHAW is surely the First Lady of Fly Fishing. Her superb book, *Fly Tying,* has for more than ten years been one of the standard texts for beginners and advanced tyers alike. She lives in New York City and restricts her fly-tying for collectors only, many of whom have framed specimens of her limited editions.

DOUG SWISHER and CARL RICHARDS are two Michigan fly-fishermen whose recent book, *Selective Trout,* received wide attention. Their careful observation of mayflies and other aquatic insects and their use of underwater photography have led to their development of the Swisher-Richards patterns now known across the country. Both men are excellent tyers who constantly experiment with new methods and materials.

DAVE WHITLOCK is an exceptionally gifted tyer who specializes in western patterns. Several of his flies, like the marvelous Whitlock Sculpin, have been singled out for special attention in national magazines. He has written articles for *Field & Stream, Sports Afield, Outdoor Life,* and *Flyfisher,* and is a Director of The Federation of Fly Fishermen. Recently he has been presenting illustrated lectures throughout the country on fly-fishing, fly-tying, and conservation. He lives with his family in Bartlesville, Oklahoma, where he directs a premium fly-tying business, specializing in his own designs.

# INDEX TO FLIES